The Last Schooner

The Remarkable Life of Captain Lou Kenedy

Joe Russell

The Nautical Publishing Company
An Imprint of Far Horizons Media Company

Far Horizons Media Company is a division of NetPV, Inc.

Published by
The Nautical Publishing Company
www.NauticalPublishing.com

An Imprint of Far Horizons Media Company
www.FarHorizonsMedia.com

Far Horizons Media Company is a Division of NetPV, Inc.
P. O. Box 560989, Rockledge, FL 32956 - www.NetPV.com

The illustration of the *Sea Fox* on the front cover was created by Rosemary Kenedy Mitchell, daughter of Captain Louis Kenedy. The sinking of *Wawaloam* on the rear cover is a picture of an original oil painting by Gloria Greco, Wild Things Studios, 134 Front St., Greenport, NY. Photo of Captain Kenedy on the rear cover courtesy of the Kenedy family. All used by permission.

Please note that charts in this book are for illustration only and are not intended for navigation.

Also note that the spelling "harbour" is used in the captain's direct quotations, whenever the word appears in the exact transcriptions of his Ship's Log, and when the word is part of a proper place name.

ISBN-10 0-9789350-0-4
ISBN-13 978-0-9789350-0-9

LCCN   2006934107

For
Leslie Dianne Russell
and
my children:

Abigail
Allistair
Cecily
&
Joby

Contents

Foreword (by Bill Bolling) **ix**
Preface **xi**

		Prologue **1**
Chapter	1	*Abundance* **11**
	2	*Adams* **33**
	3	*Sea Fox* **45**
	4	*Wawaloam* **67**
	5	*Sea Fox* (Redux) **99**
	6	*City of New York* **109**
	7	*Vema* **141**
	8	*Alpha* **151**
	9	*Aquanaut* **181**
	10	*Pikes Arm* **201**
	11	Motorsailer *Sea Fox* **215**
		Epilogue **231**

Acknowledgements **235**
Glossary **237**
Appendix 1 **244**
Appendix 2 **245**
Index **247**

Figures

Figure   **Title and Page**

          Patsy and Bill Bolling   **x**

P-1   Chesapeake pungy schooner *Amanda F. Lewis*...   **2**
P-2   Lou Kenedy, age 18...   **3**
P-3   *Tilky*, Lou Kenedy's first real sailboat   **5**
P-4   Sloop *Sarah E.*   **5**
P-5   *Tusitala*   **8**

1-1   *Abundance*   **11**
1-2   Lou's handsome 1926 Stutz Black Hawk...   **13**
1-3   Lunenburg Harbour   **14**
1-4   Chart: The transatlantic route of *Abundance*   **22**
1-5   *Abundance* hove to   **29**
1-6   Chart: The last voyage of *Abundance*   **30**
1-7   ...*Abundance* was abandoned on the southeast shore of Jamaica...   **31**

2-1   *Adams*   **33**
2-2   Stowing lumber as deck cargo   **40**
2-3   Sailing off Turks in rising wind and seas...   **41**
2-4   Chart: The last voyage of *Adams*   **42**

3-1   *Sea Fox*   **45**
3-2   Heavy going aboard *Sea Fox* on one of her cargo runs...   **58**
3-3   ...Beaufort Scale [ink sketches of *Sea Fox*]   **59**
3-4   ...Pat and Lou in full wedding finery...   **63**
3-5   *Sea Fox*...winning the Boxing Day Regatta   **64**
3-6   Captain Lou, 27, with one-year-old Brian off Barbados   **65**
3-7   Light squall   **66**

4-1   *Wawaloam*   **67**
4-2   Mate Peter Jones caulks the new deck   **69**
4-3   Captain Lou dubs...spar (1940)   **69**
4-4   New mast being hoisted aboard from ice-filled water   **70**
4-5   Sheers rigged to hoist new mainmast aboard, March 1940   **72**
4-6   Discharging salt at Clark's Harbour   **77**
4-7   Lou's brother John Kenedy painting a U.S. flag on the topsides...   **79**
4-8   *Wawaloam's* crew...   **80**
4-9   *Wawaloam* anchored in front of the Kenedy home...   **82**
4-10   The captain at the helm...   **83**

Figures (Continued)

Figure	Title and Page

4-11   With her fore and mizzen masts shot away…pencil sketch… **90**

4-12   Butch, the survivor 94

4-13   Chart: The final voyage of *Wawaloam* and route of survivors **97**

5-1   *Sea Fox* (Redux) **99**

6-1   *City of New York* **109**

6-2   Captain Lou aboard *City of New York*, 1947 **116**

6-3   Brian and ship's dog Gotlik **118**

6-4   An enormous load of Nova Scotia lumber for Boston **120**

6-5   Private labels for high class rum. [Skunk Squirt] **127**

6-6   Bath time at sea for Patsy and Pat, in a puncheon **130**

6-7   *Thomas W. Lawson*, the only seven-masted schooner ever built **133**

6-8   Twenty-seven-ton Atlas Diesel engine coming aboard at Lunenburg **133**

6-9   *City of New York* careened at Snyder's Shipyard… **134**

6-10   Gabrielle Kenedy peeks from a butterfly hatch **136**

6-11   …the *City*…burned and sank off Yarmouth, Nova Scotia **140**

7-1   *Vema* **141**

7-2   *Vema's* figurehead **144**

7-3   Agile ship's dog Gotlik…captured tropical birds… **146**

7-4   …a broken mizzen boom and gaff **149**

8-1   *Alpha* rounding Hog Island Light **151**

8-2   Beautiful main saloon **154**

8-3   Charterers enjoying a swim on Sandy Cay **170**

8-4   Lou's youngest, Rosie, aboard *Alpha* **174**

8-5   Assisted by daughter Gabrielle, Lou siphons rum from a barrel… **175**

8-6   *Alpha* blown ashore by freak storm… **177**

8-7   Friends and crew drilling holes in coral ledge for dynamite **178**

9-1   *Aquanaut* **181**

9-2   "Japanese" crew for filming of *Father Goose* **185**

9-3   *Aquanaut*, with *Esperanto* alongside… **188**

9-4   Fred Whittier sorting out his rifles… **189**

9-5   *Esperanto* sunken at Stirrup Cay, Berry Islands on May 2, 1966 **190**

9-6   Chart: Route of *Aquanaut* during Camarioca Boat Lift **199**

10-1   *Pikes Arm* entering the Miami River **201**

10-2   …*Pikes Arm* and *Cobbs Arm* one behind the other… **202**

Figures (Continued)

Figure   Title and Page

10-3   Original blue-line drawing of *Pikes Arm*   **203**
10-4   Chart: *Pikes Arm's* biweekly course   **205**
10-5   *Pikes Arm* off Spanish Wells in 1968   **206**
10-6   Fiats as deck cargo for Harbour Island, 1970   **207**
10-7   The captain with *Pikes Arm* at Miami Shipyard   **210**

11-1   Motorsailer *Sea Fox*   **215**
11-2   Chart: LaHave/Lunenburg Area   **218**
11-3   Pat and Lou at Teddy's Shipyard, Dayspring, Nova Scotia   **219**
11-4   Navigating Great Dismal Swamp Canal   **222**
11-5   *Sea Fox* tied up at Jones Fruit Company dock, Wabasso, Florida   **224**
11-6   At anchor in the Exumas, Bahamas   **227**
11-7   Lou and ship's dog Thor riding in dinghy   **228**

E-1   Pat and Lou's 50th anniversary celebration… **232**

G-1   Tern schooner sail nomenclature   **237**

Unless noted otherwise with the figure, all photographs were taken by Captain Kenedy or members of his family and are used with the family's permission. The captain, his brother John, and his sister Rosemary were all skilled amateur photographers, as are the captain's son and daughters.

All charts and the drawing of the tern schooner in the Glossary are by the author.

Foreword

Captain Lou Kenedy was an amazing guy. Lou really lived 75 years too late, as sailing ships earning their ways belonged more to the nineteenth century than to the twentieth. Success required someone larger than life. Captain Kenedy succeeded.

I'm Bill Bolling, married to Lou's eldest daughter, Patsy. She inherited her father's courage, daring, and self-discipline.

Lou grew up in Stamford, Connecticut, the eldest son of Louis A. Kenedy, whose firm, P. J. Kenedy & Sons, published Bibles, missals, prayer books, and the like for the Vatican. The Kenedy clan was a cultured, upper-middle-class family, with a Buttersworth hanging in the parlor.

Six-foot-one, 200-pound Lou left this steam-heated family manse at age 19 in 1929 for the brutish, freezing fo'c's'le of the last of the Cape Horn square riggers. *Tusitala*, a 261-foot full-rigged ship berthed in Baltimore, became Lou's school of the deep sea. He was given four days to learn 234 names of halyards, sheets, braces, slab lines, lifts, downhauls, and pin rail positions in Norwegian (the first mate was from Oslo). Failure would have gotten him a smart blow upside the head from the mate's fist.

After carrying a load of sulfate-of-ammonia fertilizer to Hawaii, *Tusitala* loaded raw sugar for the return passage to Baltimore. Paid off, Lou was now hard muscled and had learned square-rigger seamanship, navigation, and the old-time man-o-war discipline which forbids idleness. You'll read of his further adventures, so well chronicled by Joe Russell.

Maybe I can help with perspective. At sea today, ships (sail or power) have powerful engines and generators, stabilizers, refrigeration and air conditioning, hot and cold pressure water, a full array of electronic navigation and weather forecasting tools, radar, auto-pilot, radios, and endless entertainment alternatives.

None of these was aboard Kenedy's dated sailing vessels. To profit from already-low freight rates, short-handed crews were dictated. The equipment: a lead line for depth sounding; a barometer for weather forecasting; and for navigation, a sextant, a time piece, and tables when sun, moon, or stars showed (otherwise, it was days of ded reckoning). With no halyard or sheet winches, "Swedish steam" was used to manhandle huge sail areas. *Adams'* mizzen was about 3,200 square feet of double-0 duck, and it weighed nearly 1,200 pounds. The gaff, high in the air, was half a yard in diameter and 40 feet long.

Meals featured bully beef hooked from a brine cask on deck. Fresh water was at a premium; bathing and hygiene were non-existent. Consequently, Lou usually smelled like a goat. "Don't want to wash away my natural body oils," he'd say with his remarkable grin. In the 30 years I knew him he never owned a comb, sunglasses, or underarm deodorant.

But Lou was far from dour. On a visit to the captain of the Port of Halifax in 1949, he was accompanied by his daughter Patsy. "Like to get this young lady seaman's papers" he announced. The amused official said, "Can she box a compass?" In those days compass cards had only cardinal and inter-cardinal points, no numbers of degrees.

To the head officer's delight, Patsy rattled off all 32 points of the compass. Astonished, he quickly issued her a "Canadian Seaman's Identity Certificate," which under "Title" lists her as Shipping Master, a lifetime authority to command any sail or power vessel in any ocean. She was six years old.

Bill Bolling
New Smyrna Beach, Florida

Patsy and Bill Bolling

Preface

All good sailors realize the sea will always surprise them with a new twist on each voyage. But after 20 or 30 years of open-ocean sailing, a few years as a Caribbean charter skipper, and generally messing around with boats, I began to believe I had a good working knowledge of sailing. I was confident that my level of expertise would stand me in good stead in almost any offshore situation. I graded myself highly.

I must have been grading myself on the curve. As soon as I was introduced to the Bollings, my grade level slipped significantly. In the early 1990s, my old writing and sailing buddy, Fritz Seyfarth, invited me to spend a week sailing and relaxing on a small group of islands in the Bay of Honduras called *Cayos Cochinos.* (In English, that's "Pig Cays." It sounds better in Spanish.)

We met in Miami at the airport, where he introduced me to Captains Bill and Patsy Bolling. These two were the instigators of the trip and had arranged for lodging at Captain Phil Richard's dive resort on *Cochino Grande.* (In English, "Big Pig." Also better in Spanish.) We landed in Roatan and boarded the brand new 120-foot gold-plated gin palace that Phil skippered. In the middle of the night, we motored (in obscene opulence) 30 miles south to the resort.

As soon as Patsy and Bill stepped aboard, their knowledge of the sea and vessels large and small became instantly apparent, and I was in awe. We spent a wonderful week together. We settled into the resort and toured the virtually uninhabited cays by Boston Whaler and piragua—dugout canoe. I learned of the ships they have owned and restored including the schooner-yacht *Puritan* and the 120-foot Icelandic gun boat, *Albert.* Then, around the bar at the small resort, stories started to surface about some old sailor named Lou Kenedy. The tales were cryptic to me. They were being told to people who had known him, and I didn't know the connection between the Bollings and this guy Lou Kenedy. But the stories were amazing, and as a sailor, they fascinated me.

After the trip, the Bollings and I stayed in regular contact, and the next time we saw each other was in Hawaii where they visited and stayed aboard *Christina* after we arrived in the Ala Wai from the Marquesas.

It wasn't until 2003 that I received a call from Patsy. "You interested in writing Daddy's story?" It had been a couple of years since we had seen each other, but I jumped at the chance. All my writing up to then was centered on cruising guides and destination pieces for *Cruising World,* so I saw the project as a way of broadening my horizons. When I later learned that I was not the first writer to be offered the project, but only the first one to accept it, I worried there were reasons for the earlier rejections that I didn't know about. As it turned out, there was a lot that I didn't know about "Daddy."

Within a few days, boxes of photos, transcripts, magazine articles, log books, and family memorabilia began arriving at my home in Connecticut. One of the articles was a four-part, 1953-54 *Saturday Evening Post* piece I used for research. What I didn't know was the *Post* had printed four-part articles only twice in its history. One was on Winston Churchill. The other was on Captain Lou Kenedy—Daddy.

Another thing I didn't know was that Ralph Getson of the Lunenburg (Nova Scotia) Marine Museum Society—operator of the Fisheries Museum of the Atlantic—was a friend of Lou Kenedy's and as a museum curator, had a keen interest in preserving a record of commercial sailing vessels and their skippers. I received a 270-page transcript of an interview Ralph Getson recorded with the captain in the early 1980s. This record was invaluable in the writing of this book. I learned, however, there were significant differences between incidents that were covered in *The Saturday Evening Post* story and the same incidents as recounted to Mr. Getson 30 years later. Like the size of the fish I almost caught, some yarns grew in significance and excitement as the years wore on. This isn't surprising as Captain Lou Kenedy was, if anything, a master story teller, and he rarely missed an opportunity to entertain his listeners.

As a result of these discrepancies, I consulted as many sources as I could find. Most of us know the adage, *"Never let the truth get in the way of a good story, or true love get in the way of a good time,"* but I've worked to present the life of this man as true to his amazing reality as possible.

This is a story of a man who successfully pounded a square lifestyle into a round society and ran shipping enterprises in a manner obsolete a generation before his time. His magnificent sailing ships were run profitably into the 1950s in the same manner as similar ships were in the 1850s. Life aboard these working vessels demanded hard, decisive men. These men also had to have a sense of humor entwined with a certain tenderness in order to endure the day-to-day hardships—no pun intended. These softer traits may seem at odds with the demands of shipboard life, but they invariably permeated the lives of tough men who sailed even tougher ships.

Joe Russell
S. V. *Freebooter*
San Rafael, California

Prologue

When Captain Lou Kenedy pulled himself up on deck this squally morning in May, 1985, he did not reflect on the fact that it was the last day of his last command. The captain was clad in canvas deck shoes, khaki pants, and a red plaid wool shirt. A coffee mug steamed in his hand.

The 75-year-old Captain had a full head of barely graying hair that neither needed nor frequently saw a comb. His limbs were thin, and fine wrinkles ran down his once powerful biceps and calves, but he was still thick-a-chest; a sailorman. He was proud that even at this age, he never needed glasses.

He was a holdover. He was famous—infamous a few said—from the Canadian Maritimes to Barbados. He was the last captain to profit from hauling molasses, lumber, salt, and general cargo in pure sailing ships between the frozen estuaries of New England and the Maritimes and rum-soaked ports in the Bahamas and Caribbean. But Captain Kenedy was a great deal more than simply the last of his breed. His reputation as a seaman of extraordinary skill and guile, and as a captain with an unflinching sense of responsibility, is etched deeply into the maritime traditions of America's east coast. "Lou Kenedy stories" are still being retold from Nova Scotia to Barbados.

This May morning he was aboard *Sea Fox*, his last vessel, a lovely white, wooden, 68-foot Hand motorsailer that he sailed into Atlantic Yacht Basin the night before. It had taken 10 days to make Great Bridge, Virginia from his daughter's dock at Marathon, in the Florida Keys. He was up early as usual and did nothing to mute the rattling of the coffee pot and breakfast pans in the galley. No one should be asleep this late anyway. It was first light, for Christ's sake.

Finally the crew was rousted and they got under way. *Sea Fox's* old Jimmy 6-71 had a bad injector so she billowed a bit of smoke on start up—and also when she was pushed too hard. Lou was careful not to push her as she slid through the oily Atlantic & Chesapeake Canal. He certainly didn't want the crew to see the damn smoke. Captain Kenedy was the skipper but *Sea Fox's* new owners were the crew for the delivery to Deltaville, Virginia, which was a condition of sale.

By 0930 on May 3, 1985, they cleared the lock. By 1500, *Sea Fox* was abeam Wolf Trap, a 58-foot brick-tower lighthouse commissioned in the 1890s.

Built to protect the schooners that were the mainstay of coastal shipping of that era, the lighthouse boasted the name of the HMS *Wolfe*, the first vessel of record grounded—trapped—at that location. The captain, navigating yet another wooden vessel past Wolf Trap Light, exemplified the spirit, self-reliance, thrift, and skill of those schooner captains. *Sea Fox* took the light to port. At the time, of course, no one noted the sail-era congruence between the old skipper and the red brick lighthouse.

The breeze turned gentle from the east and only a slight swell rolled this deep into the Chesapeake. The course was NNE to fetch #3 at Deltaville.

* * *

The first time Louis Kenedy, Jr. rounded Wolf Trap was in 1928 when the six-foot-one-inch, well-built 18-year-old was aboard a Chesapeake pungy schooner.* He wasn't supposed to be there. He was just starting his second year at Georgetown University when, without telling his parents, he packed his bag, walked out of school, and wandered down to the old Potomac wharf. There he spotted the 35-year-old schooner, *Amanda F. Lewis,* skippered by a white-bearded captain twice her age. The ship had long before left the oyster beds, but as a full-keel vessel, she displaced 33 tons with ample room below decks for cargo in the Chesapeake tidewater trade.

Figure P-1. Chesapeake pungy schooner *Amanda F. Lewis*, Washington D.C., 1928.

Standing on the dock, the 200-pounder yelled to the old man working on board the schooner, "I'm looking for a job." Rum-flushed and heavy, Captain Gus Rice turned around. Brown tobacco juice had run down the deep creases in his chin and built up a dripping amber mess in his white

*Two-masted vessel originally designed as a Chesapeake Bay workboat.

beard. The captain wore dirty, dark trousers and an old vest over a discolored dress shirt. He looked at the young man from head to toe and figured anyone that big would be an asset to the *Lewis*.

"Can you cook?" the old timer yelled back. "If you can keep people from starving to death, you have a job." "Yeah, I guess I can keep people from starving," Lou responded. "You're the cook, 18 bucks a month." That was that. Lou heaved his sea bag over the rail and never looked back.

Lou had no way of knowing, but Captain Rice was one of the Chesapeake Bay's more colorful characters. During the 1880's "Oyster Wars," Rice reportedly exhibited his disdain for the state of Maryland's attempt to restrict his oyster-dredging rights by capturing the state's gunboat, locking the captain in his cabin, and marching the crew—stripped naked—through downtown Easton, Maryland.

Ducking to avoid clobbering himself on the companionway headers, Lou climbed down to the larder where he found only beans, molasses, salt pork, salt beef, and flour. He had seen his Mom make baked beans with molasses so he decided he would feed the five-man crew beans for lunch the next day. That evening, the *Lewis* got underway with a load of canned tomatoes for Baltimore. After a sleepless night on donkey's breakfast,* Lou went on deck for a half-watch. Most schooners didn't require that the cook stand watch at all, but the short-haul Chesapeake traders didn't adhere to that rule. At 10:00 a.m., he went below to begin preparing his first and last luncheon masterpiece.

Amidships on the starboard side, the galley wasn't much. It was only about 5 by 10 feet, and the sole was coated with grease. There was a blackened, coal-burning stove/oven against one brick-veneered bulkhead. In the forward outboard corner stood a square, deep concrete sink that could be filled with salt water from a brass hand pump. Fresh water was stored in 55-gallon drums on deck and was used only for cooking and drinking. The stove vented through a thin sheet-metal flue that glowed red-hot at night. The mesh spark arrester and chimney cap, universally nicknamed "Charley Noble," stuck up above deck

Figure P-2. Lou Kenedy, age 18, aboard *Amanda. F. Lewis*.

---

*Nautical slang for the usual bag of straw used as a fo'c's'le mattress.

next to the mainmast. It was an unlucky sailor who forgot about ol' Charley Noble and leaned against him or, even worse, sat on him.

Lou lifted an enormous cast iron pot into the sink. He filled it with fresh water from a bucket he had carried from the barrel on deck, dumping what he thought were enough beans for the crew into the pot—about half a bucket—and let them soak until he had the stove up and roaring. Lighting the stove only took 15 minutes, and he lifted the cauldron of beans onto the hot, cast iron stove plates. As the beans boiled, they doubled in size, absorbing water and molasses, and started to overflow the pot. The kid crept topside and dumped the excess beans overboard, without the skipper noticing. The trick was dumping them over the side when the skipper, who was on the poop, wouldn't see the beans floating past the lee quarter. The beans in the pot doubled in size again necessitating another trip to the rail; and then yet another. The chumming continued but the skipper never noticed. Finally the mess seemed to stabilize so he dumped out the excess water, added some more molasses and shoved the pot into the oven. Years later, Captain Kenedy recollected:

*"...they certainly looked good but, boy! When you went to eat them, they were just like eating rocks. Since they weren't soaked they were solid, and they were sweet with all the molasses I put in them to make them brown."**

He had used up the crew's two-month ration of beans for his first and only lunch. He was banished forever from the galley and almost fired, but as soon as the captain and crew found out Lou could sew, splice, and sail, he was signed as a deckhand. He advanced quickly to mate at $40 a month.

One night in the fo'c's'le, the crew, curious about how a young kid knew so much about ship maintenance and sailing, cornered him and got this story about his youth on Long Island sound:

"We lived in an area that was kind of isolated, on a bay, with water all around and lots of land. There were hardly any houses. From the time I can remember, the main thing I'd see were boats going and coming. That was my whole interest. I read about them as soon as I

---

*Unless indicated otherwise, Captain Kenedy's first-person quotations throughout this book are excerpted from the extensive interviews he gave to Ralph Getson in June 1989, under auspices of the Lunenburg Marine Museum Society in Nova Scotia (unpublished), now part of the **Fisheries Museum of the Atlantic Collection**. (Used by permission.) These excerpts have been edited for clarity.

learned to read, and talked about them and went on every one I could—oyster boats and pleasure boats, anything that floated.

"My father built me a rowboat when I was about seven and soon he rigged it up with a jib and mainsail, and I fooled around learning to sail. There were several other young fellows, more or less my own age, who were interested in boats and we all sailed with one another and against one another. We'd spend our time repairing the boats and painting them, and we learned, little by little, about carpentry and painting and all maintenance.

Figure P-3. *Tilky*, Lou Kenedy's first real sailboat.

"Then when I was about 10 or 11, the old man got me a sloop with a keel on it, a good sailing boat—I had great times sailing that around.* When I was 14, I got a Friendship sloop, 25 feet long that had been a Maine fishing boat, a lot like the Tancook sail-boats in Nova Scotia. But fishermen were getting away from them, changing over to powerboats, and their sloops could be bought for little or nothing. I think we paid around $200 for this sloop, named Sarah E.

Figure P-4. Sloop *Sarah E.*

"She was in good condition, not too old, maybe 20 years, and she became my whole ambition. I kept painting and scraping her, calking her and putting her in first-class shape. I added a little more cabin to her, and two headsails and a mainsail. I'd spend all winter working on her, after school in the afternoons, and playing hooky when I could. I'd corral

---

* Lou named the boat "Tilky," an acronym for "This Is Louis Kenedy's Yacht."

friends and put them to work. By spring we'd have the boat in fine condition. The day school closed, we'd move aboard Sarah E. and take off eastward. We'd go down to Block Island, Nantucket, Martha's Vineyard, Narragansett Bay, Buzzard Bay and sometimes we'd go around Cape Cod and get as far as Gloucester. We all wanted to see the fishing vessels and talk with the crews and talk about boats. Because all this was interesting, I learned chart work and coastal navigation.

"We did a little fishing to augment our supplies, because our supplies were pretty awful. We used to go in farmers' fields in the evening and steal corn or whatever happened to be in the field, take it back to the ship and we'd have some feasts. And we'd bum lobsters from some of the fishing boats, especially around Martha's Vineyard and Block Island. Quite a life. We hated to go back to school in the fall."

Figuring the *Amanda F. Lewis* crew would not be interested in nor appreciate the more mundane aspects of his youth, Lou left out the little detail about his being the scion of a well-to-do family. And, of course, he did not think it was necessary to explain to the crew, who averaged about $15 a month, that his father was a successful publisher, heading the firm P.J. Kenedy & Sons, and was also treasurer of the prestigious Huguenot Yacht Club in New Rochelle. And, of course, it was neither important nor seaman-like to tell the crew he raced extensively under the burgee of his father's yacht club and never lost a race.

Lou was born with a silver spoon firmly lodged in his mouth, but he spent a lifetime successfully covering it up. Instead, he radiated a constant, moderate (but fraudulent) air of financial desperation. Captain Louis Kenedy carried Yankee frugality to extremes. To put it bluntly, he was a tightwad, so tight he squeaked. He spent money only on what he thought was important—his family, ships, and cars—and he never spent a dime impulsively. He might open his wallet to help a friend or even a stranger, but he never spent money on anything he considered frivolous—his definition of "frivolous" including almost everything.

As a perfect example of his frugality, he would choose the names of ports in which to register his vessels based on the fewest number of stencils he had to buy to paint the city's name on the stern. In the Northeast he used RYE (New York) several times. "MIAMI" was a favorite because it only took three stencils. If he was forced to register in a port where too many stencils were required, he simply would not bother painting the name on the stern.

Late in life, not believing in health insurance, he paid $100,000 cash for a back operation, but he never allowed himself to be known as a person of means. It embarrassed him. He aspired instead, at times to a fault, to Yankee thrift. Thrift was central to his unique concept of what it took to run a profitable sail-based shipping company 40 years after sail was obsolete and considered inefficient.

During his time on the *Lewis*, he only wanted to live the simple life of Jack Tar. Over time that attitude evolved into a single-minded desire to be a financially-successful schooner captain and nothing else. The wealthy son of a successful publisher didn't fit the image required to earn respect from captains and crews in the schooner trade. From the very beginning and throughout his career, thrift, hard physical labor, and an even harder mental attitude were Louis Kenedy's tools for success. He was a romantic when it came to sailing, but he never ran a vessel for anything else but profit. By 1930, sailing ships were cheap, and the wind was free. For Lou Kenedy, there was little else to consider.

His berth on *Amanda F. Lewis* was Lou Kenedy's first paying job at sea. He began adhering to the complicated system of traditional sea superstitions that only became more imperative as he grew older: Never begin a trip on a Friday, whistling on board ship is forbidden (unless needed in a calm to bring the wind, and then only if the captain gives express permission). The list of superstitions is long and had a significant effect on the outcome of some of his most famous exploits.

As mate aboard the *Lewis*, he learned the cargo business while hauling pulpwood, canned tomatoes, fertilizer, and coal between Washington D.C. or Baltimore and the small ports along the Chesapeake. The Chesapeake tidewater was a perfect classroom. Lou saw the little schooner make a profit, and he started planning.

* * *

After three months, he decided to leave the confines of the Chesapeake and signed aboard a succession of miserable drogers that still eked out a living in the dwindling lumber trade between the Canadian Maritimes and the northeastern U.S. As wretched as life was aboard these ships, he was learning even more about maintaining wooden sailing vessels and running a shipping business. In a terse description of those times and ships, Captain Kenedy simply recalled that all you could rely on aboard the lumber ships was "poor food, low pay, and no heat."

The life was wearing thin. Lou wasn't happy bringing home $45 a month alternating between sweating as a deckhand on a timber droger and freezing as a watchman on wintered-down schooners on the East River waterfront. Otherwise he was living at home and saving his money. In late summer of 1929, he landed a job as a rigger at a City Island yacht club. There he became even more adept at rigging, splicing wire rope, stepping masts, and other maintenance chores.

Then, in late winter of 1930, came what seemed to be the opportunity of a young seaman's life. On March 15 Lou signed aboard the last American, commercial, full-rigged* ship, the 1,800-ton *Tusitala*. The train ride down to Baltimore to pick her up seemed to take a lifetime. Upon his arrival, *Tusitala* and her newest deckhand sailed to New York to load fertilizer for Honolulu.

Lou was in heaven. The complexity of a full-rigged ship was mesmerizing. The sea crew consisted of 40 men standing watches and two cooks.

One entry into Lou's personal log at the time reads: *"Sat. Apr.19/30: Got paid...put $40 in the bank and as my grandmother gave me check of $50 for Easter, why that makes $90, so someday sooner I'll have my own vessel, be it a ketch, cutter or schooner, large or small, fast or slow, she must be sound & seaworthy."*[†]

Figure P-5. *Tusitala.*

This was in 1930 when the Depression seemed bottomless. After the first trip [described in the Foreword—ed.], *Tusitala*'s fertilizer deal fell through, and Lou worked aboard her as a maintenance hand for months. He augmented his income by again doing rigger's work at the local yacht clubs.

In 1931, Lou met some researchers from the American Museum of Natural History. Fifteen years earlier, the Museum had made a name for itself by completing an in-depth, five-year exploration of the Congo and had decided to repeat the effort in the Amazon. The naturalists were impressed with Lou's self-confidence and maturity, and paid his expenses to search for an appropriate vessel for the expedition.

---

*Square-rigged tall ship with three or more levels of square sails per mast.
[†] Patsy Kenedy Bolling maintains a family archive of log books and other memorabilia relating to her father. All log quotes in this book are from that archive.

"So they sent me off and I headed down through Maine, and I didn't find anything. I ended up in Lunenburg [Nova Scotia], and it was a sailor's dream, a harbour full of masts and all the vessels in good condition. Beautiful vessels, not big, fat lumber carriers, but fast fishermen and trim little three-masters built for carrying fish, more like clipper ships than the big cargo vessels.

"I found that Harry Adams would sell me the Abundance, *which was laid up, for $2,200."*

This trip was important on many levels. In Lunenburg, Lou fell in love with southeast Nova Scotia and the Lunenburg-LaHave River area. He met Harry Adams, who turned out to have a significant influence on Lou's future as a schoonerman. And, above all, on this trip, he laid eyes on his first command.

Belying its historic dependence on the lumber industry, the southeast Nova Scotia coastline is as treeless, cold, and forbidding a moonscape as anywhere in the world. Rocky promontories offshore are major hazards to navigation. The tides, though not nearly as severe as the Bay of Fundy, still routinely top a seven-foot range. But it was a hub of schooner trade, and Lou was interested in its history only as a sailorman's paradise.

Harry Adams was an owner of Adams & Knickle,* a shipping agent and fishing company with several salt-bankers out at any given time. A & K was a dockside receiving warehouse and outbound freight consolidator. Years later it remains a fully-stocked ship's chandler.

Abundance was in wonderful condition. She was tied up at Adams & Knickle and was just off the ways sporting new bottom paint. Lou inspected her from truck to keelson and found her in superb condition. His dream seemed to be within his grasp; he wired the research director and told him he had found their ship. He was ecstatic and also wired his family.

Before receiving his wire about the *Abundance*, the museum didn't know exactly where Lou was and couldn't contact him. Unfortunately, a week before he arrived in Lunenburg, the expedition had been cancelled. As soon as the research director received Lou's telegram, he wired back apologizing, explaining that the Depression had dried up all their research funds, and the project would have to be scrapped. Twenty-year-old Lou Kenedy was devastated, but not for long—never for very long.

On his way back from Nova Scotia, he pondered his situation. He had never spent any significant money and had the $2,200 necessary to buy the

_____

* The "K" in Knickle is not silent: "Kuh-NICKel."

ship himself. But Lou was not an impulsive young man. Though he was confident in his future as a schooner captain, he didn't buy *Abundance* immediately. Instead, he slogged home, back to the room at his parent's place in New Rochelle. But he had, by this time, made up his mind as it concerned *Abundance*.

The day after his return from Lunenburg, he enrolled in the Seaman's Institute of New York. Though he had the necessary sea-time, he needed formal training in celestial navigation. Three months after enrolling in the institute, he turned 21 years of age. The next day he stood for and received his Master's ticket. The test was easy for Lou as he learned quickly and intuitively. It wasn't work, nor was it difficult; it was about the sea and therefore enjoyable, interesting, and easy to comprehend.

His single-minded focus built a carefully-planned foundation for all that was to follow.

The ink sketch of the tern schooner *Wawaloam* used throughout the book as a chapter divider was drawn by Captain Lou Kenedy inside the cover of the *Wawaloam* log book.

Figure 1-1.

The ship: *Abundance* (ex-*Richard B. Silver*)
Year of Launching: 1919
Rig: Tern Schooner
Official #: 231442
Builder: John McLean & Sons, Ltd.,
    Mahone Bay, Nova Scotia

Material: Wood
Length between perpendiculars: 138 feet[*]
Beam: 27 feet 8 inches
Draft: 15 feet
Depth of Hold: 11 feet 2 inches

Chapter 1   *Abundance*

When tern schooner[†] Richard B. Silver *came off the ways at McLean's in Mahone Bay, Nova Scotia, she was intended for the "milk run": the lumber, fish, salt, and molasses trade between the Maritime Provinces and the Caribbean. But no sooner had she eased her way into the cold Nova Scotia waters than Andy Volstead's law passed the U.S. Congress, over the veto of*

---

[*] Waterline length, measured parallel to the centerline of a cargo ship carrying full load.
[†] Schooner with three masts (fore, main, mizzen). See Glossary.

President Woodrow Wilson. The Volstead Act put teeth into the Eighteenth Amendment to the Constitution, which outlawed the manufacture and sale of intoxicating liquor.

Richard B. Silver's owners, who included one of the late Richard Silver's family members, decided it made more economic sense to use the new schooner for running rum to the States than running salt to the LaHave River. But Captain Silver's family certainly didn't want his name on a rum-runner, so her name was changed to Abundance. *Captain Ammon Zinck was made her master. She ran salt fish to Barbados and other Caribbean islands, returning loaded with contraband liquor to "Rum Row." This continued until the three-mile territorial limit was extended to 12 miles and larger motorized vessels took over the trade in the late 1920s.*

There were several "Rum Rows" stretching from Florida to New England waters. The largest of these depots was near New York and New Jersey, the area of greatest demand. Narragansett Bay's "Rum Row" (the main source of liquor for southern New England) was about 15 miles southeast of Block Island. As many as 13 or 14 schooners and steamers at one time would lie at anchor there, off-loading booze.

In June of 1928, Abundance *was lying off Narragansett's Rum Row when a rum lighter knocked off her bowsprit. She was forced into Newport, Rhode Island for repairs. Customs agents boarded the Canadian-registered schooner and sealed the entire cargo, including the hatches. But aft, there was a hidden hatch into the lazarette that blended perfectly with the deck and was undiscovered. It was full of rum, of course. During the nights at Newport, the crew spirited a significant amount of the booze ashore, selling it at much better prices than they got from the off-shore runners.*

Apparently word leaked out that the crew of Abundance *was up to some hanky-panky. As she was leaving Newport, a Coast Guard motor vessel pursued her out of the harbor and caught up with her several miles out. Captain Zinck hove to and overheard the Coast Guard captain order a boarding party to search her. Zinck flew down the companionway and hauled up an ancient, double-barreled 10-gauge shotgun loaded with double-ought buck. He pointed it skyward and pulled the trigger. The blunderbuss lit off with a tremendous boom—which got everyone's attention—and Captain Zinck slowly lowered it until the young Coast Guard skipper was looking directly down both barrels. Zinck roared, "On land you're the boss. Out here, I'm the boss. You see that red flag up there? This is a British vessel, and your first step on this deck will be your last!"*

Exercising the better part of valor, the Coast Guard vessel quickly departed in search of less aggressive quarry. And, of course, Abundance continued directly to Rum Row to off-load her remaining contraband.

* * *

The day after 21-year-old Lou Kenedy—CAPTAIN Lou Kenedy—successfully stood for his master's license, he and John Hubbell, an old sailing buddy, threw their sea bags into Lou's aging but pristine Stutz Black Hawk and roared off for Lunenburg, Nova Scotia.

No matter how fast he pushed the car, to Lou it seemed to chug along toward Maine at ox-cart speed. It took all the daylight to get to Bar Harbor; then they suffered an annoying overnight stay waiting for the morning departure of the Bar Harbor-Yarmouth Ferry.

It took six and a half hours for the clunky steam ferry to lurch over to Yarmouth, and when it arrived, Lou and John were still 140 miles short of Lunenburg. He knew the coast road, as he had taken the identical route on his first trip while working for the museum folks. It was late August and the weather was wonderful; the top was down on the Stutz. As with his other visits to Nova Scotia—as a deckhand on the grubby timber drogers—he didn't take the opportunity to explore the countryside.

Figure 1-2. Lou's handsome 1926 Stutz Black Hawk parked in front of the family's elegant digs in Stamford, Connecticut.

Shortly after leaving Yarmouth, John Hubbell asked Lou to stop to relieve himself and get a bite to eat. Lou was having none of it and told John to hold it in and have a cracker out of the tin in his duffel. The Stutz rumbled on bouncing over the barely discernable roadbed. John moaned at every bounce. They passed the village of Wood's Harbour without stopping, then tiny Barrington, Shelbourne, and Lockeport.

With John threatening mutiny—"If you don't stop the car, I'm gonna piss in it!"—Lou finally pulled over at Liverpool to empty a five-gallon can of gas into the car. John emptied his long-suffering bladder behind a handy bush.

Continuing without stopping to eat, they turned south at Bridgewater, directly to the Adams & Knickle wharf at Lunenburg. The 140-mile trip had taken seven hours; it was now 11:00 p.m. Idling past the A & K warehouses, Lou braked and turned off the Stutz's engine. It was a clear night with a waning moon, and all was quiet.

Lou didn't know Harry Adams well enough to wake him at this late hour, so he and John pulled their duffels out of the back seat of the car and walked down between the warehouses. By moonlight, he saw the masts of the tern schooner he came to buy. She was magnificent. Because she had just come off the ways, *Abundance* was now tied up to the dock, not out on the hook or on a mooring like the dozen or so other ships in the harbor. Her bottom was newly painted and she had just been re-rigged.

He was overjoyed. By moonlight, he walked slowly down the wharf eying her lines. He climbed up the gang plank and over the rail, walked over to the aft doghouse and yelled down the companionway, "Anyone aboard?" No answer. He didn't own her yet and thought it would be unlucky to go below so he pulled an old striped Hudson Bay blanket from his seabag and laid it down on the spruce deck close to the gangway. He motioned to John to do the same. John was hungrier than hell but knew there was no place to eat this late. He opened his duffel, pulled out the last two soda crackers from the tin and popped them in his mouth. Using their seabags as pillows, they lay down, wrapped the blankets around themselves, and tried to sleep.

At first light, they were awakened by the daybreak commotion of a fishing village. They were surrounded by the smell of coal-stoked galley stoves and the sounds made by crew aboard the anchored salt-bankers as they heaved buckets of brown saltwater up the topsides to wash down the decks. A dog

Figure 1-3. Lunenburg Harbour. In 1931 it was filled with working schooners.

yapped and a trash can rattled here and there. A few feet away from where they were lying, an Adams & Knickle worker started clanking about, flaking out shots of anchor chain on the wharf next to *Abundance*.

Lou and his mate were invisible below the rail, so when they raised their heads above it, they startled the A & K guy. "Jaysus, you scared the shit out of me and what the hell are you doin' aboard that ship, eh?" "I'm here to buy her," Lou answered. "Where's Harry Adams?" The response changed the attitude of the chain-flaker and he said that Harry didn't usually get to the yard until 6:30 or 7:00 a.m. "You and your friend want some coffee?" The dockhand's enormous gloved mitts were rusty red and full of chain, so he motioned with his chin toward a corner of a fire-engine-red warehouse where a sheet-metal chimney, puffing coal smoke, stuck at right angles out of the wall.

The two young men stuffed their blankets back in the seabags. As Lou jumped over the rail to the wharf, he turned to the chain-flaker and without smiling said, "That chain belongs to *Abundance*, right?" The flaker didn't answer and Lou turned toward the warehouse, just as Harry Adams opened a man-door inset into one of the huge rolling warehouse doors and stepped out.

"Harry Adams gave me every helping hand he could. He was a very cooperative man, a wonderful man. In fact, when all the skippers saw I wanted to work and had my mind on my business, they were most cooperative. This was unusual treatment for a stranger who has come in their town and into their very life. Everybody was having a hard time running their vessels. They wondered how the devil I was going to keep from failing on account of the economy of the times. But I was very frugal and could do everything myself, which helped me."

One of the understatements of Lou's life was when he said "I was very frugal." It bears repeating—Lou Kenedy kept a tight leash on his wallet, sometimes to the point of penury. This trait was probably not inherited from his family, but rather was self-taught, a part of his strongly-held views about the necessary qualities of a successful schoonerman. As with all of Lou's views, this one was strongly held. There was no such thing as equivocation; there were no grays, just blacks and whites.

Lou eventually carried this extreme frugality into every part of his life. He had a celebrated penchant for using one ruse or another to lower an agreed-upon price or to avoid paying altogether. He was proud of his success in negotiating prices, especially pilot and tug fees.

The purchase of *Abundance* was no different. On September 5, 1931, Lou settled the purchase with Harry. Of course, the original "where-is-as-is" price had been $2,200. But Lou pointed out the ratlines were not installed and demanded $100 be deducted to install them. Harry reluctantly agreed. So Lou and the mate got busy and rattled her down. The job took over a week; afterwards they bent on the sails.

It was not until the onset of the Nova Scotia winter, the middle of November, that *Abundance* was, in all ways, ready for sea. Unfortunately, she had no cargo charter and thus no crew. But Lou used this downtime to explore every cranny of his new ship.

"She had a fo'c's'le house for the crew and a galley forward. Aft she had a paneled cabin divided into a saloon for the skipper and a messroom, along with a head, a chartroom, and an extra stateroom. Off the messroom was a mate's cabin, a cook's room, and a pantry. She had no wheelhouse—the wheel was outside. She had three topmasts and a big spread of sails. She had a coal stove aft and a galley stove forward, kerosene lights all around, and a gasoline deck engine which hove the anchor, worked the cargo winch, and hoisted the sails."[*]

Finally, in December, Harry Adams again showed his helpful nature and put Lou in touch with a Nova Scotia agent who arranged for a lumber cargo to be loaded in Halifax for New York. But it was not to be an auspicious beginning.

Lou formally signed on his crew. When he sailed from Lunenburg, his crew list named L. Kenedy, captain; J. Hubbell, mate; J. Selig, cook; L. (Windy) Mason, seaman; and R. Mayo, seaman. By now it was December 17, 1931, and the Nova Scotia winter had set in with a vengeance. All the lines and sails aboard *Abundance* were frozen. Undaunted, Lou had the crew thaw the rigging and sails temporarily, using pails of heated salt water. The schooner, without a tug or pilot, sailed out of Lunenburg that afternoon.

Arriving in Halifax two days later, Kenedy immediately signed on the first of a score of ship's dogs that would play notable roles in his future adventures. The new puppy was a boisterous German shepherd called Hans.

That afternoon, a tug pulled *Abundance* up and across the Narrows to Dartmouth to load 2-by-10-inch planks. This was before the days when lumber was run through planers at the mill, and these rough-sawed planks— which numbered in the thousands—were a mass of slivers. Tough gloves and

---

[*] Thruelsen, Richard, "The Incredible Captain Kenedy," *The Saturday Evening Post*, December 1953, 19. (Used by permission.)

tough men were needed; Lou's crew did the loading. By now it was Christmas and work was halted for two days. Lou claimed demurrage, which he wasn't worried about getting for Christmas day, but the day after Christmas might be a reach.

The hold was finally topped off on December 29, and they loaded a ton of coal for heat and cooking and 1,100 gallons of water, then prepared to load the deck cargo. They battened down all the hatches, cleared the deck, and started to load in the afternoon. By the end of day of December 30, the deck was loaded to the pin rails. They were towed back down to Halifax to load smaller-dimensioned lumber—two-by-fours and one-inch boards. With only a bit more loading to do the next day, three more crewmen were signed for the trip to New York.

Lou had learned a trick when loading the lumber drogers, and now it came in handy. It was a system of deck loading lumber that let him get rid of the standard eight-inch-square timber stanchions that were used to brace the lumber load against and above the rails. These stanchions stood on end against the rail, generally extending about four feet higher. Once the lumber was loaded close to the rail, these stanchions were placed on the deck every 10 feet or so. As the load rose above the rail, the stanchions held the lumber in place. The problem was that these dunnage stanchions took up valuable width on deck (16 inches times 100 or more feet) that could be used to carry more cargo. An added problem was that when the voyage was over, what did one do with the stanchions? Nobody wanted them.

Instead, Lou loaded the lumber as high as the rails, then draped three-quarter-inch wire cables over the load, allowing the ends to hang down the topsides of the schooner. He then continued to load on top of the cables. When the load was four or five feet above the rail, he brought the loose ends up and over the load, clamped eyes on the ends, and tightened the cables with big turnbuckles. Lou described another advantage later:

> "...if you ever wanted to let the deck load go in a gale of wind, all you had to do was unfasten the turnbuckles and the lumber would take care of itself. It would fly off in the gale. I only did it once, but it was a very handy way to do it."

By 4:00 p.m. on New Year's Eve, 1931, the tug was alongside. Lou went ashore to clear customs. An hour later he returned and was about to order the lines singled up and prepare for the tug to tow them out, but all was not well before the mast.

Attempting to take advantage of imminent departure, the three new Halifax crewmen strode up to Lou, looked him right in the eye, and threatened to quit if their wages weren't increased on the spot. They figured they had the upper hand because Lou was young, it was his first voyage as skipper, and *Abundance* had already cleared out of Halifax. The most aggressive of the mutineers was the new deckhand, Harvey Mason (no relation to the Windy Mason signed in Lunenburg). He stood toe-to-toe with the skipper, screaming, "This ship ain't movin' if we don't get a raise! We need more money to sail at this time of year!"

Lou didn't hesitate. As soon as the first words came out of Mason's mouth, he dove below and pulled his old frontier model .45 out of the chart table drawer. Taking the companionway steps three at a time, Lou marched directly at Mason with the pistol cocked and pointing at him.

The crewman was so startled that he backed up two steps, turned around, and without thinking of the water temperature, belly-flopped into the Narrows. The Narrows describes itself: a constricted arm that connects Halifax Harbour with Bedford Basin to the north. In December that freezing bottleneck sports floating ice.

Mason thrashed as fast as he could around to the wharf side of *Abundance*. Underneath the wharf, he slogged out of the water, dripping, leaving his right boot stuck in the mud, and made for a nearby house. Lou slapped the pistol into his mate's hand. "Keep 'em here," he said. John nervously pointed the old pistol at the other two mutineers and motioned to them to sit down.

Jumping the rail on the dockside, Lou sprinted up to the house. He hollered at Mason to come out and go to work. Hearing the commotion, the local constable arrived and Lou told him the story. Desertion, even from a private ship, was a crime in Canada at the time, and the constable asked Lou if he wanted to swear out a warrant for the deckhand. "Goddamn right I do!" he said, so Lou and the constable grabbed a cab to the local police station. The warrant was sworn and they took the same cab back to the house where Mason was holed up.

The constable bellowed at the upper floor of the house, "Mason, you goin' sailin', or goin' jailin'? I have a warrant on you for desertion." There was a commotion in the house, and shortly thereafter the front door opened. Unseen occupants pushed a wet, poorly shod, crewman Mason backwards through the door into the cold night air. Once more, the constable gave him the choice of sailing or being hauled to the calaboose. He finally elected to go sailing. The officer escorted Lou and the shivering deckhand back to *Abundance* and once more, he was before the mast.

During the fracas, the other two new crewmembers sat on frozen coils of rope. John Hubbell leaned casually against the aft deckhouse waggling the ancient .45 at them. Of course, Hans had to make the situation even more annoying by maintaining a continuous yap-yap-yapping while straining at the end of his tether, his paws up over the rail while he looked shoreward for his master.

Back aboard, Lou yelled at the crew, "You gonna work?" Their eyes were lowered but they all nodded, including a half-frozen Mason. Finally, at 7:00 p.m., after Lou had spent a carefully-accounted-for $7 in taxi fares and a $1 warrant fee, *Abundance*, without a pilot, was under tow outbound. In the last hours of 1931, the tug cast off *Abundance* abeam Maughers Beach Light. Twenty-one-year-old Captain Lou Kenedy was at sea aboard his first command.

This wild start to Lou Kenedy's maritime career was only the beginning of his tumultuous life aboard *Abundance*.

The weather on the first trip was terrible. At 2:30 a.m.[*] on January 2, it was blowing a gale when the outer jib parted, the mizzen boom lift parted, and the fore-gaff splintered. It only got worse. On January 5, the wind died completely, the schooner wallowed, and the constant slatting of the frozen sails caused wide-spread damage to the canvas. The mizzen was ripped badly by the chafing. The next day it was again blowing a gale. Lou was about to heave-to when he spotted Montauk Light, and he kept moving under reduced sail. And, by the way, *Abundance* needed 100 strokes a day on her bilge pump to dry her out.

He finally dropped anchor off City Island on the 6th of January, 1932, but *Abundance* got stuck in the mud while being towed to her berth for unloading. Harvey Mason deserted as soon as the vessel touched the dock in New York. He signed aboard the tern schooner *William Hall* and sailed back to Nova Scotia. The reasons for Harvey's precipitous departure are the stuff of conjecture. Perhaps, just perhaps, it had something to do with Lou's inexperience. Maybe it was the bizarre events prior to departure from Halifax, or maybe it was the equipment failures caused by the foul weather on the way to New York. Whatever the reasons, Harvey ran like hell as soon as *Abundance* arrived with her first cargo under the command of Captain Kenedy. Nonetheless, the skipper was pleased.

"We got to this basin in Brooklyn. Those were the days when it was fun to be at sea. Here were about eight three-masters and four-masters,

---

[*]Prior to World War II, logs of commercial vessels were kept in conventional 12-hour a.m.-p.m. time, converting to the now-standard 24-hour system during or after the war.

all in one basin. All the crews could get together and talk about ships and so on. The skippers and mates and all got together; it was very colorful."

The crew had cheered up a little because there was little to do for the next few days except sit around the stove in the galley and jaw. Ship's work couldn't be done as it was cold and snowing, and they couldn't unload.

As would become a theme, Lou claimed demurrage for a few of the waiting days, but it was refused. He finally unloaded after five days on the hook. He spent some time trying to sign a return cargo but couldn't even find a coal charter due to the deepening Depression.

So after nearly a month repairing the damage from the trip down, on March 8, 1932, *Abundance*, in ballast,* set off back to Halifax. She didn't get out of Long Island Sound before being hit by another storm. Kenedy dropped the hook off Falkner's Island, Connecticut in a Force 10 nor'easter.

SHIP'S LOG
SCHOONER Abundance FROM: New York TOWARDS: Halifax
DATE: Tues. 8th day of March 1932
REMARKS: Dawn finds us lying near Goose Islands 1/4 mile south of us and Falkner's Island's 1/2 mile east, wind and seas dragging us onto the beach.

The winds howled out of the northeast peaking at Force 11 but never subsiding below Force 9. By nightfall *Abundance* was only 100 yards from the breakers. They put out a small kedge anchor as a "last straw." In the log a young Lou Kenedy wrote, "It's blowing a terrible gale." The lack of visibility during the night, the wind roaring through the rigging, and the smashing of breakers a stone's throw away made the ordeal even more terrifying. The crew didn't sleep at all, anticipating the first spar-rattling contact with the beach. But it never came.

On Wednesday, March 9, the sun rose clear, with not a trace of red. The wind had eased and backed to the west, and the tide had taken *Abundance* toward the deep. This good news, however, was tempered by Lou's inability to get the anchors aboard. After setting the foresail, main, and mizzen, he had to endure the sight of the lighthouse keeper at Falkner's Island leaning against the tower rail pointing and grinning at the schooner as it rounded close to the ice-covered light with anchor chains angled aft from her bows.

---

* Empty of profitable cargo, carrying only the weight required for stability.

A hellacious effort finally got the anchors home, and *Abundance* sailed directly to New London to lick her wounds. After days of hard work in New London, she cleared for Halifax, arriving March 19, 1932.

To summarize the first voyage of Captain Louis Kenedy, Jr., it started with a desertion controlled only by police and the threatened use of firearms. Then the mizzen boom lift parted, followed by the parting of the outer jib. Then the flying jib ripped to shreds, and the mizzen tore from chafing. Let's not forget that Harvey successfully deserted and, of course, *Abundance* returned to Nova Scotia in non-revenue-producing ballast. Lou nearly lost his ship on the beach at Falkner's Island. Finally, the anchor stock was bent beyond repair while dragging past an amused lighthouse keeper.

It might be difficult for anyone at the time to recognize this trip as the beginning of a legendary maritime career. Objective observers would probably consider it a disaster at sea. But Lou Kenedy was elated at his "successful" voyage and was as convinced as ever that he had made the right career decision.

On the day *Abundance* was towed back into the Narrows in Halifax Harbour, April 11, 1932, what was left of the crew began loading lumber for Madeira. The same Halifax agent who had arranged the New York voyage signed this load. The only problem was Lou didn't know where the hell Madeira was. He got out some books and finally found it, then:

"I went down to Bert Battson and he had everything from a needle to an anchor; they were selling charts for 10 cents apiece. These were out-of-date charts but they were perfectly good and I got a chart of Madeira for 10 cents. I should have got some more at that price. I did get some, but not as many as I should have."

Abundance was being loaded at the same wharf with the tern schooner *E. C. Adams* under Captain Howie Corkum. Both ships were loading lumber for Madeira out of railroad cars parked on a spur at the wharf. Meanwhile, Lou had hunted up an old flying jib to replace the one blown to ribbons on his last trip and made repairs to the mizzen.

After loading seven railroad cars of lumber into the hold and onto the deck of *Abundance*, on April 23, 1932 she cleared for Madeira with John Hubbell again as the mate; John Evans cooked. Two ABs* and an ordinary seaman also signed on.

---

* Able-Bodied seaman, i.e. a seaman qualified to stand watch, steer the ship, and perform similar responsible tasks.

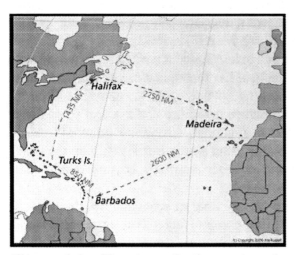

Figure 1-4. The transatlantic route of *Abundance.* **She arrived in Madeira in 14 days and 19 hours, a record at the time.**

Frequent heavy winds made for a fast trip. Once again, equipment aboard *Abundance* started to fail. John Hubbell's precise handwriting in the log indicated that she was leaking due to her hull working in heavy weather. The captain, ever the optimist, thought it was leaking through the deck near the forepeak as she buried her nose in the seas. This disagreement went on from watch to watch for several days. Lou finally told his mate to cut it out and stop writing references to a leaky hull in the log and just keep pumping.

During the trip, the fore and mizzen staysails ripped and the old flying jib that Lou found in Halifax was holed, but *Abundance* arrived in Madeira after only 14 days, 19 hours, a record at the time. She had averaged seven knots. *E. C. Adams* left a few days after *Abundance*, but took 28 days to make the same trip. *Abundance* was a fast vessel and Lou Kenedy was a racing skipper.

The arrival, however, was plagued again with crew problems. The three deckhands—Schwartz, Whynacht, and Boettcher—simply went on binges. The day after arrival, Schwartz was found with liquor in the fo'c's'le, too drunk to work. The next day, Whynacht stumbled aboard at 8:00 a.m., pie-eyed, and couldn't work. Two days later, Boettcher was found in town smashed and was locked up. The same day, Schwartz, again (or still) inebriated, tried to start a fight with the skipper in town and was also locked up. Kenedy bailed them out of jail three weeks later, the same morning *Abundance* cleared for Barbados with a load of onions and wicker chairs. It was June 2, 1932, and *E. C. Adams* had still not arrived in Madeira when *Abundance* sailed.

The three tippling crewmen continued to give Lou problems all the way to Barbados, where they arrived on June 24. Lou off-loaded as fast as he could. In early July, taking only a few days to make repairs, he departed Bridgetown in ballast for Turks Island. He had been telegraphed by his agent in Lunenburg to load salt for Clark's Harbour, Nova Scotia. Again, Lou didn't know where

Clark's Harbour was and had to carefully search his large-scale chart of Nova Scotia to find the tiny inlet.

On the day after they left Barbados, a stowaway, Reginald Reid, a 17-year-old Bajan,* was found in the forepeak. The skipper best describes the incident; his account also sheds light on his temperament and the prevailing racial attitudes of the time:

"We left Barbados in Abundance *on a Saturday evening. Next morning at breakfast, the mate came to me in the mess room and said, 'We have a stowaway aboard—we've got trouble now.' Now a stowaway is a liability because, when you get where you're going, they won't let him land. He has to be sent back to his own country, which would be an expense—a tremendous expense in our minds.*

"So I went on deck and they dragged this colored boy, or young man, back to me on the poop and I said, 'Boy, are you a sailor?' And he said, 'No Sir, I'm not a sailor.' I said, 'Do you know anything about a ship?' He said, 'No!'

"Well, what he was escaping from was poverty in Barbados; it was a pretty hard time for a young fellow to make a living at anything because there was only working in the sugar fields. I said, 'Boy, I'm going to make a sailor out of you now. So the first thing—can you steer?' 'No, I can't steer.' 'Well,' I said, 'you're going to learn.' So I said to the mate, 'Get me two reef-points.'

"Now a reef-point is a line about three-quarters of an inch in diameter and about five feet long. So he gave me two reef-points. And I grabbed this kid by the neck and I shoved him back to the wheel. And to the man at the wheel I said, 'Move over. Let this boy take over.' He said, 'I can't steer.' I said, 'Well that's where you're learning.' So I said, 'Mate, you stand on that side and I'll stand on this side.' And I said, 'Hold it to north by east.' He said, 'I don't know where that is.' I said, 'It's right there!' I pointed at it and I said, 'Now keep it there!'

"So when he was off on one side, the mate would whale him across the back with a double reef-point and when he was off on my side, I'd whale him—flog...

"Well, you know that boy was some smart. It didn't take very long before he learned to steer and he was right on. But the best part of it was, by the time we got to Lunenburg and even long before that, he was pretty able. He learned to do things—how to shift the topsail and the whole works. And then he became a faithful—oh, I wouldn't call him a

---

* Native of Barbados.

servant, but he was more than a sailor. He was faithful to me and he would do anything I wanted him to. He stayed with me as a crew member for several years. He turned out from being nothing into a good, able man. He learned something which did him good for the rest of his life."

The captain's attitudes toward the Caribbean and Bahamian islanders—patriarchal, condescending, and sometimes adversarial—would probably offend people these days. However, in the 1930s the British West Indies was no more than a Raj, and the French and Dutch colonies in the Caribbean and South America were considered dead-end hell-posts for the civil servants and bureaucrats consigned there. The prevailing attitude of whites toward those descended from slaves was little better than contemptuous tolerance. Lou Kenedy, though still a man of his times, treated the individual islanders with significantly more respect than they received from the average white man of the era. His attitudes should be judged by the standards of his own time and place.

Carrying salt up to the Maritimes from pans in the Caribbean and Bahamas was a mainstay of the schooner trade, one of the cargos that kept the schooners in business past their time. Salt fish from Nova Scotia became a staple of the Caribbean population and is still so today. "Sal'fish and rice" is on the menu of most native restaurants, and Caribbean children from Grenada to Grand Cayman are raised on it. Salt fish and lumber down brought salt, rum, and molasses up. This was the "milk run."

As soon as the *Abundance* arrived at Turks, salt lighters immediately started toward the schooner. The captain explains the salt loading process:

"We got to Turks, a little coral reef island in the Bahamas Archipelago. Loo'rd were the Caicos Islands, part of the same group. Sometimes we loaded there. Salt was made in Turks Island, in ponds. They called them pans and they were about 2 feet deep of water, man-made pools, and they pumped from a big lake that came in from the sea. The water was evaporated through the wind and the tremendous sun there and the wind rippling the water. When it came to a certain salinity, it was then pumped up into these pans at a high salt content.

"It was pumped by windmills that were all made from spars from wrecked ships—homemade windmills with cogwheels and other parts made out of the windlasses and things from old ships. Very inventive contraptions that were built by the local people there.

"*These pans got so heavy with salt that the salt wouldn't stay in solution. It would fall to the bottom and build up from the bottom until it would just be a dampness on top of it. Then they'd go in with wagons pulled by mules or donkeys or whatever they were and shovel it up. They brought it to a big windmill where it would be ground into either fisheries size salt or coarse salt. Then they would pile it in mountains. There were hills there 60 and 70 feet high, just salt that they had piled up. They would load ships from these salt hills.*

"*The way they loaded it, they made little cotton bags, like canvas, that would hold half a bushel (about 43 or 44 pounds of salt) and they tied a knot around the neck of it. They had sailboats that were modeled from old lifeboats of wrecked ships, now reinforced and made much stronger with sawn frames and heavier planking. The boats were sloop-rigged and they'd load them right to the deck with these bags of salt, and the water would be almost washing into them. Then they'd sail out to the schooner. We'd sling hatch covers over the side, half way up. Two men would stand on these hatch covers and take bags being passed up from the sloops to them and they'd lay them on the rail. There'd be two fellows grabbing them from the rail and taking them to the hatch, pulling the drawstring on the neck and dumping them in the hold loose, then piling the bags up in bundles of 10. Now after they got through this with each sloop, those bundles were all counted. A government officer there would oversee the counting and that was the way the tally of the salt was made. In other words, the total of bags from that boatload would be added to the sum total. And that's how it was all counted.*

"*There were a few fellows in the hold later, when she was nearly loaded, shoveling—what you call trimming it—out in the wings so the hatches weren't blocked and giving the ship the right trim. We were careful that the ship didn't get loaded by the head* or anything like that.*

"*To carry salt, you need a tight ship. You couldn't have a leaky ship with salt or you'd lose a lot of salt or maybe the salt would get in a solution and plug the pumps, and then you were finished. So many vessels were lost with salt, especially in the latter days when ships were getting older because they weren't fit really to carry salt. It's a dangerous cargo and it was a heavy strain on the ship with such concentrated weight.*"

---

* Out of trim, with excessive weight in the bow.

Sailing from Turks, in fine weather, on July 16, *Abundance* arrived loaded in Clark's Harbour on August 1, 1932. Much to Lou's disappointment, John Hubbell signed off, but his future was bright. He went on to become a leading New York attorney.

Abundance returned to Lunenburg in October and took on a load of lumber for Barbados, and finally Lou had a relatively uneventful outbound voyage. In Bridgetown, as soon as the schooner was unloaded, the crew, of course, got loaded. Several of them couldn't or wouldn't work. But other than that, all went well. They loaded six molasses puncheons and 26 tons of ballast and cleared Barbados for a Turks Island salt cargo on the 26th of October. This return trip, however, would be fateful.

On the 27th, *Abundance* was sailing under six lowers in heavy squalls with only three miles visibility. Her course was NW by ½ N. She blew out her outer jib, and her spanker was ripped but repaired. As quickly as the squalls came up, the wind died leaving a very heavy swell. The noon DR* was 14° 45' N and 61° 50' W. At 3:00 p.m., *Abundance* sailed between St. Lucia and Martinique.

The 28th came in clear, and a moderate breeze sprang up from the northeast. All sails were set including the flying jib and the topsails. In this fine weather, the crew was set to work on the ship. They installed flooring in the holds to take on salt at Turks Island.

The next two days—October 29 and 30—*Abundance* sailed between St. Croix and St. Thomas and headed north toward Grand Turk. She had good weather and uneventful runs. This soon changed:

SHIP'S LOG
SCHOONER Abundance FROM: Barbados TOWARDS: Turks Island
DATE: Mon 31st day of Oct. 1932
REMARKS: This day comes in fine and clear with moderate trade wind.

6:45 a.m. Rudder gear broke and disabled due to broken steering quadrant† casting, clewed up topsails, lowered sails, commenced breaking down wheel box to rig tillers.

7:30 a.m. Rudder unshipped, probably broke pintles from banging.

---

* Ded Reckoning, short for "deduced reckoning": Estimating position based on sailing speed, direction, and elapsed time, when weather does not permit finding position from a sun or star shot. Also called "dead reckoning."

† Metal fitting on the rudder head to which steering cables or ropes attach.

9:00 a.m. Anchored in 10 fathoms in sight of NE breakers, Mouchior Bank [southeast of Grand Turk]. *Lashed oak beams athwart the rudderhead and put steering tackles on.*

Squalls etc. and hard wind*

Hoisted sail and at 12 noon tried to beat to windward, rudder post broke at waterline as soon as strain came on rudder, which floated up astern. Anchored again in bad position.

The next day, November 1, dawned with a northeast gale, and *Abundance* was shipping seas over the bow while at anchor. At 11:00 a.m., Lou finally realized he would have to make a move, as it became clear *Abundance* would eventually drag her anchor. Port-au-Prince was the nearest place to leeward that had the facilities necessary to replace the rudder, so Lou made the decision to go. The crew set the headsails and hove the anchor. They were off to Haiti.

But of course, there was no rudder, so Lou designed an innovative but minimally effective system. He attached a long line on each side of one end of a spare mizzen gaff.† On the opposite end of the gaff he attached a line 30 feet long and tied it off to a cleat on the stern. With difficulty, the crew lowered the gaff astern, leading one of the two long lines to port and the other to starboard. The gaff now streamed behind *Abundance* in line with her keel. When a course change was needed, the crew hauled on the line that corresponded with the desired direction of turn. The after end of the gaff slewed in that direction and the increased drag turned the boat. Then the sails were trimmed to allow the gaff/rudder to be returned (more or less) in line with the keel on the new course. At least that was the theory. Notwithstanding difficulties with tacking and jibing, it worked fairly well.

The waters in this area are usually gin-clear. When the bottom is hard coral and not sand, water visibility can exceed 30 feet even in inclement weather. As *Abundance* began drifting down through the coral heads to the southwest, she had no steerageway. The crew could easily see the brown stalagmites of brain and antler coral awash to port and starboard. Making things even more difficult was the jury-rigged steering system which needed an inordinate amount of speed to function. The gaff banged into the shallower pieces of

---

* *Abundance* was beginning to feel the force of the storm simply named "1932 Hurricane Number 10." The slow-moving storm later wreaked havoc on Cayman Brac, destroying almost every home, with the loss of 109 lives. Estimated wind velocity was 150 to 200 mph.

† Spar that controls the head of the mizzen sail. On tern schooners the mizzen usually had larger sails than the mainmast, with a long, heavy boom and gaff.

coral as it swayed from side to side in the choppy seas. Even at five knots, the steering system didn't allow *Abundance* to dodge coral heads. It was only luck that in the two hours it took to reach deep water, she never struck an obstacle.

Wednesday, the second of November, 1932, came in "very squally." At 6:00 a.m. the fore and main were set, and after spending the night heading southwest, the course was set to WNW. The Monti Cristi light on the northwest corner of the Dominican Republic was bearing southeast, 10 miles distant. At 10:00 a.m., the wind was blowing such a gale that Lou was forced to lower the main and foresails. By noon he logged the wind blowing hard out of the east and northeast "all the time." By 2:00 p.m., Tortuga was barely visible to the south, and his course was due west. At 11:00 p.m. that night, in very heavy seas and wind, St. Nicholas light on the northwest tip of Haiti was sighted.

By midnight, *Abundance* had wobbled abeam St. Nicholas light. At 2:00 a.m., the winds had abated enough to reset the main and set the trysail in order to get a bit more to windward. The course at this point was SE by E½E. At 4:00 a.m., Faux Pointe was six miles east. *Abundance* was closing in on the target and spirits were high. By 8:00 a.m., the seas were calm, a nice east- northeast trade piped up, and Faux Pointe had receded; it bore 10 miles northwest. An hour later, however, the seas turned choppy, and the breeze veered south of east. *Abundance* could not lay the weather side of Gonave Island. If Lou took it to leeward, there were no anchorages, and it would be impossible to make Port-au-Prince. So with Gonave Island only six short miles due south, *Abundance* squared away for Kingston, Jamaica.

The next day brought rough seas from the northeast and southeast. By 7:00 p.m., the crew, tired from battling the sea and cold from the constant spray, sighted the old cast iron lighthouse at Point Morant on the extreme eastern point of Jamaica. The rolling and strain on the gear was terrific. By midnight, *Abundance* was abeam the light.

At the time *Abundance* rounded the lighthouse, the wind was off the port quarter. She was on a port tack with only the trysail and main set. As she turned the corner to head west toward Kingston, Lou called his mate aft. The wind was deafening and the seas were blowing hard white blasts of water over the deck. He yelled, "We gotta jibe. Get to it." The mate and crew worked their way forward to carry out the order. Lou stayed close to the shore to take advantage of the protection the island should provide from the northeast gale.

But within minutes of jibing and rounding Point Morant, the Force 11 gale clocked south and then varied between southeast and southwest. Because of the wind shift, the main gaff suddenly jibed before the make-shift steering gear could correct the course. The mainsail leech boltrope

Figure 1-5. *Abundance* **hove to.**

parted, and the sail tore from the strain. The wind now blew Force 12 with hard rain. Abruptly, the main boom jibed, and the violence of the jibe pulled the main-sheet padeyes out of the deck.

Abundance was now abeam Rocky Point and was tossed around like a toy. Lou desperately tried to hold her course toward Kingston under nothing but the trysail. Then, without warning, the hurricane-force winds veered to the west of south and tore the trysail to shreds.

The din of the wind, rain, and sea now overtook all senses. Green water broke over the port topsides, flooding the deck. Lou and the mate had to holler into each other's ears to be heard. With no sails, *Abundance* was at the mercy of the storm and was shoved by the white-capped rollers toward the coral beach, now only a couple of hundred yards to leeward.

We'll let 22-year-old Captain Louis Kenedy finish the description of that day, Saturday, November 5, 1932:

SHIP'S LOG

SCHOONER Abundance *FROM: Barbados TOWARDS: Kingston, Jamaica*

DATE: Sat 5th day of Nov. 1932

REMARKS; Midnight – Terrific squall and rain; split foresail and blew it to ribbons. Drifted down in to SE point into breakers. Could not keep her off under main and headsails or make any headway to get around the point. Vessel ashore at 1 a.m. on coral beach studded with sharp coral rocks; nearly worked us all off! Finally washed well up onto the beach. One side stove in. Hurricane blowing. Abandoned ship at 8 a.m. left her with the colors at masthead.

Several keels nearby. Schooner Copperfield lost.

So ends the career of one of the fastest 3-masted schooners ever built.

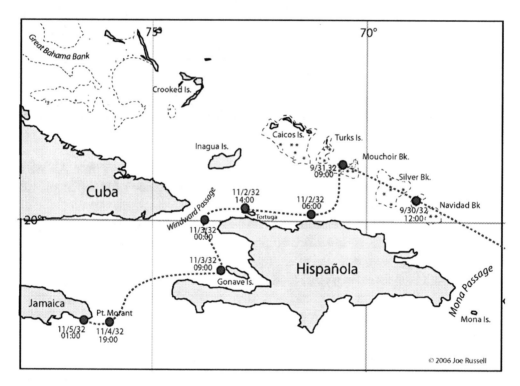

Figure 1-6. The last voyage of *Abundance*.

The skipper told the crew to collect one bag each of their personal belongings, and they abandoned ship. Lou, always the trader, chose to fill a suitcase with bottles of rum hoping to turn the liquor into some badly needed cash. He also stuck that old frontier .45 in his belt, the one that John Hubbell had used to keep the deserting crew in line during the first trip to New York.

They started walking west down the beach and were soon picked up by a donkey cart that took them most of the 30 miles to Kingston. Here's where things started to get a bit complicated.

As if losing the ship weren't enough, during the trip to Kingston, Lou, the mate, and the now fully-grown Hans somehow became separated from the crew. Without warning, they found themselves surrounded by a gang of Jamaican robbers-salvagers in a small town just east of Kingston. Lou and the mate didn't know where the crew had gone and spun around desperately looking for them.

The members of the gang were all carrying large sticks. Two of the biggest men demanded money and the suitcases. True to form, Lou told them to go to hell. He was clubbed on the back from behind. He dropped his suitcase to confront the attackers, and another one picked it up and started running. Lou pulled out the old pistol and shot the fleeing thief in the leg. The thief fell

Figure 1-7. On November 5, 1932, rudderless, with a hurricane howling, *Abundance* was abandoned on the southeast shore of Jamaica with her starboard side stove in.

screaming and dropped the suitcase full of booze. It was immediately picked up by another gang member who hightailed it for a nearby stilt beach shack with Lou and the mate in hot pursuit. The remaining gangsters followed close behind. The situation had some flavor of the Keystone Kops, mixed with real menace.

The rum thief entered the shack leaving two cohorts on the front porch to stop anyone from entering. Lou side-stepped them and crashed through the front door. He pulled out the .45 again just as a half dozen more gang members stormed in and joined the fracas. He swung his arms and fists, wildly and sporadically firing the gun, once nearly shooting the suitcase thief in the face. Lou was bleeding freely from a superficial scalp wound and blood was spattered on everyone and everything. He shot the cabin up pretty well and a tense standoff ensued. The sight of blood seemed to cool the ardor of the gang, as each member took time to inspect himself to find out if he was the bleeder.

Outside, the mate finally got the attention of the local constabulary, and the brouhaha was put down quickly. The gang, notorious for previous problems, was soon rounded up. The police were so pleased to get the gang in jail and under control that the leg shooting was officially overlooked.

Hans was no help during the fracas. He headed for the hills as soon as the first shot was fired and came back wagging his tail as soon as things calmed down.

Finally arriving in Kingston, Lou sold what was left of *Abundance* to a salvage company and arranged passage for the crew, including the stowaway Reginald Reid, back to Nova Scotia.

Each day's page in Captain Kenedy's ship's logs ends with the same simple phrase, which seems appropriate here:

So ends this day.

Figure 2-1[*]

The ship: *Adams*	Material: Wood
Year of Launching: 1929	Length between perpendiculars: 164 feet
Rig: Tern Schooner	Beam: 32 feet
Builder: Arthur D. Storey, Essex, Massachusetts	Draft: 16 feet
	Depth of Hold: 13 feet
Designer: Edwin C. Perkins	Cargo capacity: 500 tons

Chapter 2   *Adams*

Arthur Storey built the schooner Lincoln *in 1919. She exemplified the yard's tradition of building the finest fishing and trading schooners of the time, which included the* Gertrude L. Thebaud.[†] Lincoln *was an immediate success in the eastern coastal lumber and coal trade. This success prompted Storey to begin work on* Lincoln's *sister ship,* Adams, *in the fall of 1920. The two ships were of identical design except that* Adams *had a clipper bow and* Lincoln *had a rounded "spoon" bow.*

---

[*] *Adams* at LaHave, Nova Scotia, with a hold full of lumber and a full, 10-foot-high deck load (1933).

[†] See note about *Gertrude L. Thebaud* at the end of this chapter.

Work continued through the winter of 1921, but schooner shipping was declining along with the economy of the whole country. By 1922, Arthur regretted ever beginning construction of Adams. *The nearly-finished hull languished for years in his shipyard. She became a landmark, with her weathered breast hooks overhanging the street in front of Arthur's office.*

During this time, Adams *acted as nothing more than an imaginary ship in which Arthur's children and their friends would play pirate games. But occasionally, during slack times, workmen would chase the kids out and finish a project or two on the ship. Eventually, the foredeck was framed and her designer, Ed Perkins, completed the massive aft deckhouse. Then she lay fallow for another few years.*

Lincoln *was still marginally profitable when, in 1928, she was put out of service by a collision in Boston Harbor with the steam collier* Sewall's Point. *This prompted Arthur Storey to finish* Adams *as a replacement. But now, after so much time in the weather with rain water draining into her, many dry-rotted planks had to be replaced, along with virtually all deck planking.*

Not named after the second president, but rather for the family name of Arthur's wife, Adams *finally slid into the Essex River on April 13, 1929, nearly eight years after her keel was laid. She was towed to Gloucester where she started a relatively successful career under Captain William H. Kelson, the former master of* Lincoln. *Though no one realized it at the time, this was the last launching of a wooden, three-masted cargo schooner in North America. Hundreds had been built before her, but their time had passed.*

One incident that was to be of vital importance to Lou Kenedy was that in October of 1929, Adams, *with Kelson in command, struck Dry Ledge at the mouth of the Latele River near Eastport, Maine. She carried a full cargo of coal, and the receding tide left her lying on her port side with both her bow and stern overhanging the ledge. This abuse caused a severe hog in her port sheer[*] from which she suffered for the rest of her days.*

Arthur Storey died in 1932, and Adams *was returned to Gloucester to face an estate sale.*

Captain Kenedy didn't write or speak much about the Adams, *and the brevity of this chapter reflects that fact. The logs went with the vessel, and he owned her for a relatively short but turbulent time.*

* * *

---

[*] The sheer line is the fore-and-aft curve of the plank just below the gunwale. A "hog" is a displacement from a proper, smooth curve, indicating the original hull shape is deformed.

At the end of February, 1933, Lou and the *Abundance* crew arrived safely in Nova Scotia, except Reginald Reid, the stowaway, who was sent back to Barbados directly from Jamaica due to "irregularities" in his documentation. Lou insisted that all the other hands work their way back if they were able. Lou worked as an AB on a four-master. As soon as his feet touched Canadian soil, he was off looking for another schooner. The crew signed on to other ships in LaHave or Halifax. Lou promised to notify them as soon as he bought his next schooner and assured them they all had berths aboard any ship he commanded.

In Lunenburg, Lou heard that the well-known shipbuilder, Arthur Storey, had died. More to the point, he heard that Arthur's tern schooner *Adams* was up for sale. Lou was aware of Storey's reputation as an excellent shipwright, and the young skipper had first-hand knowledge of some of the legendary ships he built. He got the Storey family on the phone and expressed his condolences, then immediately turned the subject to the *Adams*. Over the phone, they agreed on the price—$2,500—that Lou would pay if she was in good condition as described. Jumping in the Stutz, Lou made the trip down to Gloucester in two days and negotiated the deal. Always finding a reason to lower the agreed-upon price, he bought her for $2,000 and set about getting her ready for sea.

Within a month he had her reasonably seaworthy and hoisted the Stutz aboard as deck cargo. He signed on a crew to take her to Meteghan on the "French Shore" of Nova Scotia where it was cheaper to have her caulked. She leaked like a sieve and needed caulking from stem to stern, including every deck seam. She was a large vessel, and Lou, not wanting to hire more men than necessary, took several months to get the job done. But he finally cleared Meteghan for Bridgewater in May, 1933:

"Took me 14 days! People thought I was lost. It was flat calm the whole time. We drifted with the tide coming down to Cape Sable. When the tide would flood, we'd anchor; and when the tide would ebb, we would haul up the anchor and drift. And that's all the progress we ever made in the Bay of Fundy.

"Eventually we got around the Cape and I thought, well if we get a sou'west wind, there would be nothing to it. We drifted and slatted and banged and we finally got in sight of Cape LaHave. Then the wind came east—a gale of wind. So I stood her off to the south under short sail and waited till that was over. Then there was a couple of calm days and eventually, in 14 days, we got into Bridgewater. Finally we had a fair wind. We sailed up to Bridgewater, right to the wharf, and loaded for the West Indies. Then we went back to Clark's Harbour and we made another trip."

On this second trip, in late July, 1933, *Adams* made the 900-mile run from Bridgetown to Turks Island in four and a half days. This is averaging 200 miles a day, or better than eight knots. That's a hell of a fast trip. *Adams* arrived at midnight, and the pilot came out in his sloop with his two sons as crew. It was blowing hard out of the northeast. As *Adams* jogged along toward the anchorage, the pilot's sloop followed behind. Suddenly, a meteor crossed the sky lighting up the deck with a brilliant green light. The old black pilot said, "Cap, that's something—every time you see something like one of those, it comes a hurricane." Lou patiently explained, "Well, a hurricane is only over a small area down in the West Indies, but a meteor can be seen for hundreds and hundreds of miles." The pilot answered, "I don't know, but that's what happens." Lou, tired of the conversation, replied, "Well, I'll believe it when I see it."

The next morning the northeast wind increased to a gale. Black clouds, "minister's eyebrows," descended and scudded past the topmasts. The pilot was supposed to stay aboard until loading began, but out of nowhere he said, "Cap, I gotta go tend to my chickens." Lou responded, "Can't your boys take care of the chickens? I need a pilot aboard when we start loading." Of course, no loading was going to take place in the gale, and while Lou thought the wind would abate, the pilot knew better. He wanted to get ashore before the winds made it impossible to get home. "I don't trust dem to do da job right," said the old black man with finality. An hour later, under a scandalized* main and a working jib, the pilot sloop arrived, again with the pilot's sons aboard, and took the old man ashore. Lou never did find out how the pilot notified his sons that he wanted them to pick him up.

And the glass was dropping like a stone.

Adams had only one anchor down, because if she dragged both anchors over the ledge, it would demand a tremendous effort to bring them both up. The gale swung the schooner close by a steamer mooring, and the crew quickly attached two heavy hawsers to it. They let out a shot of chain, and the mooring shared the load with the anchor.

When the pilot first arrived, the crew took the tarps off the hatch covers in anticipation of loading salt at first light. But by midmorning, the wind had piped to such a point that any conversation had to be shouted, and the hatch covers were starting to lift. The crew immediately battened everything back down and held on. *Adams* slued violently, changing tacks while "sailing" on the mooring. She would take a port tack until the hawsers tightened, then jerk

---

* Sailing in high winds with the peak halyard partially lowered and the clew raised, which spills air from the sail and reduces the effects of the wind force.

to a starboard tack and fall off until the hawser brought her up short. She repeated the maneuver hundreds of times. Finally the hawsers frayed and parted, leaving *Adams* abeam to the wind, laid over 30 degrees to starboard and dragging her single anchor seaward. This bit of bad news gave the crew the final clue: They were in a hurricane.

The nearest land to leeward was Caicos, 22 miles northwest. Lou was gripped by *déjà vu*—the specter of *Abundance* being thrown ashore in Jamaica haunted him. It wasn't going to happen again, by God!

The first problem was that *Adams* was drifting sideways, with 40 or 50 fathoms of chain dragging an anchor that would alternately catch a coral head, then break loose. This caused the chain to jump the wildcat with a tremendous racket and, slowly but surely, the anchor chain was ripped from *Adams'* chain locker.

"So we rigged relieving tackles onto the chain under the fo'c's'le head. We could retrieve a fathom or two of chain at a time, then we would re-rig the tackles. And after several hours, we got the anchor up, which we were some glad of. But, in the meantime, you could only work on deck under the lee of rails—she was heeled over so much..."

Then the spanker blew up, literally. It was stopped down but not well enough and when the stops failed, it blew up like a piece of bubble gum. For an instant the sail stayed inflated, then exploded. The shriek of the wind was now matched by the popping of whiplashed canvas.

After two hours fighting the storm, it fell absolutely quiet. From indescribable and deafening violence to absolute calm took less than two minutes. Lou knew they were in the eye of the hurricane, and they had precious little time to get things in order. He needed steerageway so she'd be heading north when the eye went through and the wind turned south. They immediately pulled up the forestaysail and then began raising the foresail which was in fairly good condition. But when it was only halfway up, the wind backed to the south, piped to 50 knots, and tore the bolt rope out. They were lucky to get the sail down without shredding it. With only the forestaysail set, *Adams* ran off before the wind. The log was streamed but it blew out in front of the schooner. Later, Lou figured *Adams* was doing 11 knots with only the forestaysail set.

The skipper was at the helm; he didn't trust anyone else to steer under these circumstances. If she broached, there was no way to get her back underway with the short rig. The wind had risen to over 100 knots, and Lou was concentrating on guiding *Adams* between Turks and Caicos Islands, when he felt a sting on the back of his neck; then another; and another; then something hit him in the back and in his hair. Abruptly, *Adams* was aswarm with moths. They were being blown by the storm and were so thick the windward side of the deckhouses and spars were carpeted with layers of fuzzy squashed insects.

Then the pigeons started—hundreds of them. They slammed into the deck, the rigging, and the crew. The poor crew, all but Lou, hunkered below or leeward of the deckhouse to avoid being pelted by them. There was no wheel house on *Adams,* so Lou stayed at the helm and got pummeled every so often by storm-blown fowl. A 100-knot pigeon felt like a fist hitting him, a fist that blew up into a cloud of fluff when it struck. Feathers blew everywhere. The captain had wrapped himself in a blanket when the moths started and that helped blunt the pigeon blows a bit. The epic seemed to be directed by both DeMille and Hitchcock. First the moths, a pestilence of Biblical proportions, followed by a scene from *The Birds*. Someone figured out later that the hurricane winds had picked up the moths and pigeons in Haiti or the Dominican Republic and simply dragged them northeastward to the sea.

But the problems weren't over yet. As Lou scraped the bugs off his face and neck, the mate popped his head up through the aft deckhouse companionway and yelled over the storm, "Cap! The cook is cut and he's bleeding to death!" Disgusted, Lou just said, "Jesus H. Christ. What the hell is this shit?"

"So I told the mate to take the wheel and I went forward the best I could. I got in the galley and here sat the cook with his foot in a bucket that looked like it was half full of blood. His calf had a big gash in it, and it was pumping blood right out. A cooking pot made of china that he used to mix bread in—a big one—had fallen off a shelf and come down and hit the table, and broke, and then came down on him and cut his leg badly.

"And so I said, 'Boy oh boy,' and grabbed a dishcloth or a towel and made a tourniquet and put it on. And I said to the fellows, 'Keep that tourniquet on him and lay him down on a settee in the galley.' I had no more time to look after that. So I went aft.

"An hour or so later, one of the fellows came back and said, 'The cook is dying!' So I went up again and here he was—he was a colored man and he was a great cook. He was with me, eventually, for 12 years..."

Neville, the Bajan cook, didn't look well. At the time, Lou was afraid he had lost too much blood and wouldn't make it. His color, usually a glistening blue-black, turned gray as if he had been powdered. He was having trouble speaking. Lou, always handy with a needle and sail thread, stitched up the gash and bandaged it tightly to stop the bleeding. They carried Neville to his bunk where he finally recovered, but only after several days of bed rest. This was an unfortunate turn of events on several levels as Neville was the best cook Lou ever had and no one else aboard could even boil water.

That night, the wind abated. They had been blown 100 miles north of Turks and had no usable sails to power *Adams* back to the harbor. The wind returned to normal northeast trades, and Lou set the trysail. They hove to for days while repairing sails. The spanker was torn up badly. It was a big sail as the mizzen boom was 70 feet long. The foresail and mainsail were also a mess. By the time they repaired the sails and got back underway, the trades and current had pushed *Adams* south of Turks. With the light breezes that seem to follow hurricanes, it took another week for *Adams* to beat back up to Turks Island.

"We got back there and everybody came out from the Island, hollering and yelling and they said, 'Oh, we thought you were gone. We had a church service for you. You're the first ship that was ever caught in a hurricane here that survived.' So that made us feel pretty good. And they were happy as well. Several people ashore were killed during that hurricane. Two or three were blown right off the Island into the water and drowned, and some were killed—tin roofs were flying around and cutting them. It was quite a tragedy and it was very local. That hurricane, I heard later from a meteorologist, was only about 60 miles wide and we were right smack in the middle of it. Although I had been in others, I had never been in the middle of one before. I have great respect for a hurricane compared with a northern gale. A gale looks just like a squall compared with a hurricane."

This episode started with the admonition by the old pilot that a hurricane always blows in after sighting a large meteor. From that day on, Lou never scoffed at island juju.

After loading the salt, the remainder of the trip to Clark's Harbour was routine. In December of 1933 *Adams* slid down to Barbados loaded chock-a-block with lumber out of Halifax. It was an uneventful voyage; she off-loaded and quickly cleared Bridgetown sailing in ballast for Turks. There she again

Figure 2-2. Stowing lumber as deck cargo.

loaded 500 tons of salt for Clark's Harbour. However, north of Bermuda and only 300 miles south of Cape Sable, a combination of heavy Gulf Stream seas and a series of gales caused *Adams'* hull to start working.

It was nothing alarming at first, because *Adams* always leaked more than most schooners. But it grew worse as the gales strengthened and the seas rose. Salt was no cargo to carry in a leaking ship, and the hand pumps clogged quickly. Lou ordered the donkey engine fired up to run the big pumps. This deck engine was used to handle cargo and raise sails. She was also rigged to run the two main pumps, and the powered pumps kept up with the inflow for a day. The second day of the storm, two great, green-water seas were taken over the bow, and the donkey engine was swamped out of service.

Later that day, the seas abated but not before *Adams* had settled in the water and her decks were awash. The respite gave the crew time to get the engine working again. But no sooner had the pumps started than another gale blew up, and the Gulf Stream again became a maelstrom. The string of gales continued for nine straight days. On the morning of the tenth day:

> "...we saw a steamer through the spindrift and haze. He was hove to and drifting sideways, unable to make any headway against the weather. By this time, Adams was almost awash and it was blowing a 50-mile-an-hour gale from the nor'west."[*]

The tramp steamer *Blairesk* out of Glasgow, under the command of Captain John MacFayden, was the only salvation for the crew of *Adams*. It was Lou Kenedy's expert seamanship that maneuvered the logy schooner close in the lee of the steamer so the crew could scramble up the lines and rope ladders draped over *Blairesk*'s rails. Acting fast, four of *Adams'* crew

---

[*] Thruelsen, Richard, "The Incredible Captain Kenedy," *The Saturday Evening Post*, 19 December 1953, 83. (Used by permission.)

Figure 2-3. Sailing off Turks in rising wind and seas before most of her canvas blew out.

caught a heaving line, jumped overboard, drew themselves hand over hand to the steamer's topsides, clambered up the rope ladders, and were safe aboard. Now the only ones left aboard *Adams* were Captain Kenedy, mate Paul Johnson, and Neville the cook, the same cook who was cut so badly during the previous voyage.

When it was time for Neville to jump, the Bajan cook froze. He didn't know how to swim and wasn't about to cooperate in any rescue effort that included jumping in the cold briny. He simply got down on his knees, wrapped his arms around a stanchion, and refused to budge. As Lou and the mate pulled one of his arms free, he grabbed onto something else with the other hand.

The freighter having substantial freeboard[*] where the foundering *Adams* had none, drifted to leeward faster than the schooner, and the tables were turned. *Blairesk* was now 50 yards downwind. Lou concluded that the only way to escape was to use the *Adams'* dory. Lou and the mate again slogged the schooner down close by the freighter. The dory was chocked on the poop hatch, just forward of the mizzen. Though it was too heavy to lift,

---

[*] Distance from the waterline to the deck.

the decks were awash as *Adams* was sinking, so the men were able to tip the dory over the rail as *Adams* rolled.

Quickly, the three men jumped in and rowed over to *Blairesk*. The steamer was rolling rail under, beam to the seas as they closed in. The idea was to jump directly from the dory to the ropes along the side of the steamer. The leap had to be coordinated with the roll of the freighter and the violent pitching of the dory. The cook was the first to jump but lost his grip on the rope ladder when the ship rolled and ended up in the drink after all.

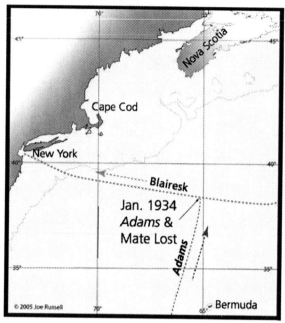

Figure 2-4. Chart: The last voyage of *Adams*.

Flailing his arms, he caught a life ring thrown from the deck and was pulled over to the ladder for a second try. This time the cook was successful, and the mate went next. Lou made sure Paul was climbing the rope ladder before he belly-flopped out of the dory himself and swam to the freighter's topsides. He grabbed the ladder just as the mate reached the rail. Then *Blairesk* rolled heavily, taking the ropes, Lou, and the rail under water for what seemed like an eternity.

Unfortunately, it *was* eternity for Paul Johnson. When *Blairesk* rolled back, there was Lou, dangling from the rail, dripping but hugging the rope ladder with all his strength. The mate was gone. He had been straddling the rail when the steamer rolled gunnels under, didn't have a proper grip, and was washed free. He was never seen again.

Finally, at sundown, *Adams* sank while *Blairesk* was still hove to fighting the gale. The little dory that had saved Lou and the cook splashed about untethered in the lee of the freighter until late the following day when *Blairesk* could finally make some headway against the storm and toward New York.[*] Captain Kenedy rarely spoke of *Adams*, but much later he said:

---

[*] *Blairesk* was sunk by a German U-boat on the day after Christmas, 1939, with the loss of all hands.

"Unfortunately, she was built on a shoestring and she had plenty good wood and equipment, but poorly fastened, which I didn't realize or I overlooked, because she was so new. She was a fine looking vessel and a good sailer."

First, *Adams* wasn't that new. Captain Kenedy always referred to her as being only five years old, but she was lost in 1934 and her keel was laid in 1920. Admittedly, 14 years is not old for a schooner, but for almost nine years she was laid up, enduring the elements while under various states of construction and disrepair. In retrospect, the comment that he "overlooked" certain faults was accurate but probably referred more to the port sheer hogging than faulty fastening. His disregard for *Adams'* faults reflected a young man's blind love of and ardent desire to return to the sea as master of a schooner.

Though Lou Kenedy was not one to dwell on his own shortcomings or feel guilty about any past action, he probably felt some pangs of responsibility for the loss of *Abundance,* so we might cut him some slack when he blamed the loss of *Adams* on poor fastenings. But there is no evidence *Adams* was "built on a shoestring." The fastening of *Adams'* planking was begun prior to any sailing industry or national economic downturn. According to records, she was fastened in the same manner as *Lincoln* which, to anyone's knowledge, never had a problem with her fastenings. Further, the Arthur D. Storey yard had a first-rate reputation and was responsible for constructing some of the most famous schooners of the time.

The most likely reason that *Adams* worked and leaked as she did is that the Latele River grounding damaged her frame timbers and stringers far more than was realized—or admitted. Those years of abuse in the Storey yard, the grounding in the Latele, along with a week or more of fighting gales in the open Atlantic were the obvious reasons for her excessive working and resultant leaking.

As an aside, the port sheer hog offers a pretty good clue as to why every snapshot of *Adams* was taken of the starboard side.

So ends this day.

Gertrude L. Thebaud: In New England and the Maritimes, the America's Cup managed a poor second in excitement, publicity, and anticipation to the "International Fishermen's Race." The race was sailed by the two fastest Grand Banks schooners—one from Canada, one from the U.S. Run in intermittent years beginning in 1920, the last of these classic regattas was held in October, 1938, off Gloucester, Massachusetts.

Decided by the best out of five races, the final series pitted the 17-year-old Lunenburg schooner *Bluenose* against *Gertrude L. Thebaud,* the last fishing schooner built in the Gloucester area. This U.S. entry was built in Arthur D. Story's Essex yard in 1930. Partly completed *Adams,* Lou Kenedy's second command and the last tern schooner built in America, languished a few yards away.

With thousands of people and the press watching, *Gertrude L. Thebaud,* skippered by Ben Pine, lost the fifth and last race by six minutes. Captain Pine's dream of returning the International Fishermen's Race trophy to Gloucester never came to pass. A wonderful description of this race is retold in Chapter 43 of actor Sterling Hayden's classic biography, *The Wanderer.* Captain Hayden was a young maintopmastman aboard the *Thebaud* during that historic contest.

Figure 3-1

The ship: *Sea Fox*
Year of Launching: 1888
Rig: Schooner
Official #: 118216
Builder: Harlan & Hollingsworth,
　　Wilmington, Delaware

Material: 7/16-inch Swedish iron plate
Length between perpendiculars: 115 feet
Beam: 23 feet 11 inches
Draft: 12 feet
Displacement: 100 ton

Chapter 3   *Sea Fox*

Captain Kenedy's first non-wood vessel, Sea Fox, *was a magnificent yacht, but she was small compared to* Abundance *at 138 feet and* Adams *at 169 feet. She was designed by her first owner, A. Cass Canfield, at that time the commodore of the Seawanhaka Corinthian Yacht Club, and she served as the club flagship.*

In 1889, in a howling sou'wester, she won the Goelet cup race that ran between Brenton Reef, Block Island, West Island, and back. In that race, she beat the America's Cup defender, Mayflower.

She was then purchased by Dallas B. Pratt, a rear commodore of the New York Yacht Club who, in 1912, was elected commodore, and Sea Fox *became his flagship.*

NYYC's annual cruise of 1913 started at New London on to Newport, Vineyard Haven, and around Cape Cod to Provincetown. A $500 cup was presented to the winning vessel built before 1900.

In the NYYC's report of the race, "...some 30-odd yachts competed on this cruise, including over a dozen schooners; Elena *was notably successful at the outset but did not continue beyond Newport. A Marblehead schooner,* Taormina, *designed and built by Lawley in 1906, owned by William S. Eaton, was a winner, as was* Endymion, *the* **flagship** **Sea Fox** *[author's emphasis] and* Irolita..."

During World War I, Sea Fox *was pressed into service as a West Indies freighter. In 1929 she was refitted as a yacht, owned by Mrs. R. D. Upham, a widow from whom Lou bought her in 1934.*

* * *

After the loss of *Adams* and upon reaching New York aboard *Blairesk*, Lou was essentially broke. He paid off the crew and sent Paul Johnson's family his wages, along with a letter of condolence that Lou never thought was written with an appropriate sense of sorrow.

Reginald Reid, the former stowaway, was competent enough by this time to catch a berth on any sailing vessel in port. He signed aboard another schooner in the West Indies trade. Lou, an expert rigger, took seasonal work at a Stamford, Connecticut beach club. He didn't have the least doubt that he would soon skipper another trading schooner.

He soon found one: *Sea Fox*. She was built along the lines of *America* and other racing yachts built in the late nineteenth and early twentieth centuries. She was laid up on blocks at the same City Island boatyard where Lou worked after the *Tusitala* days.

Lou's net worth at the time was next to nothing, so for the first and only time in his life, he took a partner. Lou Kenedy's lifelong love of fast and unique cars led him into a friendship with a Stamford, Connecticut garage owner named Frank Muzzio. Frank was a schemer who lived on the periphery of legal and proper society. Lou's enthusiasm and talent for self-promotion convinced Frank to invest in the "Sea Fox Shipping Company," naming Lou as managing partner and captain of the vessel. With this backing, Lou was able to convince Mrs. Upham she should sell, and with Frank's investment, Lou had enough cash for a proper refit.

Sea Fox was a yacht, and below decks she was magnificent. Lou and Frank figured she would be perfect as a research vessel and for the charter trade, while avoiding the vagaries of the schooner cargo business, which by this time (1934) was in dismal straits. A group of college friends had already voiced serious interest in taking a winter cruise to the Caribbean.

Meanwhile, the City Island boatyard owner was not happy to see his long-standing storage fee disappear and tried to enforce his rule against owners working on their yachts in the yard. Yard employees were supposed to perform all labor. *Sea Fox* was in dire need of bottom paint. Of course, even if Lou had the money, he wasn't about to shell out $400 to have the schooner's bottom painted by the yardmen. And Captain Lou Kenedy couldn't bear the thought of paying to have her hauled again when she was already on the hard. Unthinkable! So he and a few friends snuck into the yard after dark, slapped 20 gallons ($25 worth) of ablative paint* on her bottom and stole away into the night. When the boatyard owner confronted him, Lou explained that *Sea Fox* was a working schooner, not a yacht, and at any rate, he was broke. His excuses fell on deaf ears; the yard owner kept threatening legal action. Finally, Lou just declared, "I can't pay you. If you want to wipe the goddamn paint off, go ahead." That ended the argument. *Sea Fox* was launched and towed to Stamford, Connecticut, where Lou continued working at the beach club while slowly bringing *Sea Fox* up to yacht condition.

The widow Upham had been anxious to get rid of the vessel and agreed to take payments. The $100 plus food that Lou earned at the beach club just covered the $90 monthly payment. With Muzzio's financial help, by the fall of 1934 she was all Bristol fashion except for the mainmast, which was rotted at the deck. She also needed some rigging changes that could be done easier—and cheaper—in Lunenburg. Lou signed Frank Muzzio as the mate, enlisted a group of friends as crew, and they cleared for Nova Scotia.

> *"We wanted to put a new mainmast in her and make various other rigging repairs, so that fall I gathered a crew of friends and various unemployed who were willing to take an October ocean trip for free. We ran the* Sea Fox *down to Lunenburg in Nova Scotia. At the time my entire capital was $150. With that money we had a new Douglas fir mainmast stepped in her—it had been shipped east as a derrick boom and hadn't been used—and replaced some of the rigging. Then we brought her back to Stamford."†*

---

* Since she was iron, he couldn't use copper paint due to possible electrolysis damage.

† Thruelson, Richard, "The Incredible Captain Kenedy," *The Saturday Evening Post*, 26 December 1953, 23. (Used by permission.)

The departure from Lunenburg illustrated yet another example of how Lou was convinced that a bit of tough love could straighten out a wayward soul. A young AB, Jerry Wendell, signed articles in Lunenburg for the trip back to Stamford but wasn't on board when she sailed. As *Sea Fox* ghosted away from the wharf, Jerry showed up, hollering and waving his arms, so Lou sent the tender back to pick him up. He was uncontrollably drunk, and Lou, being cautious, put him on the captain's watch to keep an eye on him.

The procedure at night aboard a schooner was that every 30 minutes, the helmsman, hearing the ship's clock below, copied the ring on the main bell at the wheel. Upon hearing this, the bow watch returned the same number of rings on the bow bell. This way everyone knew the time and that the helmsman and bow watch were awake and alert. The very first night out, Lou rang four bells at 10:00 p.m., but there was no return from Jerry on the foredeck. The skipper yelled for the mate to come up to take the helm and went forward to find out what the hell was going on. As he approached the fo'c's'le companionway, he smelled smoke and dove below. There was Jerry, dead asleep on a smoldering bunk caught afire by a cigarette that had dropped out of his mouth when he passed out.

"I knocked him the length of the fo'c's'le and he ended up on the anchor chain. When he got up, he said, 'Yes, sir. I'll go right up on deck.' And from then on, he was my bird dog. He'd do anything for me. It didn't matter whether I had money to pay him or not. He and I were buddies. It took just one good whack to change everything."[*]

* * *

Here's where the famous *"Battle of Sea Fox"* begins.

During the time Lou and *Sea Fox* were in Lunenburg, his partner, Frank Muzzio, temporary first mate for the trip, had heard that the value of the lead in *Sea Fox*'s keel, some 35 tons of it, was more valuable than the vessel herself and even more valuable than any short term profits that might accrue from the new charter business. So when *Sea Fox* returned to Stamford, Muzzio informed Lou he was going to sell her for scrap.

"The hell you are!" Lou went through the roof and reminded Muzzio who the managing partner was. Instantly, the relationship between the two men deteriorated into chaos and intense dislike. Unfortunately for Lou, some of the crew who he hired to sail *Sea Fox* back from Lunenburg were *persona non grata* in the U.S. and had been deported several times in the past for working

---

[*] Thruelson, *op. cit.* 23.

illegally in the country. During the Depression, all undocumented foreigners were tossed out in order to preserve jobs for U.S. citizens.

Muzzio took advantage of the illegal status of the aliens aboard *Sea Fox* and forced the authorities to prohibit Lou from sailing her away. The disreputable Muzzio called his even more disreputable lawyer, and with help from friends in the courthouse, had *Sea Fox* seized and a deputy marshal put aboard to preserve the government's evidence and (coincidentally) Frank Muzzio's 35 tons of lead. The legality of this action is suspect, given she was a documented vessel, but we'll leave that up to the sea lawyers—like Lou.

Fat Nicholas Cerulli, the hapless deputy marshal the court consigned to guard *Sea Fox*, also was known as "Two-Gun Nick." The poor bastard didn't stand a chance against Lou. But ol' Two-Gun always dressed well. He moved aboard *Sea Fox* in all his finery: gold-rimmed glasses, a fedora, patent leather shoes, a big shiny badge, and holsters sporting two lemon-squeezer Smith & Wesson .38s, one on each side of his belly overhang.

On the 18th of January, 1935, Lou met with Jerry, the mate Windy Mason, and Old Man Ryle, the harbormaster at the Getman & Judd wharf at the end of Graves and Strand Streets. Ryle was a long-time friend of Lou's father, and he helped concoct and execute a plan that would become legend and the subject of years of off-duty fo'c's'le gabble.

Lou assigned the harbormaster two missions: first, to spread a rumor around the docks that Lou was a trigger-happy thug, infamous in the Caribbean for casually shooting innocent islanders, and second, at the right time, to announce that *Sea Fox* must be moved from her berth immediately. Oddly enough, it was easy to convince the locals that Lou was a random murderer of Caribbean islanders, as New Englanders at the time were ignorant of that area and its inhabitants. The West Indies were considered wild, uncivilized, and as far away as the moon.

Meanwhile, the Connecticut winter had set in, and in order to soften up Nick, Lou and Windy decided they didn't need any heat. It was colder than hell, and the court had not provided Two-Gun with any coal, nor did he have any right to use the stove. Lou and Windy, of course, went about their business as if everything was normal and pretended they couldn't understand why Nick was so uncomfortable. They cooked their food but Nick got none of it; he had to wait for the unreliable daily vittles delivery from the sheriff's office. Two-Gun took to staying in his cabin, bundled up in all the blankets the sheriff would supply.

After a couple of days of this misery, Lou arranged for the owner of *Massasoit*, the only motorboat in the harbor, to come alongside when the harbormaster "kicked him out" and tow them out of Stamford. Instead of just moving *Sea Fox* off the wharf and onto a mooring, as everyone would think, he intended to keep on going and take the vessel—with Two-Gun aboard—out of Connecticut waters. At that point, Cerulli would be powerless. Anyway, that was the plan.

On the appointed morning before Two-Gun arose, Lou quietly locked the deputy in his stateroom by jamming a four-by-four between the cabin door handle and the bulkhead on the other side of the companionway. He hoped this would slow Nick down a bit when he realized the boat was being moved further than the anchorage.

At ebb tide, Old Man Ryle showed up, and in a voice that was heard throughout the area, dutifully instructed Lou that *Sea Fox* would have to move off the wharf. Right on cue, the little underpowered *Massasoit* sputtered up to the bow, but *Sea Fox* was backwards in the estuary and had to swing 180 degrees to head downstream toward the ocean. The dredged channel was narrow, and the schooner was too long to negotiate a U-turn without being backed down about 200 feet to a wider spot. Lou's plan was to let the tide take her down to the turning basin while the little motorboat guided her away from the shallows. Once in the basin, *Massasoit* would turn her and she'd sail on the tide. Again, that was the plan.

It didn't work out that way. Even though Nick had been told of the move, he got suspicious that more than a simple move to a mooring was planned. Just as the motorboat arrived and Lou was on the dock trying to pull the bow line off the bollard, the deputy began crashing around in his cabin attempting to bust out. He was shouting and raising hell, and finally broke through the skylight butterfly hatch and marched down the gangplank toward Lou, both guns drawn.

"...he saw me there struggling with this line, to get it off the bollard; and he hauled out his .38s and he says, 'I'm here to keep this ship and I can't let it go and that's illegal,' and so on. I said—I said, 'Boy, put those things away before you hurt yourself,' and he said, 'No! No! No! I'll lay you down.' And I said, 'Boy, you're going to hurt yourself, sure as hell.' And I said, 'You haven't got the balls to shoot anybody anyway.' So he put them in his overcoat pocket and he hauled out a billy sap with lead in it. And he said, 'Well, I can lay you out,' and he went to lay me out.

"I hauled out my .45, which was a big frontier model; and I pulled the hammer back and it went Click! Click! She clicked and I said, 'You goddamn pirate, I'll blow your bloody brains out,' and he saw those

leads looking out of the chambers. Why, he laid down when I said, 'Lay down!' and he laid down right on the dock; and I reached down and took his eyeglasses and pitched them overboard, took his badge and put it in my pocket. Then I took his guns and put them in my pockets...one in my belt and the other in the pocket and I kicked him in the ribs and I said, 'Now get running.'"

Two-Gun got running. He ran as fast as he could to the Sheriff's office, only a half mile away. And now it really hit the fan.

Lou, Windy, and Jerry got *Sea Fox* clear of the dock but *Massasoit*'s engine quit just as a gust of wind hit *Sea Fox*. She fetched up in the mud at the opposite side of the canal, only five or six yards from the shore, still facing inland.

Out of sheer frustration, Windy Mason yelled, "Sweet bleedin' jaysus, skipper, what the hell'd we do to deserve this shit?" Jerry Wendell then confided with uncanny timing, "You know I'm out on a rum-running charge with a bond up, and if they know about me and if I come up into this racket, I'll be in real trouble."

Lou sighed, and just said, "Crap." He told Windy to take Jerry ashore in the dory. Jerry was to contact a few of his friends in town and have them out to the boat at 8:00 p.m., and until then, to lay low.

Massasoit's 80-year-old Irish skipper finally restarted her engine but didn't have enough power to pull *Sea Fox* off the mud, and at any rate, there was no crew. All Lou could do was wait for the higher tide later that night. Lou called the Irishman over to the rail and asked him to come back at 8:00 that night. The old man said he'd as soon stick around now and watch the fireworks. "But I'm not paying you a goddamn cent more than the 10 bucks we agreed on," warned Lou. The old man replied, "No problem, we never get any excitement around here. This is fun. I like to see the Irish beat the shit out of the Guineas!" Except for a short break to eat, the old man stayed on his boat in the estuary during the entire "Battle of *Sea Fox*."

That afternoon the *Stamford Advocate* picked up the story and ran it under the heading, "POLICE TO ARREST OWNER OF YACHT." This prompted a stream of the curious to flow towards the estuary. With the onlookers came a phalanx of law enforcement officials which eventually included the chief of police, the district attorney, obese Two-Gun Nick Cerulli, the state police, and the co-owner of *Sea Fox*, Frank Muzzio, with his lawyer in tow. As they arrived, in turn, they all formed up on the banks of the firth and the discussions proceeded.

"Two-Gun Nick had left his shotgun behind, and so I propped that up against one mast and my high-powered rifle against the other. I had my two 45s strapped around my waist and I just walked up and down the deck while this constantly growing group of officials and cops and curious bystanders argued and talked with me and each other across 20 feet of mud. I was determined to hold the fort until the next high water, when my friends had promised to come back."*

First, a policeman stepped forward from the crowd and asked, "Is Mr. Kenedy aboard?" Lou replied, "If you're looking for CAPTAIN Kenedy, you're talking to him." The cop explained that they would like to see him up at the police station. This prompted Lou to emulate rum-running Captain Ammon Zinck.† "Well if you come to get me, be sure of your rights before you come over the rail, because the first step over the rail, you'll be a dead man." The cop blinked once, blinked again, his Adam's apple bobbed a couple of times, and he just stood there.

Then Frank Muzzio sidled up and urged the cop to do his duty. "Well, go and get him, you got your warrant. Go get him!" The policeman wasn't happy with Frank's butting in and simply said, "You and your lawyer got yourself in a fine bollocks. I ain't burning my hands." Then he turned and walked away. Muzzio, open mouthed, watched him leave. A sprinkling of applause was heard from the growing crowd.

The bystanders siding with Lou and the cop didn't make Muzzio any happier, and he yelled, "I'll go and get my brothers!" His brothers—Amil, Andrew, and Clarence—were known by the police and were gangster wannabes, kind of "Mafia light." He continued, "I'll get my gang, and they'll come with shotguns, and we'll get that ship." The cop was not impressed. He said, "We don't want any shooting around here. You stay away! You're not allowed here." Muzzio was incredulous, "That's a hell of a thing—I'm not allowed on my own ship?" The cop replied, "That's it! We'll put you in the clink if you start any rough stuff."

Muzzio was beside himself. He turned on his lawyer shouting, "I told you, you son of a bitch, a ship was different than a house; and now you find out you're in a mess!" The lawyer, flushed with rage, yelled back, "Well, I've been practicing for 40 years!" Muzzio, not a master of *bon mot*, yelled, "Well, it's time to stop practicing and get to work!" The assembled crowd apparently felt some obligation to acknowledge Muzzio's old chestnut and tittered.

---

* Thruelsen, *op. cit.*, 38.
† Page 12.

Then, without further provocation, Frank wheeled, grunted, and socked the lawyer on the side of his head with an awkward punch that did more damage to his own hand than to the lawyer's head. The crowd broke into applause. Rubbing his temple, the lawyer's response to the punch was predictable. "I'll see you and Kenedy in the jail right together." And he stormed off. Muzzio, nursing a broken right hand, gave the lawyer the customary Italian chin gesture with his left.

About this time, a convoy of 10 cars drove into the area, and the size of the assembly doubled. Among the newcomers were Chief of Police John Brennan, and Harbormaster Ryle. The chief, another big guy like Two-Gun, walked to the edge of the mud and said, "Come on now, Kenedy, you got to come ashore with us. You're under arrest." The "Ammon Zinck Gambit" worked for the morning show, so Lou pulled it out for the matinee. "That's fine," he said, "But I'll tell you what I told the other fellow. The first fellow over the rail here better be sure of his rights cuz he'll be a dead man."

This caused some consternation, and the group of officials just huddled together and mumbled. At one point, Chief Brennan turned to Ryle—not knowing that he was a friend of the Kenedy family—and asked, "Why—is he as tough as they make out?" The harbormaster, in a New England twang, replied nonchalantly but loud enough for all to hear, "Oh why hell, I hear he used to shoot islanders for fun down in the West Indies. Yeah, yeah, he'd shoot the brass buttons off your coat just as soon as look at you." This was food for thought.

To complicate things even more, if it were possible, a few state trooper cars arrived. The chief rolled his eyes, sighed, and said loud enough for Lou to hear, "What now?" Immaculately dressed, the head trooper marched up to the chief and asked, "Well, you got a situation you can't handle?" The chief replied, "When we need you, we'll let you know. We can handle anything. We'll handle it."

A jurisdiction dispute ensued and it lasted for hours. The officials on shore broke into four or five football huddles which changed team members every so often but no headway was made. They figured the ship wasn't going anywhere because she was stuck in the mud so there was no sense of urgency. They just argued on and on. Meanwhile, Lou strode up and down the deck cradling his shotgun like a hunter, occasionally chatting with the crowd. He tried to look tough but it was hard not to laugh at the cop's predicament. Now and then, to reinforce his new image as a cold-blooded killer, the big, shaggy-haired skipper would fondle the pistols in his belt.

The whole affair started at 10:00 a.m. and at 5:00 p.m., it was starting to get dark. At 8:00 p.m., Chief Brennan and the head trooper were still in a pissing contest, which is just what Lou needed. He had picked the right day for the caper, for it turned into a cold but beautiful night with a full moon. The tide was at its highest at 8:00 p.m. Right on time, he heard a dory bump against the deep-water side of *Sea Fox*. Four of his old pals, along with Windy Mason and Jerry Wendell, tumbled aboard. Darkness helped hide the shipboard activities from the shore.

The bickering between officials was unabated. Frustrated, at one point they even came up with an implausible threat to use a machine gun to sink *Sea Fox* in the mud.

There was no perceptible movement at first, but then the relative position of the shore landmarks seemed to change slightly. Earlier, Lou stood near the mainmast when he threatened gunfire if police came aboard. Now, he stood next to the foremast to face the same piece of real estate. *Sea Fox* was afloat and silently inching her way backwards down the channel, drifting with an offshore breeze and an ebb tide.

No one ashore noticed anything until Windy and two other crewmen quickly hauled up the outer jib. They backed it to windward by hand, Lou threw the wheel hard to starboard, and the breeze took the bow slowly 180 degrees. Soon she was underway down the channel. Lou saluted and yelled, "So long, boys." The shore crowds hushed; no one yelled; the officials didn't utter a word. In a very few minutes, *Sea Fox* was nothing but a vanishing ghost, silently heading out to Long Island sound. The congregation ashore, open-mouthed, simply watched her disappear. The entire incident seemed as if it had never happened.

Lou ordered all hands to man the throat and peak halyards, and they hauled up the foresail. By the time she surged to the swell of the sound, she carried four lowers under a full moon and countless stars. He took her up 15 miles to City Island where his Stamford buddies and Jerry Wendell wished him farewell. Jerry wanted to stay aboard but Lou was afraid his own troubles would spill over and Jerry would be caught in the same net. The rum-running charges were serious, and no one would look forward to languishing in a stateside prison. So Jerry went over the rail with the other temporary crewmen, leaving Lou and Windy Mason alone aboard *Sea Fox*.

"The next day I called up my harbourmaster [Mr. Ryle] *and asked him how things were going. And he said it was very bad; all the government fellows, they had made an indictment against me and the government fellows were looking up and down the coast for the vessel*

and there would be hell to pay. Also, your Dad's lawyer told the sheriff and the newspaper that you'd be here to answer charges. So I said that was all right with me. So I said, 'Windy, I'm bound for Barbados. Do you want to come along?' And he said, 'Anywhere's better than here.'"

The next morning, with $20 his grandmother had given him, the skipper bought a bag of potatoes, a case of bully beef,[*] some canned milk, and a few miscellaneous items.

Windy and Lou collected driftwood to fuel the stove. When they catted the anchor, it was a cold winter's night with a nor'west breeze making it even colder. They got the foresail and forestaysail set, and *Sea Fox* began jogging around City Island with a crew of two men and Hans, the German shepherd.

As they cleared City Island, the two men fought the main halyard while a massive four-master passed to weather. Out of LaHave, Nova Scotia, she was the *Laura Annie Barnes* with Jim Publicover in command. Publicover, on the poop, pulled his mate aside and said, "Look at that damn yacht there. Two poor fellows struggling there on a bitter January night, going out on a big yacht. No power to hoist sail or anything, and all the owners and yacht people down below having a good time. Snug down in the cabin."[†]

"... to get the mainsail up, now that was a job! She had no power for hoisting. It was all hand, she was a hand heaver and we'd get the throat hauled up with a handy billy, little by little; and then we'd get the peak up a little. Then we'd get the throat up and it must have taken way over an hour to get the mainsail on her. Then she flew down Long Island Sound."

As they passed Montauk Light, it started to snow. *Sea Fox* was icing up as a nor'east gale blew in. The nor'easter increased in intensity during the night, so Lou and Windy lowered the main and *Sea Fox* ran off under foresail and forestaysail. It got so bad that eventually they lowered both the fore and forestaysail and ran only under a storm trysail jury rigged from a spare topsail. The air temperature was only eight degrees Fahrenheit. Windy and Lou alternated watches every half hour. When one was at the wheel, the other stole below for a bit of warmth and a cat nap.

The storm worsened as they crossed the Gulf Stream. Near Bermuda, *Sea Fox* hove to under bare poles for a couple of days. They finally got across the stream and into the horse latitudes, where they were becalmed for two days.

---

[*] Canned (tinned) corned beef.
[†] Thruelsen, *op. cit.* 38.

That's when Lou discovered the steering gear had shattered when they were hove to. He lashed a long beam athwart ship to the rudder head, attached tackle to each end and steered her with a tiller. It was hard work but it kept them on course and the weather gradually warmed. A few days later, they caught a big dolphin fish and the ensuing feast raised their spirits as much as the sunny weather.

*"We got into the trade winds and set all sail on her just as if she had a full crew. We rattled her off down the trades for Barbados doing 250 miles a day, and made it in just over two weeks."**

The arrival in Barbados was pure Kenedy. They brought the ship into Bridgetown, dropped the hook, and dutifully raised the yellow "Q" flag requesting free pratique. They awaited the visit from the government sawbones who would examine the passengers and crew for disease and inspect the ship's clearance papers from its last port.

Lou Kenedy's recollection of the conversation with the doctor:

"Morning, Skipper, where's the crew? Have them all line up please."

"They're all lined up, sir," said Lou.

Squinting, the doctor said, "Two men? With all this vessel? Come now…well, let me see your clearance and your bill of health."

"Well," said Lou, "I'm sorry, we have no clearance and no bill of health."

"Really, Skipper, supposing you tell me about that," said the doctor.

Lou, trying to seem cooperative, explained, "Well, doctor, it was this way: The two of us were shifting my schooner here along the coast, from Boston down south a ways, and we got blown off in a big, howling northeast snowstorm. When we shook ourselves loose from the storm, the nearest place I knew anything about was Bridgetown here."†

All the doctor could say was, "Oh, really?"

Lou's old Barbados contacts from *Abundance* and *Adams* trips held him in good stead, and they vouched for *Sea Fox*'s crew. Windy and he were finally adjudged to be of good character and physical health and were allowed ashore.

Lou had two problems. He couldn't return to the States for the duration of the seven-year statute of limitations, and *Sea Fox* was too small for the Nova

---

* Thruelsen, *op. cit.*, 38.
† Thruelsen, *op. cit.*, 38.

Scotia/Caribbean milk run. Lou immediately began setting the schooner up for local shipping. In those days, Bridgetown was the hub for Caribbean shipping, just as San Juan is today. Steamers of the Harrison Line hauled—and still haul—goods from England to Barbados. There the cargos were transferred to warehouses, then finally consigned to local schooners for distribution to the other Caribbean islands. St. Kitts and Antigua were the best runs, as they had the largest populations. The rate for inter-island freight was fixed at $5 per ton. There was no negotiation. Lou, ever confident, figured he would be more efficient than the locals; he had a faster ship and should be able to deliver more tonnage over the long run.

Lou and Windy threw themselves into tearing the beautiful teak and mahogany interior out of *Sea Fox*, converting it back to the freighter it was during World War I. They ripped out five and a half tons of interior accoutrements and ballast. Of course, Lou carefully stored all the wood and fittings ashore just in case he would ever need them again.

Forty days after Two-Gun Nick Cerulli seized *Sea Fox* for the Stamford court, on February 25, 1935, *Sea Fox* cleared Barbados loaded with 400 barrels of bread for Guadeloupe and a small amount of cargo for Dominica.[*] Windy Mason was mate and a Bajan crew was signed. Things were happening fast.

This first trip set the tone for the years that Lou and *Sea Fox* plied the West Indies. When they arrived at Guadeloupe, the French consignee wasn't prepared to receive the 400 barrels of bread. Lou wasn't about to cool his heels or pay his crew for sitting around, so they unloaded the barrels themselves, leaving them helter-skelter in a field next to the quay. The Frenchman screamed like a stuck *cochon,* but Lou replied with the main sheet and cleared for Dominica to off-load the remaining cargo.

When converting her back to a freighter, Lou left one spare cabin in *Sea Fox* for the occasional traveler who might pay for passage to the other islands. This was the case upon leaving Guadeloupe on this first trip. An incredibly fat West Indian lady booked passage from Guadeloupe to Dominica and was ensconced in the little cabin below decks.

"We had one spare cabin and I put her in there. The ship was very light— just a small amount of cargo for Dominica. And I'm going across the passage there, in the trades. It was blowing hard, and next thing, we heard her screaming. We went down to see and here this big fat woman had fallen. The cabin had a closet. She went to the closet, the ship made a roll, and she went in and jammed in the closet and she couldn't get out.

---

[*] Pronounced "dohm-ah-NEE-kah".

Figure 3-2. Heavy going aboard *Sea Fox* on one of her cargo runs to Dominica.

Well, she was about 350 pounds. Between me and the mate we had quite a job hooking her out of there because we couldn't get in the closet with her; she was down on the lee side and it was like taking an elephant out of a pan. Anyway, we finally got her loose, somehow. She thanked us very much for saving her life. She thought she was going to suffocate in there. We got to Dominica okay."

Lou, Windy, and *Sea Fox* settled into a regular weekly routine. The runs were usually about 700 miles round trip, and being in the trades, the trip was usually completed in five days. General cargo carried north would include anything from "tombstones and schoolbooks to lard and tins of paint."* Depending on the season, cottonseed was brought back to Barbados for refining into oil but usually *Sea Fox* returned empty. A couple of times a year, Lou ran up to Turks for salt and brought along some trading items for the local Turks and Caicos population.

Lou grossed an average of about $900 per month, hauling between 60 and 140 tons of cargo on each trip. He paid his crew $10 per month each, which netted him between $200 and $300 a month after maintenance costs. To limit

---

* Thruelson, *op. cit.*, 38.

his personal expenses he lived aboard *Sea Fox.* There was a three-year period when Lou never slept ashore.

Windy Mason was more than Lou's mate. He was also his best friend. And Windy was 100 percent loyal, reliable, and competent—until he had a drink or two. The serious trouble started late in the first year of *Sea Fox*'s inter-island shipping career. During one trip to Dominica, Lou was ashore in the customs office when he heard gunshots. The schooner was anchored a couple of yards off the quay, and Windy was on the foredeck firing Lou's .45 at some kids in a dugout canoe. The kids jumped out of the canoe, swam like hell toward the shore, and were not hurt. Lou jumped into the dory, rowed to *Sea Fox,* and wrested the pistol from Windy yelling, "What the hell are you up to?" Windy, in his cups, answered, "Well, they were bums—they were bumming cigarettes off of me, and I won't put up with that." If Windy had wounded or killed any of the kids, Lou would have been held at least partially responsible and might have lost his vessel.

Figure 3-3. In the front of the first *Sea Fox* Log Book, Captain Kenedy pasted a hand-drawn Beaufort Scale, annotated with the associated ship and sail conditions, with statements such as, "Most advantageous for sailing with leading wind. All sail set" (notation for Force 3 and 4). In the right margin, he sketched (in ink) these four remarkable views of the *Sea Fox* configuration under the various wind conditions. The top sketch was beside Force 1 through 3, the second beside Force 4 and 5, the third beside Force 7 and 8, and the bottom sketch was for Force 10 and 11. His final notation (for Force 12—hurricane) was "No sail can stand when running."

After a few more trips, Windy became a real problem. In Barbados, the locals enjoyed giving Windy free rum because he would get smashed and start fights with the police. He was six-feet-two-inches tall and as strong as a bull. The police, who weren't allowed to carry firearms, couldn't arrest him. If they tried, he just threw the constables off the nearest dock into the water. The last straw was when Windy took Lou's .45 and drove all the officers under their beds in the police barracks in Bridgetown. He had captured it. It was his.

Lou arrived in time to defuse the situation, avert physical damage, and convince Windy of the wisdom of a tactical retreat to the schooner's fo'c's'le.

The day after the "Capture of Bridgetown Barracks," the Canadian consul contacted Lou, and they decided that in order to prevent a real tragedy, Windy must be sent home. This was going to cost Lou a lot of money, but he agreed it was the only way to solve the problem. The only hitch was the chief of police wanted to talk to Windy before he left. The consul said the meeting was scheduled at 2:00 p.m. that day. The consul also made it Lou's responsibility to have Windy present. Returning to *Sea Fox*, Lou explained the situation to Windy. He seemed to take it well and promised to be at the police station at 2:00 p.m. Lou went ashore to find a new mate.

The appointed hour came, and Lou walked into the office of Colonel Dickens, the long-winded chief of police. The consul was there, and of course, the colonel. Windy was absent. Colonel Dickens was the archetypical Raj-era English colonial bureaucrat. He was proper, fat, sported a pith helmet, and when perturbed, smacked his riding crop on the side of his desk. He was outraged that Windy wasn't on time and started to slap the crop and "Harrumph" a lot when a commotion was heard out in front of the station. It was Windy, of course, drunk as a lord, in a horse-drawn carriage, yelling at the driver to yell at the horse to stop. He fell out of the carriage before it had completely halted and instructed the driver to wait for him as he would be right back. He dusted himself off and weaved his way into the station and into the colonel's office. He gave the chief the best British military salute he could muster, his open left hand touching his left ear. His right hand was braced against a chair to keep himself from falling over. "Reporting as ordered, sir," Windy lisped.

Lou smiled and stifled a laugh. Colonel Dickens ignored the lack of military polish and launched into an endless tirade explaining how Windy had upset the yin and yang of the island; he could be put in jail for an indeterminate number of years, and he was very lucky to have friends who take care of him, blah, blah, blah.

Halfway through the speech, Windy held up his hand and sputtered, "Stop, for the love of God, stop, for Christ's sake. I have to piss!" He staggered to the head and returned promptly, snapping another one of his unique salutes. Dickens harrumphed some more and bored everyone by repeating most of the speech. When finished, he made the amateur's error of asking Windy, "Do you have anything to say for yourself, my good man?" Windy said, "Yes," his eyes wandered around the room for a moment and he continued, "My God man, what do you eat that makes you so goddamn fat?"

Well, that was it. Dickens bellowed for Windy to be taken out and held under guard until passage could be arranged to Canada. But the officers were afraid of him and wouldn't arrest him, so Lou stepped up and promised that Windy would be kept under house arrest aboard *Sea Fox* until his departure for Canada aboard *Lady Boat* later that evening. Having no other choice, Colonel Dickens agreed, and Lou and Windy rowed out to the schooner.

Lou gave Windy's back pay to the purser aboard *Lady Boat* with instructions not to dole any out to Windy until they sailed. Windy, however, talked the purser out of a few bucks before they left and took a bum boat into town. He arrived back aboard drunk and happy, toting a bag full of rum bottles for the trip. As *Lady Boat* pulled out of Bridgetown, Lou waved to his pal who was standing on the fantail with a bottle in his hand. Windy saluted by hoisting the bottle. That was the last Lou saw of Windy for many years. He was sorry to see his old friend go, but he had become a liability, and Lou had his own problems.

Lou was now without a mate. To add to that predicament, the American consul summoned him to the consulate to inform him that he had received a "very disquieting letter—from Washington." Lou knew what the letter was about but asked politely, "What letter might that be?"

"[The consul] said, 'They want to know how long you're going to be out of the country, that they have an indictment against you.' And I said, 'Well that's interesting, but you tell them, if you're in communication with them, just tell them I'll be here seven years.' And he said, 'Uh huh, that's what I thought,' and he laughed."

That was the extent of any efforts to extradite Lou back to the States.

As sad as Lou was to see his old friend leave, this was a turning point in Lou's life. A chance meeting with Peter Jones was a windfall. Peter was a Saban who had been working aboard sailing ships for years. The Dutch island of Saba, little more than a lava cone southeast of St. Maarten, was—still is—renowned for the sailing skill of her native sons. Peter had sailed square-riggers around the horn several times and was as good a seaman as Lou had ever known. He was ageless; once he turned 53, his age never changed. His birth year just increased by one on each birthday. He sailed as mate aboard Lou's ships for over 10 years.

In 1936, however, Lou was to begin a lifelong relationship that became infinitely more significant than all others before it. Patricia Greenidge, the beautiful daughter of a Scottish physician, lived on Barbados with her parents. She was slim with short dark hair and ever-smiling eyes; some later said when she married Lou, she resembled Fay Spain, the 1950s actress.

Pat was educated in Scotland and returned to Barbados only two years before meeting Lou. Twenty-six-year-old Lou met her at a typical, stuffy British tea party, which they blew off as soon as they could. At that time, Lou had an old English Morris that was almost completely rusted out. He covered the whole car with pieces of canvas sewn together with twine, glued to the remains of the body with paint. Sneaking out of the soirée, Pat, Lou, and some friends swarmed the tiny Morris, rumbled to the wharf, and rowed out to *Sea Fox* for a nighttime swim.

As the relationship became serious, Pat's parents were not overjoyed with the prospect of their beautiful daughter, a society belle and the most sought-after young woman on the island, marrying a sailor of unknown quality who might be away for months at a time. Also, on such a small island, it would have been difficult to keep Lou's stateside legal problems secret. Though Pat's parents never let on, they were probably aware of the "Battle of Sea Fox" and its repercussions before the couple were married. To add to the marriage problems, Lou's side of the family, until they arrived on Barbados, all thought Pat was a black Bajan. Because of this perception, his mother refused to attend the wedding at all and stayed in Connecticut.

The wedding was an all-island event culminating in a huge reception at the Ocean View Hotel and a parade down to the wharf where the couple boarded *Sea Fox* for a revenue-producing honeymoon: a cargo voyage to Antigua.[*]

Though raised on an island, until her honeymoon Pat had little sailing experience except in small boats. The transition to an off-shore life was difficult at times. Her attempts to bring a bit of femininity to the skipper's quarters on *Sea Fox* were met with equanimity by the new groom, but when an old friend, Captain Dawsie Geldert, lowered himself down the ladder to be met by a pink and powder blue cabin motif, he blurted out, "Jaysus Christ, Lou! What do you have here, a fookin' French whorehouse?"

---

[*] Pronounced "ahn-TEE-gah."

Pat overheard the remark, took the hint, and immediately set to work restoring the cabin to its original battleship grey color scheme. Much later in life, Lou admitted he was ever so thankful to Dawsie for the remark that prompted the redecoration.

These were the salad days for Pat and Lou. During this time, Lou organized the now famous annual Boxing Day Race around Barbados, which he never lost in four years.

"[We organized] *a schooner race around the island of Barbados on Boxing Day for any of the schooners that were in port. They were mostly in at*

Figure 3-4. A strikingly handsome couple, Pat and Lou in full wedding finery were married at the seaside Ocean View Hotel (run by Pat's mother) in 1936. Photo by City Studio, Bridgetown.

Christmastime. The race ran for several years until I left the islands. In one or two of the races, some 15 or 18 schooners took part. But unfortunately for them and lucky for me, we won it every time. The first time we won it over three hours ahead of the second boat, the Mona Marie *which used to come from Riverport. And there was* Marian Belle Wolfe—*she came from LaHave. I must say the* Mona Marie—*after awhile I never beat her by much. She got within three-quarters of an hour of me.*

Figure 3-5. *Sea Fox*, **carrying every bit of canvas she owned and with a gala crew of guests aboard, winning the Boxing Day Regatta. Photo courtesy** *Bridgetown Advocate.* **(Used by permission.)**

"But the race around Barbados—around 70 miles—was a good race and it was beating, reaching, running, and then reaching again; and they were some interesting. The whole island would go crazy; they'd follow it around in cars and buses, all around the island watching the schooners. When we'd come in, I'd sail right in the careenage and tie up and the crowds would be solid. Sometimes they'd pick me up on their heads and walk down the street and I'd think, 'Ah, I'm gonna get dumped now,' but no, I never got in any trouble. The prize generally was $300 for the first one, $200 for second, $100 for third, and a case of beer for the last schooner as a consolation prize. I went home after one race and the next day we were going down to work on the schooner, when I looked out and here were two schooners racing for the last place. They were out overnight, each trying to hold up so they could get that case of beer."

Sea Fox's racing success was immortalized in the calypso song, "*The* Sea Fox *beat up the* Mona Marie." To this day, one historical feature of the main hall of the Royal Barbados Yacht Club is a large photograph of *Sea Fox* under full sail racing around the island.

In 1937, a year and a half after they met, Pat and Lou were presented with the first of their four children. Brian Kenedy's arrival prompted the renting of a house on the beach in Barbados and Lou's first shoreside home in five years. Though there was always a warm and inviting home ashore, Brian grew up on the ships. His first recollection of his baby days is sitting in a cold pond under a waterfall in Dominica, while on a cargo voyage in *Sea Fox*.

Figure 3-6. Captain Lou, 27, with one-year-old Brian off Barbados.

Lou received an unexpected wedding present from his grandmother. She contacted Frank Muzzio, bought out his interest in *Sea Fox,* and presented it to Pat and Lou. A condition of this payment was that Frank Muzzio would relinquish all claims against *Sea Fox.* She also convinced Two-Gun Nick to drop the assault charges against Lou. So now, Lou was able to return to the States whenever he desired, but he continued the shipping business out of Barbados for several more years.

Figure 3-7. Light squall.

As the rest of the world was deafened by European war drums, Lou noticed that long-haul freight rates were inching up between Nova Scotia and the Caribbean. Also, he longed to get back into larger schooners. *Sea Fox* was a wonderful ship and she didn't owe Lou a cent. She had done her job profitably and was still in excellent condition. In October of 1939, he found a buyer for her in Baltimore. Just a month after Hitler's ruthless and trumped-up attack on Poland, Lou packed all their belongings into *Sea Fox* and sailed Pat and little Brian up to the States, straight into the worst winter of his life.

So ends this day.

Figure 4-1.

The ship: *Wawaloam*
Year of Launching: 1918
Rig: Tern Schooner
Official #: 227006
Builder: Waterhuizen, Holland
Material: Steel

Length between perpendiculars: 134 feet 8 inches
Beam: 25 feet 4 inches
Draft: 9 feet light, 12 feet loaded
Displacement: 336 tons
Power: Originally steam. Gray Marine Model
    6-71 installed by LK

Chapter 4 *Wawaloam*

Wawaloam *was the name of a New England Indian princess. Since the ship was built in Holland, it is unlikely she was launched under that name. At her launching, Lou was only eight years old and was sailing* Tilky *around Long Island Sound. Also eight years old at the time was Walter Schug, a gentleman who will loom large in the future of* Wawaloam *and her skipper.*

Wawaloam *was built for the Scandinavian lumber trade but was soon sold to a wealthy Brit who had her converted to a yacht. She served her owner well until the early 1930s when, destined to reenter the lumber trade, she was bought by Sam Loveland, the owner of a fleet of coastal carriers out of Philadelphia and Baltimore. As diesel ships quickly became the more efficient, Sam didn't complete the freighter conversion, and she never saw service under the Loveland flag.*

She was abandoned and anchored in the flats off the Loveland wharf in Riverside, New Jersey. Lou and Sam Loveland were friends from the Abundance *days, and he was happy to sell* Wawaloam *to Lou for only $200. Lou bought her, sight unseen.*

* * *

The new owner of *Sea Fox* was anxiously awaiting her in Baltimore. Meanwhile, Captain Kenedy's new command was stuck in the muck in Riverside, New Jersey, just north of Philadelphia.

On the trip north in October of 1939, *Sea Fox* hove to, allowing a hurricane to pass, but then she shadowed the storm, making excellent time up to Hatteras. She sailed up the Chesapeake and was within view of Baltimore when a 50-knot gale hit. She was forced to anchor for two days waiting for the storm to abate. Once ashore, Lou handed *Sea Fox* over to her new owners. The Kenedy family, with all their worldly belongings, piled into a truck and rumbled up to Jersey to survey their new home.

The only *Sea Fox* crew member still with Lou at this point was the mate, Peter Jones. Neither of them had seen *Wawaloam* before, and what they saw was a mess. The locals called her "The Ghost Ship," as she had been mired in the black Rancocas Creek mud for years. She dripped rust and her rigging draped in festoons. She'd been on the mud for almost half of her 20 years. The list of rotted spars, tattered rigging, and rusty, inoperable gear was as long as your arm. Her condition hardly lived up to the image of *Wawaloam*, an Indian princess, but the pitch-pine main deck and steel hull were sound and seaworthy.

Trees three-feet tall were growing in the rotten fir poop decking. All the spars were rotted and no rigging was usable. The 22-foot main hatch had been decked over in England during her yacht life and had to be rebuilt. The steel hatch coamings were stowed below and required reinstallation. She had a wonderful windlass but it was designed to be run by an electric motor which, of course, didn't work. Her steam engine had been pulled out years before leaving only the propeller and its shaft attached to a 20-inch flange. Her hull, though sound, streamed rust from every scupper and rivet.

And poor Pat? The winter was upon them, she had little Brian to tend, and there was no heat in her new cabin. In fact there was no cabin, just a cold steel box in the stern where she, Lou, and Brian slept those winter months. But even though the east coast winter closed in, the crew rolled up their sleeves and got to work.

Figure 4-2. Mate Peter Jones caulks the new deck.

First, the stove in the galley was repaired. Pat quickly mastered the art of cooking with wood fuel. She had trouble getting the stove hot enough at first but finally got the hang of it. The stove fuel was ripped from the very guts of the ship.

Two high school boys were hired, one seconded to Peter, the other to Lou. Their first project was to tear up the rotted fir poop deck. A new deck was bolted to the steel frame; as Lou and his helper laid down the deck, Peter caulked it.

Next was the main hatch. After the opening had been re-cut, the old coamings were riveted in place. To cover the 22-foot hatch, more than 30 hatch cover planks (two inches thick) were cut from other parts of the ship, banded with steel and bolted together. A deck engine was installed and rigged to run the windlass to raise sails and work cargo.

Figure 4-3. Captain Lou dubs with his adz, shaping a four-sided timber towards eight sides; eventually, this ends up as a round spar (1940).

Tearing out the remnants of the cabins took a hellacious effort. Once all the floors were removed, the men hauled 15 tons of sand from shore in five-gallon buckets, to make concrete to coat the interior of the lower hull. It was standard procedure during this time to "cement" the bilge of steel vessels. While Peter plastered the bilge, Lou converted an existing tank for water storage. Once the bilge was coated, the two-by-eight-inch cabin sole planks were bolted down as flooring for the hold.

Before leaving Barbados in *Sea Fox*, Lou had sent a wire to his New York agents to order new masts for *Wawaloam*. He specified the masts be 88 feet long, about 9 feet longer than the old ones. When the masts arrived, they were towed through the ice-clogged Delaware and coaxed ashore by sliding them over the mud of the Rancocas Creek flat. Even during snow showers, Lou dubbed the masts on the beach, squaring them, knocking off the corners to make them 8-sided, then 16, and finally 32-sided. Then he rounded them using a draw knife and other prehistoric tools.

Peter Jones single-handedly designed and rebuilt the massive rigging to fit the new spars. The rigging was installed on the ground and when the masts were raised, every stay and shroud fit perfectly, just as if they had been measured in place. Peter's teenage helper was trained to worm, parcel, serve, and seize as well as to cover the turnbuckles with protective canvas.

Figure 4-4. New mast being hoisted aboard from ice-filled water.

The skipper and the mate made a trip to nearby woodlands to mark Jersey pine for use as gaffs, booms, and spars. A woodsman charged them five bucks a spar and delivered them for free.

"They were of Jersey pine, which is a cross between Nova Scotia spruce and southern spruce but lighter than southern pine. It's a breed that just grows around Jersey."

As *Wawaloam* was reborn, every day a cadre of regulars lined the shore at the foot of Stewart Street to watch and comment on the work. The size of the crowd ebbed and flowed with the weather, but when Lou started building the masts and spars on shore, the crowd increased. Speculation was rampant as to how the masts would be stepped. There were only four workmen and no crane. It was impossible, they said.

Two of the tallest trees were erected as sheers, a primitive A-frame used for stepping the masts. Each time it was moved, the A-frame had to be rigged and stayed as thoroughly as the masts themselves. The donkey engine that had been installed early in the work was, of course, invaluable:

"...we took the longest ones and used them for sheers, which we rigged up to haul the old mizzenmast out. I had made the new mizzen-mast, with the iron works and crosstrees and all that already mounted. Once we had hauled the old mast out, we launched the new one and took it out to the ship, and used the sheers to step the new mast. Then we moved the sheers to mid-ships, took out the old mainmast and stepped the new one. Finally we moved the sheers along the deck until we got to the foremast. We took that old foremast out, and that one went down through the fo'c's'le house. That mast had to be hoisted up very, very high to get the heel of it above the top of the house."

Lou's description made it sound a hell of a lot easier than it was. But now, with the masts stepped, he got to work finishing the gaffs and booms. He carved and bent the gaff and boom jaws out of pasture oak found nearby.

She had a suit of sails that had been stored properly and were in good shape. However, since the new spars were significantly longer than the old ones, the sails didn't fit at all.

"When we went to bend them, they weren't cut like Canadian sails. The gaffs were much shorter than the booms, so they only went half way out the new gaffs, which was a funny looking rig."

Figure 4-5. Sheers rigged to hoist new mainmast aboard, March 1940.

Though *Wawaloam* was not completely ready for sea, J. F. Whitney cabled Lou that a load of coal was ready in Philly. Unconcerned, in the first week of May, 1940, Lou hired a tug to pull *Wawaloam* off the flat, then down and across the Delaware to load 600 tons of anthracite for Killiam in Yarmouth. No additional crew were signed. The two high school kids, Peter Jones, and Lou ran the ship with Pat as cook and medic and little Brian as supervisor.

After loading, a tug pulled the schooner out past Cape May and cast off. That day the breeze promised a fast and agreeable voyage. Lou spun the helm to bring *Wawaloam* off the wind—but she didn't respond. He spun the wheel the opposite direction. Again, no response. She was so under-canvassed she couldn't gain steerageway, and she had been loaded by the head, which lifted the stern and further degraded the efficacy of the rudder. The tug was long gone back to Philly, and here was a big tern schooner, bobbing around aimlessly in the busy east-coast sea lanes. It was both dangerous and costly. *Wawaloam* was no more than an ark that moved at the pleasure of the tides and currents, no pleasure for the crew.

Although the schooner was fully loaded, most of the rudder was out of water and was completely airborne when the bow dipped the least bit. Lou immediately ordered the men to begin shifting the cargo aft. It took the four-man crew two days to move enough coal to keep *Wawaloam*'s rudder immersed. This annoyance, coupled with the slow, clumsy progress toward Yarmouth, raised crew frustration levels to the boiling point. Inevitable disagreements arose. Pat and Peter, normally best of friends, got into it because Peter cast accurate though unwelcome aspersions upon the sailing characteristics of *Wawaloam*; three-year-old Brian got his head stuck in a hawsehole; at the first sign of a decent breeze, the rotted bowsprit disintegrated; and continuous deck leaks made the galley a sizzling hell as water splashed into the bacon grease.

To top it off, upon arrival at Yarmouth after nine days of misery, the tow boat demanded 40 bucks to take the schooner into Killian's wharf. Of course, Captain Lou blew his stack. By the time the argument ended, the price was lowered to 10 bucks, but by then *Wawaloam* had closed handy to the dock. This is one of the only times that it isn't crystal clear who won a negotiation with Lou Kenedy.

As the Jeremiahs gathered on the wharf, they made book on whether the bowsprit-less, rusted hulk would sink before it docked, overrun the wharf, or run aground. The laughter and amusing asides were easily overheard aboard *Wawaloam* and weren't received cheerfully. Lou muttered expletives within earshot of little Brian. When Lou successfully tied her off at Killian's, his three-year-old son, standing on the poop, yelled, "There, how do you like that, you bunch of bastards?"

Smiling at the crowd, Pat lifted Brian by his belt loops and hauled him below to spare him the inevitable response from the shore.

After unloading, Lou hired a small motor-fishing boat to tow *Wawaloam* to Meteghan where French shipwrights were known worldwide for the quality of their work. First her decks were caulked; the hull was painted shining black with brilliant white rails. A new bowsprit was rigged and deckhouses built.

"Now the ship originally had cabins aft. They were all ripped out, no cabins—just a steel box. So they built the new cabin with birch paneling and hardwood floors, really a good rig. We put a bathtub in and a head. Put some new decking on top of the cabin where it needed renewing. A nice companionway made a ship-shape job of it. For'rd of the fo'c's'le house they put in new decking, and we dried out and painted the bottom."

Lou was understandably worried about *Wawaloam*'s sailing abilities, so for the first and last time, he borrowed some money. He used it to buy a brand new 160-horsepower Gray Marine Model 6-71 diesel.[*]

Except for the little donkey engines used on deck, Lou knew next to nothing about marine engines. Nevertheless, he immediately set about preparing the engine bed and adapting the coupling. He installed a wooden bed between the huge steel beams that made up the original steam engine mounts. *Wawaloam* had a 20-inch flange attached to a five-inch-diameter shaft swinging a 54-by-24-inch prop. The little diesel had a seven-inch coupling aft and a seven-inch flange on the forward end of the crankshaft. Lou connected the existing shaft to the engine with a steel adapter plate. At full speed, *Wawaloam* was now capable of spinning her prop at 535 rpm, through a three-to-one reduction gear, with her engine running at 1600 rpm.

When it was all hooked up, the rig became the topic of choice for the quayside wags. "She'll do a knot in a calm," they said. You couldn't blame them. The engine, compared to the enormous *Wawaloam*, looked puny. It was incongruous—an engine that looked like it would fit in a steamer trunk installed between the massive bed-plates where a mighty steam engine once pulsed. But the last laugh belonged to Lou and *Wawaloam*. Even the skipper was surprised to see that she did seven and a half knots light in flat water. But more important, the little 6-71 substantially improved the ability of the schooner to sail to weather. In any significant seas, however, running the diesel without the sails was useless.

At Meteghan, workers fitted a new jib-boom, along with new topmasts, but there were no sails for them. It would be cheaper to have a suit of sails made in Barbados, so Lou had bolts of inexpensive but high-quality Japanese canvas shipped directly to Bridgetown.

By August of 1940, work was completed on *Wawaloam*. The war thundering in Europe had a marked effect on the freight rates for lumber between Canada and the Caribbean. They stood for many years between $5 and $6 per 1,000 board feet. One thousand board feet is about 37 two-by-eight-inch planks 20 feet long. Not counting deck cargo, which Lou delighted in overloading, *Wawaloam* held 270,000 board feet. The deck load was about half the amount in the hold, so *Wawaloam* carried around 400,000 board feet per trip. At $5 or $6 per 1,000, a trip clear down to the Caribbean with deck

---

[*] Gray Marine had designed a marine conversion kit for the GM 6-71. Thousands of them were converted during WWII under the Gray Marine brand. After the war, General Motors bought the rights and designs from Gray and the marine GM 6-71 diesel was born. Subsequently, the GM Diesel unit became Detroit Diesel.

cargo loaded five feet above the rail might only earn $2,000. But freight rates spiraled up to $12 and then $15 per 1,000 by the time Lou loaded in Bridgewater for Barbados. It was prepaid freight, and the first load paid for most of the cost of the new engine even before she left the dock.

"...we finished work on the Wawaloam, *and freight rates were going sky high. We loaded lumber at Bridgewater, Nova Scotia—loaded her 'til she was so cranky that a stevedore walking from one side to the other would rock her. With that load we couldn't even use the skimpy sails we had—the gaffs would swing over to one side and* Wawaloam *would heel over to that side and stay there."* *

Lou was not looking forward to this trip. Without proper sails, *Wawaloam* would be at the mercy of the trades if they piped up. But luck was with her, and the 6-71 clattered away for 14 days over oily, windless seas. Even the ageless trade winds never put in an appearance. Once there, Lou arranged for the new suit of sails, including the missing topsails.

The Bajan sail makers were experts and inexpensive. Of course, Lou would design his own sails and the sail-makers would stitch them together:

"One special thing was to get the sails cut properly. They'd cut a sail down there just a square, flat, and it had no draft† and was inefficient to my mind. So when we went to have sails made, we'd go out in a field with a bunch of long six-inch nails and we'd put one down at the tack, throat, the peak, and the clew of the sail with all the right dimensions and angles in between. We'd run a codline between these nails, and then I would experiment with the amount of draft. We'd keep moving the lines out maybe a foot or so and put nails in to keep them that way so that they'd have a nice round to them. When you made the sail, then it had a good draft and you had drift‡ in the luff, a little bit on the gaff and quite a bit on the boom. That gave the sail a nice drawing power.

"We'd lay down two adjacent strips of canvas, starting at the leech. We'd cut the outer strip of cloth, then lay out another strip next to the second one, and cut the second strip. We'd repeat this until we finally got to the tack.

---

* Thruelsen, Richard, "The Incredible Captain Kenedy." *The Saturday Evening Post*, 2 January 1954, 76. (Used by permission.)

† A sail with proper draft is cut so it curves into an aerodynamic shape for optimum sailing efficiency. See glossary for terms for parts of a sail.

‡ Outward curving of the edges of the sail that were attached to mast and spars, to provide draft.

"The sail makers would take all these cloths—they'd numbered every one. And first they would sew two and two and two; and after they would sew them all together. It was all hand done, and the remarkable part is that it was done for 10 cents a yard. So a whole sail, a big sail, say fishing schooner size, 400 square yards, would only cost $40. However, the owner of the ship supplied the canvas and the boltropes, the sail twine and the clew irons. This beautiful hand-sewn sail for $40 was unbelievable. And yet they were happy to do it. They could do it fast because they didn't have just two or three men, they had about a dozen all sewing at once, and they sewed from daylight to dark, more or less. So a big sail could be done in a few days.

"And then the topsails—we experimented with them and got them gore* cut, not just along the leech but along the leech and the foot similar to the way a jib is put together. That made a much better draft for pulling them out. They didn't get hogged and out of shape when you were sheeting them out."

After the new sails were sewn and bent, *Wawaloam* sailed up to Turks to load salt for Clark's Harbour, then on to Lunenburg to load lumber for Bridgetown again. This circuit was made time and time again and became the standard run.

"We also made a contract in Barbados that every trip we would carry 10 or 20 tons—minimum of 10 tons—of dynamite for a big price of good, heavy freight.

"She was a remarkable little vessel. She was long and narrow, built on the lines of a steel square rigger. She went through the water very, very easily. She wouldn't go to windward very well when she was light. Because she was steel, she didn't draw much water and hadn't much grip, but the engine made up for that. Under power with 550 or 600 tons of salt aboard, she could do six knots with that engine. Nobody could believe it—it ran like a clock."

With a good suit of sails and proper loading, *Wawaloam* turned out to be a wonderful sailing vessel with few faults. But Lou, as we know, frequently overloaded her with lumber, making her "cranky" and almost impossible to sail to weather without the engine.

---

* Cut on the diagonal bias of the cloth, which allows the canvas to stretch into a curve.

Figure 4-6. Discharging salt at Clark's Harbour.

The events of one particular trip landed Lou and the *Wawaloam* into the technical manuals of Gray Marine and into the hearts of improvisers everywhere. In January of 1941, out of Lunenburg with a load of lumber for Barbados, *Wawaloam* reached 35° north when Pat mentioned she heard an unusual whine in the engine room. Lou investigated and discovered water had found its way into the starter motor and the motor was spinning unchecked. There was no fuse or shut-off switch, and as Lou was trying to disconnect the battery, the starter motor flew to pieces. Without the starter, the 6-71 couldn't be cranked up and without the diesel, the over-loaded schooner was impossible to sail efficiently to Barbados, so lumber would have to be jettisoned. Lou's natural inclination couldn't accept throwing perfectly good lumber overboard, so he tried something else.

The 6-71 had no compression release, so they couldn't hand crank it. But it did have that seven-inch flange on the front. In the hold, there were some eight-inch diameter spars. Lou cut a foot off one of them and bolted the cut end to the front flange with long 3/8-inch carriage bolts. As luck had it, this new wooden extension of the crankshaft was located directly below the engine room skylight, a removable hatch. Lou removed the butterfly hatch and rigged a series of blocks starting from the mizzen boom, forward to a padeye on the starboard rail just forward of the mainmast, then on to a block temporarily tied to the foremast. He then ran a two-inch manila rope over 100 feet from the deck engine through the blocks and straight down through the skylight. He wrapped the rope several times around the wooden flange extension, in the same direction as the engine's rotation.

Once the line was run, Lou waved a blow torch for several minutes at the pan at the bottom of the engine to thin out the engine oil. Meanwhile, the crew drained the water from the engine's cooling system and refilled it with boiling water. This wasn't easy. First the water had to be boiled on the stove in the galley up forward and then schlepped back to the engine room in buckets without spilling and scalding the carrier. Remember, this was all being done in a seaway. As soon as the cooling system was filled and the oil heated, Lou went topside. Standing over the engine room hatch, he held the tail end of the two-inch line. He motioned the mate to take up the slack. The line tightened and Peter put three wraps around the deck engine's windlass drum. Lou waved his index finger in a circle signifying that the mate should engage the donkey engine.

Gilbert Plumb, a friend and sailorman in his own right, retells Lou's description of the procedure:

I remember Captain Lou telling me the line was getting tighter and tighter and wondering if the new wooden cat head [on the 6-71] would hold the strain. All of sudden the line went "zing" and the engine turned over and was running. He didn't shut it off for 10 days until they reached Barbados. *

This was the first time a 6-71 had been started like an outboard motor.

When *Wawaloam* arrived in Bridgetown, there was no one who could repair the starter, so the same procedure was used on the return trip up to Turks. It couldn't be fixed in Newfoundland when they got back so they just kept starting the engine with a rope.

"So we went on and ran it with a rope. We got to Bridgewater [Nova Scotia] *and the Agent in Halifax had wired or telephoned Detroit, telling him how I needed this bad because I was starting it with a rope. And down came two engineers and they wanted to see how one of these engines was started with a rope. They'd never heard of a 6-71 being started with a rope like an outboard motor. They got Johnny Knickle to*

---

* From a personal letter to Patsy Kenedy Bolling. (Used by permission.)

come over and take photographs of the whole process. I showed them how it was done, and they made a shop manual, telling people how they could start their engine with a rope if they had some kind of a winch with enough power to pull the rope. So it became quite a talked-about affair, but fortunately we never had to use it again."

By this time, the U.S. was gearing up for war and manufacturing small landing craft, generators, and trucks by the thousands, many of them powered by 6-71's, both the earlier Gray Marines and GM's. Lou's method of rope-starting ended up in a service bulletin distributed to military personnel world-wide.

* * *

The prewar *Wawaloam* trips were some of the most enjoyable of Lou's career. The schooner was profitable and a big carrier. Pat, Lou, and Brian made many trips during that time with Pat as the cook. She quickly became accustomed to keeping the stove hot in sweltering tropical calms or violent storms. The dual meal schedule became second nature. The first breakfast was served to the off-watch crew at 0730. At eight bells, the watch changed and the rest of the crew clambered down the companionway for pancakes, oat meal, bacon, and eggs.

After the first few days out, there were no more fresh vegetables or fresh meat, so meal planning was easy. Lunch was the main meal of a sailor's day. First lunch was served at 1130 followed by the noon watch change. It usually consisted of soup, salt fish or salt beef—fresh fish was frequently available—along with potatoes, a veggie, and a sweet dessert of some type. Often, pudding and pies were the after-dinner treat. A huge pot of coffee stayed piping hot on the stove for the night watches.

Figure 4-7. Lou's brother John Kenedy painting a U.S. flag on the topsides of *Wawaloam,* as the captain watches. Clear vessel identification was a wartime necessity.

Figure 4-8. *Wawaloam's* **crew, 1941**

As Germany wrapped a partial quarantine around the Caribbean islands, only neutral ships were safe from the U-boat threat. Until December 7, 1941, the U.S. was neutral, and Lou, running *Wawaloam* under U.S. registry, took advantage of the skyrocketing shipping rates to load enormously profitable cargos. He always carried personal trading goods and knew what shortages existed in the islands from intelligence gathered on the previous trip. Though Lou admits to intermittent rum running on a small scale, there is well founded conjecture that *Wawaloam* was a main supplier of Mount Gay and other brands of Barbados rum to the LaHave River waterfront.

Even the most mundane products became prohibitively expensive. Consumables—rubber products, newsprint, clothing, food, and the like—were particularly costly. During this time, Lou carried hundreds of items such as tires and fan belts on his own account to earn extra profit. Fan belts sometimes sold for $50 or more in the islands; these fan belts cost Lou only a buck or two in Canada.

When the Japanese attack on Oahu finally allowed the U.S. to drop the pretense of neutrality, Pat and Lou had to reappraise their living arrangements. Brian was approaching school age, and the U-boat danger in the Atlantic and Caribbean was palpable. The shipping business was wildly lucrative, too profitable for Lou Kenedy to abandon, but it was too dangerous for his family to live aboard. The couple bought a lovely old white colonial facing the LaHave River in Conquerall Bank, Nova Scotia. When at home, *Wawaloam* was anchored in the front yard. They had little furniture; most was still in storage in Barbados. Lou would haul it north on a succeeding trip.

This change in venue brought with it a startling change in management. Aboard *Wawaloam*, Lou was a strict authoritarian. Such a disciplinarian wouldn't be tolerated today—it was barely tolerated then. But the moment he stepped through the front door at Conquerall Bank, he passed all authority to Pat. She was the undisputed captain of the Nova Scotia hearth and home. Whenever *Wawaloam* returned from a voyage, and once the maintenance chores aboard were complete, the crew members who stayed on salary between trips knew Pat had now become the skipper. Lou was at her beck and call to tend to chores and child-rearing tasks that had gone wanting since his departure.

When the little house was purchased, it had no front walk. Once, while *Wawaloam* was home, Pat asked one of the crewmen, a hardworking Newfie named Leonard Sober, to get some flat stones and set them into the grass leading to the front steps. Leonard was a better sailor than a handyman, and picked rocks that were much too rough for a walk. After several hours of work, Pat went to check on him. He was about to lay the last stone adjacent to the first step. When Pat saw it, she said, "Leonard, that won't do at all. It's much too rough. People will trip on it. Can't you find a smoother stone, at least for the one next to the step?" Leonard, not known for quick responses to anything, stared at the lumpy old rock he was holding and said, "Yes, Mum." A couple of hours passed and Pat went out to check on his progress. There she beheld a beautiful rectangular piece of granite with only a little texture to it. It fit perfectly and ran the entire width of the step. "Why Leonard, it's perfect!" gushed Pat.

"Thanks, Mum," said Leonard, rocking on his heels while holding his hat in both hands behind him. Pat then noticed that one small corner of the stepping stone seemed polished and had some writing engraved in it. Pat bent over to look at it, looked back up at Leonard, and said, "Leonard, what's that writing on the stone?" "Don't know Mum," he replied, "but the other side has a bunch more of it. And if you don't like that one, Mum, there's a lot of them rocks up by the cemetery." No one on the LaHave ever found out who stole that headstone, or where it ended up.

* * *

Figure 4-9. *Wawaloam* anchored in front of the Kenedy home in Conquerall Bank.

Back in August of 1941, while Pat and Lou still blithely enjoyed unprecedented financial success and a happy married life aboard *Wawaloam*, the 220-foot steel shark, U-86, was commissioned. Built at the Flender-Werke yards in Lübeck, Germany, she was a Type VII-b submarine, one of five VII-bs built at Flender. She was commanded by only one skipper during her life, Walter Schug. Handsome and easy-going, Walter was born within a few days of Lou Kenedy in 1910. Throughout several training voyages around Kiel and in eight combat missions, Schug's career was totally unremarkable. So undistinguished was his service, one can only believe that he might not have possessed the necessary blood-lust for which the *Unterseeboot Kapitänen* were famous. It seems that Schug, much to his credit, was more concerned with getting his crew home safely than sinking Allied tonnage. By all accounts, he was a gentleman and would have been better suited for service in a less violent branch of the military. This conjecture is verified by the fact that during her entire two-year career, consisting of eight missions, U-86 sank only three ships, totaling a little over 10,000 tons.

Though there were other relatively unsuccessful U-boats, most of those had short lives and relatively few missions. For example, between February and June 1941 during two patrols—one was a training mission—U-556 sank six vessels totaling almost 30,000 tons. U-701 sank nine ships of 28,000 tons and damaged another five ships of 38,000 tons in eight missions, and U-94 sank 25 ships in 10 patrols, totaling 137,000 tons. By comparison, U-86's paltry

10,000 tons makes one wonder if Walter Schug didn't spend most of the war parked at the bottom of a comfortable fjord, surfacing only to plink at net floats and hoping that Karl wouldn't call.

But Karl did call. Admiral Karl Dönitz, in July, 1942 ordered Walter and U-86—among others—to join Group Wolf to reestablish U-boat supremacy in the North Atlantic.

* * *

One advantage schooners had over other blockade runners was that in those days, submarines couldn't pick up the sound of a vessel unless it had a running engine. In fact, during the first months of the war, the British Admiralty was still under the impression that the Germans did not yet possess any type of underwater listening technology. Most schooner captains, having their own jungle telegraph as to the capabilities of the Germans, and having no trust in the Admiralty, used engines only to pull themselves out of calms or into harbors.

Figure 4-10. The captain at the helm of *Wawaloam*.

In the middle of June of 1942, *Wawaloam* cleared Bridgewater for Barbados with a cargo of mixed products and trading goods, arriving in good time, 16 days later. It took longer than usual to reload her for the return trip, because Lou had to make repeated trips back and forth to Pat's parents' old house to haul furniture with a tiny truck. His absence from the dock slowed the loading of the paying cargo. Finally, after two weeks on the island, *Wawaloam* cleared for St. John's loaded with a couple of hundred puncheons of molasses and all the furniture given to the couple by her parents. In addition, the old canvas-covered Morris was aboard as deck cargo.

On this trip the crew included Butch, his newest German shepherd. He was a big impressive-looking pooch weighing in at 85 pounds, and he adored Lou. Black-as-coal Peter Jones was mate.

"*...we got a telegram from Halifax saying the war risk insurance was running out and did we want to renew? Now war risk was a separate insurance from marine risk and it fluctuated with the way the war was going; and it was terrible at the time. It had been 10 percent for three months, which is 40 percent for a year. And the telegram said that the new rate was 15 percent for three months—60 percent a year. So I looked at that telegram for awhile and I studied it and I swore if the odds were that bad, it looked pretty hopeless. So I wired them back and said, 'Insure the vessel but double the value.'*

"*Well, we took off and we had a great run up to 39° N.*"

* * *

In 1942, England and the U.S.S.R were spared an ignominious German rout solely because vast quantities of men and materiel arrived in lumbering convoys that streamed from the Americas to British ports and northward to Murmansk. German U-boat packs were dispatched to destroy the convoys and stop this flow.

The day after *Wawaloam* cleared Bridgetown for St. John's, July 26, 1942, U-86 commanded by *Kapitänleutenant* Walter Schug, rendezvoused with the other members of Group Wolf. This is the group that inspired the name of the entire program of dispatching organized packs of submarines to prowl the North Atlantic.

The stalking grounds of the wolf packs were bordered by the limits of the flight ranges of cover aircraft based in Newfoundland, Iceland, and the British Isles. The unprotected area southeast of Greenland, called the "Black Pit" by the Allies, was U-boat heaven. The subs formed up in lines and simply waited for the convoys to swim into the net. So in late July of 1942, Group Wolf was shadowing convoy ON 113 made up mostly of vessels in ballast returning from Britain to reload in American ports.

* * *

At 0300 on August 6, *Wawaloam* was drifting in a dead calm. The sails were slatting, and the mate ordered the engine started. They rocked along on a glassine sea through the end of the watch at 0800, with the sails sheeted in tightly to help control the rolling and to minimize the sails beating themselves up. At 0815, Lou cradled a cup of coffee in his hands when he came topside into the cold air. He had already done a DR position. *Wawaloam* was 489 miles south of Cape Race. For a trip to Halifax or Lunenburg, he would never sail that far to the east, but this trip he had cleared for St. John's, Newfoundland to unload the molasses before returning home to Conquerall Bank.

The sun rose fine that morning, but the wind stayed dead calm. Only the groan of the diesel broke the silence. The mate had eaten breakfast and was already asleep. The morning watch was kept busy with holystoning the deck (scrubbing with sandstone) and other maintenance chores while Lou took the helm.

* * *

At first light, August 6, 1942, U-86 submerged to periscope depth after spending the night on the surface charging batteries. At 1145 the hydrophone operator reported an engine sound 5,000 meters off the starboard bow. It was closing on the sub. Walter ordered the periscope raised. He reversed his cap so the visor was out of the way and through the eyepiece saw the hull of a sailing ship rolling on a slick sea. She was black with white deckhouses and wore only the fores'l and the forestays'l. A large American flag painted on the topsides stood out starkly against the dark hull. In the calm, the slow speed supplied by the engine alone made the schooner seem motionless on the water. Blue smoke blew out the exhaust pipe aft and black smoke circled up from Charley Noble. Without lowering the periscope, Walter ordered his executive officer to load both forward torpedo tubes.

* * *

At 1200, Lou and the three members of the 0800-to-1200 watch tumbled below for lunch after the mate, Peter Jones, and his noon watch arrived on deck. As is customary, the new helmsman loudly repeated the course ordered by the captain as he took over the steering station.

Below, lunch consisted of a plate of raw Spam and mayonnaise sandwiches, a wartime creation, and French-fried potatoes with a pitcher of reconstituted milk to flush it all down. The three men ate quickly, and the Newfie cook, Mitchell Paige, took the plates away.

* * *

After 15 minutes of confirming bearings and speed, Walter Schug slammed the periscope handles up and ordered it lowered. "Torpedo – los!" he commanded. With a burst of compressed air, the noisy G7aT1 *Ato* torpedo squirted from the submarine's starboard bow tube. The six-bladed prop churned the water and left an exhaust trail of bubbles behind as it flew toward the schooner at 40 knots. Schug waited five seconds before raising the periscope again to view the sure destruction of the obsolete freighter.

* * *

The dead flat sea offered none of the normal sailing ship sounds. The Gray Marine 6-71 droning deep in the bilge and an off-watch sailor holystoning the deck was all that was heard. *Wawaloam* rolled heavily, and the mess-room lamp swung from a deck beam above the table.

After the meal, Mitchell sat at the mess table with Lou and poured himself a cup of coffee. Reginald Reid, the Bajan stowaway discovered aboard *Abundance,* now in his mid-twenties, read a week-old edition of the *Bridgetown Advocate.* The Newfie cook asked, "Cap, we got a big dolphin we hooked yesterday for dinner tonight. OK?" "That's all?" Lou asked. "No sir, provisions* too along with…"

The cook never finished his statement. A whining sound in the distance attracted everyone's attention. No one spoke as the sound grew and became a louder scream that began to reverberate within *Wawaloam*. Within seconds, the shriek of a high-speed train ran from port to starboard nearly deafening the men. The Doppler shift made the sound more menacing as the train passed under the keel and the noise and vibration faded to starboard and out into the Atlantic. The whole event had taken less than 30 seconds.

Reginald Reid jumped to his feet and looked terrified. The cook looked at Lou with huge eyes and asked, "What the hell is that?" Lou answered quickly, "That, boys, says it's time to hit the dories."

When Lou, Reginald, and Mitchell scrambled on deck, Tannis, the Bajan bow watch, was screaming incoherently about a torpedo. Two hundred yards to port, U-86 surfaced, and German sailors popped up from a bow hatch and manned the deck cannon.

Lou cut the engine. Then he ordered the dories over the side as he hustled below to retrieve his sea chest containing a sextant, timepiece, almanacs, and charts. Peter Jones, who had loaded a couple of cases of bully beef and another cask of water, was already aboard a dory with two ABs. He yelled at Lou to hurry up just as the first shell landed 50 yards ahead of the ship. Peter

---

* Provisions are cooked vegetables.

would have been more frantic if he had known that Lou was wasting time below searching for his camera. He wanted to take snapshots!

Lou finally gave up looking for the camera and hauled his chest and a seabag up on deck. Butch, the German shepherd, met him at the deckhouse hatch. Lou ordered Peter to push off and row away from the schooner as he wrestled to lower Butch into the remaining dory.

Reginald Reid and Mitchell Paige manhandled Butch into the dory, and Lou scrambled down a Jacob's ladder the mate had rigged.

* * *

On a previous voyage, weather cloths had been installed to keep Brian from falling overboard from the poopdeck. These had not been removed and hid a significant part of the deck from view. This might have been taken for an attempt to hide weapons. Ever cautious, Walter Schug considered the possibility that *Wawaloam* was an armed combatant—an unlikely Q-boat. At first, he didn't bring U-86 any closer than 200 yards, and his first shot across the bow didn't land close enough to endanger the ship or its crew. Walter Schug was not much of a warrior and definitely not a murderer. It wasn't until the dories were visible on the wave crests 500 yards from the schooner that Schug began shelling *Wawaloam* in earnest. This, of course, begs the question as to why he fired the torpedo in the first place.

* * *

When the first shell was fired for effect, *Wawaloam* was an abandoned vessel, with her crew pulling hard to put distance between themselves and the ship. The mate was in one dory, and Lou commanded the other. The boats, each black with white gunwales, were 19 feet long. Each had a compass and a set of sails with the necessary rigging.

* * *

Walter's crew wasted five shots on the old sailing ship without hitting her. Either they were the worst shots who ever sailed a U-boat (a theory that is not without some merit given their battle record), or they didn't realize *Wawaloam* was jogging ever so slowly northwestward, because the crew had never lowered the two steadying sails. Undaunted, Schug ordered yet another volley of cannon fire. This was it! *Wawaloam* was doomed. Three shots were fired, and then another three shots; there were nothing but splashes, far and wide.

It was embarrassing. The cost of the ineffective torpedo exceeded the value of *Wawaloam* and her cargo, and now ammunition was also being wasted.

The crewmen in the dories were beginning to hope that out of sheer humiliation, the U-boat would simply give up and go away. No such luck. The U-boat turned and headed for the dories, leaving *Wawaloam* unharmed, rolling in the seaway. A picture of the archetypical U-boat captain, actor Conrad Veidt perhaps, fleetingly passed though Lou's mind; "Vee vill now surface, und machine gun zuh survivors." But he needn't have worried.

The U-boat was not a large ship and was easily maneuvered windward of the dories. Walter Schug, a handsome young man in his thirties, was a few days younger than Lou. He spoke passable English and shouted down from the conning tower, "You haff everysing you need?" Lou yelled back, "Flashlights!"

Walter couldn't hear him over the engine noise and the sound of the sea washing over the sub. He motioned for the skipper to climb aboard. Lou caught a line from a German crewman and stepped directly from the dory to the deck of U-86. He climbed the steel ladder of the conning tower and stood face to face with Schug and two other officers.

"So he [Schug] asked, 'Haff you to eat? Haff you to drink? Do you need anysing?' And 1 said, 'I need lights.' I meant flashlights. But he said, 'I'll send a fellow below,' and he came up with an aluminum box full of flares and rockets. I still have part of it at home here, which I saved as souvenirs. It says on the box, 'flickenfluckensickensunder.' They tell me it means, the lights are burning under the water even if they're wet. All in one word."

Lou thanked Schug for the flares and asked, "How did you pick us up?" "We heard your engine running; if you didn't haff your engine running vee vouldn't haff picked you up." Curious about his future, Lou asked, "What are you going to do now?" "Vell, I must destroy your ship," answered the sub commander. "That's a hell of an out, she's not winning the war for anybody. You could let her go," said Lou. "No, I cannot do zat, *C'est la guerre*," replied Walter in his best accented English and French. Lou was surprised to hear a French *bon mot* pop out of the German's mouth. But without hesitation, Lou looked the captain in the eye, and as if he were asking a buddy for a ride to the next gas station, said "How about giving us a tow?"

Incredulous, Schug said, "A tow, a tow to vere?" "To Bermuda," Lou answered. The German just shook his head in disbelief, smiled, and said, "Vee are not going to Bermuda." "Well, wherever you are going is a hell of a lot better than here," Lou replied. Schug translated Lou's unusual request, and the other U-boat crewmen started to smile. One young officer grabbed his crotch and said, *"Er hat Messingtestikel"* and they all laughed.

"What did he say?" Lou asked. "Your balls are made of brass!" said Schug. Lou smiled broadly. When it was obvious to the Germans that the American captain understood the joke, the submarine officers laughed even harder.

* * *

"I was 489 miles south of Cape Race and about 500 miles northeast of Bermuda and 1,000 from the Azores. That was a hell of a place. Couldn't be worse. So, then's when he said, 'When I'm gone from here six hours, I'll radio your position and somebody will come and get you, maybe.' I said, 'I'll thank you, if you did.'

"And by God, the next day my mother down in Connecticut picked up the New York Times *or the* Herald *and there it was—a notice from Headquarters: A submarine had sunk an American sailing vessel in Latitude and Longitude so and so. So he was as good as his word. He must have got word in and it was right on the news the next day."*

Lou thanked Schug and his officers for the flares and climbed down from the conning tower. He threw the box to the mate and timed the surge to step directly into the dory. Butch, the big German shepherd, was glad to see him, stood up to lick Lou's face, and wagged his tail, thumping it against the inwale.

The men pulled away from the sub and Schug maneuvered in a large circle to put *Wawaloam* in closer range of the deck gun. It took another three shots to finally fell the mizzenmast and another four to finish off the foremast. The downed rigging draped over the mainmast shrouds and stays. The scene was surreal; because he hadn't been able to find his camera, Lou sat in the sternsheets of the dory and sketched what he saw.

Finally, a shell hit amidships on the port rail and continued though the main hatch. This ignited the molasses in the hold, and molasses burns like bunker oil.

"After awhile it was a tremendous plume of black smoke and it was calm by this time and it went aloft for maybe two miles... I don't know, it went straight up and it burned and burned and burned."

At 1400, Walter Schug and U-86 passed close by the dories, snapped a salute to Lou and motored off to rejoin Group Wolf. As he left, Schug let several of the crewmembers come topside to take souvenir snapshots of the burning schooner and the two dories full of survivors. There was no wind; the sub slid out of sight northeastward.

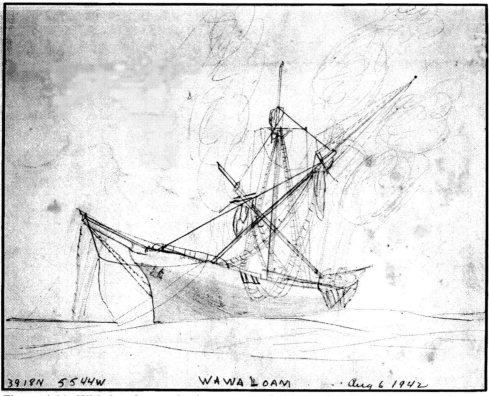

Figure 4-11. With her fore and mizzen masts shot away by the deck gun on German submarine U-86, *Wawaloam* is now afire. Pencil sketch drawn by Lou Kenedy while in the dory after abandoning ship.

Walter Schug was a gentleman who didn't conduct the unlimited submarine warfare that was practiced by most of his contemporaries. Even early in the war, the U.S. sub fleet in the Pacific sank ships without warning and didn't pick up survivors. Kapitän Walter Schug was made from a different bolt of canvas. Lou tried for years to find him after the war. He believed he was successful 22 years later when an ex-German naval officer told him Walter was teaching at the German Naval Academy in Flensburg. He wrote to the Academy and received an answer from a Commander Walter Schute.

"Eventually I got a letter back and it said, 'I'm not the man that sank your beautiful schooner Wawaloam; *but I've looked up in the archives and the name of the man who sank you was Lt. Walter Schug.' So the spelling was wrong but the pronunciation was just about right. And he and his crew were all killed, sunk and killed 15 months later off the Azores. He was attacked by planes from the U.S. carrier* Bogue *and that*

was the end of him. Now he was a good man and he treated me like a man and I'm very sorry that he was lost; I would have liked, after the war, to get together with him over a couple of beers and compare notes of our adventures. That's life I guess; it looks so futile after 40 or 50 years, all these things that men lost their lives over."

There is some controversy over whether U-86 was the sub sunk by planes from the *Bogue*. Some historians are now stating that on November 22, 1943, the *Bogue*'s planes actually dropped depth charges on U-764 in an unsuccessful attack. Nevertheless, the last word from U-86 and her crew was on the 28th of November, 1943 as they were stalking convoys MKS-31 and SL-140 in the North Atlantic. But she never answered the regular radio transmissions scheduled for the 14th of December, 1943.

* * *

The first night in the boats the wind and seas were building, and Lou tried to keep the dories close to the burning *Wawaloam*. The fire was visible for miles, and he figured it might attract a rescue ship. But just after 2200, the fire abruptly went out. The schooner had sunk.

Lou ordered the crews to rig the dory sails as sea anchors to hold the bows to windward. They were in the Gulf Stream, which added to the nasty sea state. Unknown to Lou, they were skirting the edge of a hurricane that was battering Bermuda at the time. The storm was so strong, it broke up several convoys bound for England.

At 1000 the next morning, the wind backed to the south with cresting seas. One crewman in each dory manned the oars, constantly rowing backwards to keep the line to the sea anchors tight. If they didn't row backwards, when a sea passed under the dories, the lines would slack allowing the boat to broach beam to the seas. If they allowed a breaking sea to catch them sideways, the boats would be swamped. Lou rowed the first, second, and third watches, 12 hours without relief. Finally, a rogue wave caught the mate's boat and it pitchpoled.

"...she was thrown end for end, bow over the stern and all hands in the water. And I thought, boy, here we got a good drowning party. The mate couldn't swim, the two boys that were with him—colored boys from the West Indies—they were good swimmers and they grabbed hold of him and put him on the bottom of the dory, or hanging onto it. The dory plug had a thong in it and he was able to hold onto that. We started easing her over to us while we maneuvered to keep bow on. Of course I kept rowing astern and we got over and one by one we got them

into my dory. I didn't let them all in at once because I wanted to make sure the dory could hold us all. We ended up with seven men and a dog, which was a lot, along with our food and a barrel of water."

All the loose gear in the mate's dory was lost and the water in the keg was spoiled as the bung wasn't tight. But Lou kept it for emergencies. The next day was calm, and they spent time righting and bailing the mate's dory. The sails and oars were still there but the sailing thwart was missing. Without the sailing thwart with its hole for holding the mast, it would be difficult to sail to safety.

Amazingly, after an entire night and half a day of stormy weather, one of the West Indians stood up to stretch and said, "Dere she is." "There who is?" asked Lou. "De sailin' hole bahd," said the crewman. It was only 100 yards away. It's a wonder it stayed so close after the hours of huge seas and heavy winds. They retrieved the thwart and re-stepped the mast.

The wind settled sou'west and both boats made sail. Lou wanted to make Newfoundland, the closest point of land to their position, but was afraid he might miss it to port due to the northeasterly set of the Gulf Stream. So instead of heading north, he steered northwest toward Nova Scotia, so if he got headed or the Stream was particularly powerful, he would still make Newfoundland.

At night, Lou coupled the two dories together with light line so they wouldn't lose each other. He had a hand compass that was luminescent so he took the lead at sundown, and the dory astern would reduce sail so not to ride up on the leading boat. On one of the first nights Lou was steering and felt the dory vibrating like an outboard engine with a rough idle. He looked overboard but saw nothing. It turned out to be one of the young West Indian crewmen. The poor, terrified sailor, curled up in the bow, was shaking uncontrollably. Lou calmed him down with a few words and a funny story and the shaking stopped.

On day one, Lou instituted a rigorous rationing regimen.

"I decided that for rations we'd eat very little and drink very little the first week because we could live on our fat, so to speak. That way we'd have plenty of grub. We could always increase the allowance rather than shorten down on it because it's hard to shorten down but it is easier to increase. So each boat got one can of food a day between all hands; one boat had four men, one had three and a dog. We tried bully beef, but that was too dry and miserable. The best thing we liked was a tin of fruit, which was juicy and nourishing too. We allowed one glass of water a day a man, which wasn't near enough. But by the time we were

picked up, we were pretty dry in the mouth and the poor old dog, he was having a bad time."

Butch also got his glass of water each day but was much more sensitive to dehydration than the men. Three days after losing *Wawaloam*, they got a respite when they replenished the water supply from a passing front that produced heavy rain squalls and high seas. The dories hove to for the entire day. The resultant drenching probably saved Butch's life.

The dories were not equipped with tillers or rudders; all steering was done with an oar pivoting in a half-round cutout in the taffrail on the stern. It's not easy steering this way for extended periods. Before long, Lou promised himself if he survived the ordeal, all his dories and lifeboats would have proper tillers and rudders, pintles and gudgeons.

Lou took sights everyday and pinpointed their position exactly. One day they made 96 miles! That's an amazing run for two sailing dories. If the wind was high, they scandalized the main. If it got too high, they'd take in the jib. But they stayed underway day and night. The seas and breeze were generally off the port beam, and the crew always sat with their backs against the port rail. Nobody wanted to look at the size of the endless string of monstrous rollers that ran down on them. The seas didn't look quite as intimidating from the backside.

At 0200 on the sixth night, Lou spotted a star in the west that didn't set. He said nothing to the crew as the light—now obviously a vessel—got brighter. He took out the box of "flickenfluckensickensunder" and fired one off without informing the sleeping crews. They were awakened with a start from the swoosh of the rocket as it soared west and at about 600 feet, exploded into a bright red parachute flare.

The vessel closed on the two dories and Lou fired another rocket. She hove to handy to the dories and Lou yelled, "Give us a lift?" An Irish brogue answered back, "T'would be a pleasure." Lou yelled, "Throw some lines down so we can hoist some gear aboard." Three 3/4-inch lines uncoiled as they dropped down to the dories. The little boats were held off the fouled boot top of the surging freighter by two men standing in each dory fending them with their arms outstretched. The deck lights on the freighter barely illuminated the scene, and from the freighter's deck, the black and white dories surged in and out of shadows.

The mate grabbed a line and attached Lou's sea chest that contained the sextant, chronometer, and log book. He had wrapped the instruments in clothes inside the chest and they never got the least bit damp, even in the heaviest gales.

Next was Butch. Butch was accustomed to being hoisted aboard. Lou would prepare a quick rope sling that went around the dog's chest and the big German shepherd would "walk" right up the topsides as he was pulled aboard. On this evening, Lou wrapped Butch in the harness as usual and yelled, "Heave away." Butch, true to form, walked effortlessly up the side of the ship. But just as the dog's head cleared the freighter's gunwale, a crewman screamed in terror, "Oh, Lord Jesus, 'tis a great beast," and let go the line. Butch tumbled into the water and splashed around, wondering what the hell happened to the normal boarding procedure. Except for the surprise of falling back, the pooch was no worse for wear, but Lou was livid. And with the Captain Louis Kenedy voice that was never ignored, he hollered back to the Irish crewman, "You dumb sonofabitch, haul this dog aboard or I'll personally come up there and beat the living crap out of you. This dog's a survivor, for Christ's sake." The dog was brought aboard with no further delay.

Figure 4-12. Butch, the survivor.

A ladder was finally lowered for the men. Many of them had trouble climbing as their legs weren't working well after six days curled up in dories. One by one they struggled aboard, Lou being the last to board the freighter.

True to form, not wanting to waste perfectly good dories, Lou's first request was that they haul them aboard. They cost good money, dammit. At this point the captain appeared out of the shadows and explained it was very dangerous for them to stay here just to retrieve dories. The ship was lit up like a carnival and even if she was a neutral, it was dangerous. "Neutral?" asked

Lou. "Irish, this here ship is the *Irish Rose*," answered the ruddy faced captain.

"So her name was the Irish Rose *and she was from Waterford, Ireland, outbound from Saint John, New Brunswick, with a load of wheat or grain for Waterford. She was an old Hog Island steamer of about 3,000 tons. She was very slow, six knots was her pace. I looked over the side. I said, 'I could be going a hell of a lot better in a schooner than this.' But anyway they were very kind and wonderful men and full of humor."*

Built in 1918, *Irish Rose* originally sailed under the Latvian flag but was spirited out of Riga when the Russians marched in. One of the few coal burners built at the famous Hog Island shipyards, she was sold to an Irish shipping company, and she was manned with a black gang of hard drinking, coal-dust-covered Irishmen.

The crew of *Irish Rose* sank the dories with rifle fire, and the survivors were led below to the crew's mess. Lou finally got around to letting the Irish captain know that the *Wawaloam* crew was thirsty as hell. The old Irish skipper said, "Water? Jesus, you want water? That'll be a problem." Lou was incredulous, "You don't have any water?" "No," replied the old man, "All our water comes from the condenser and we used it all up, there won't be any until morning when we fill the jugs."

Just then one of the Irish sailors handed Lou a cold, label-less gin bottle just like the ones Lou filled with water and stuck in the ice box when he had ice aboard. So Kenedy, thinking it was water, took a huge slug of what turned out to be pure gin. His mouth was "as dry as an old piece of ham" and it burned the hell out of his tongue and throat. The famous Kenedy temper started to boil. But the pleasant buzz caused by the gin adjusted his attitude, just as trays full of cold fruit juices were delivered from the galley. The survivors drank and drank; they drank more than they should have and several got sick but there were no long-lasting ill effects.

The *Irish Rose* crew found a bucket-full of rusty water and Lou told them to give it to Butch, who was on deck looking for a place to relieve himself for the first time in six days. Soon afterwards, one of the schooner's crewmen ran into the mess room where Lou and the crew had congregated and shouted, "Cap, what do we do now? The dog's drunk a bucket of water and he's all swole up." Butch had no lasting ill effects from over-drinking, but he certainly didn't need water for quite a while thereafter.

* * *

Lou didn't want to go to Waterford. Pat and Brian were waiting for him in Newfoundland, his original destination, and it pained him to think about sloshing over to Ireland in a six-knot tramp steamer, then having to hitch or, God forbid, pay for a ride back to the Maritimes. The crew of one dory, when they heard their new destination, wanted to return to the life boats. Hell, they were only 120 miles south of Sable Island. They could be there in two days. Lou reminded them the dories had been sunk, so they continued rolling east.

On the third day after the rescue, HMS *Campanula*, a British corvette that had lost her convoy in the storm (the same storm that had capsized the mate's dory) happened upon the scene. After exchanging blinker signals, the warship approached *Irish Rose* only to ask for some bread. They were out of flour and besides the cook was lousy and didn't know how to make bread. As *Irish Rose*'s captain was about to answer the request, Lou pulled the megaphone out of his hands and asked the Brit where he was going.

"Argentia, Newfoundland" was the answer. Lou yelled back, "We got seven survivors aboard heading in the wrong direction, can you take us?" "I suppose so," replied the British skipper, "but we'd get there somewhat faster if we had 20 loaves of bread." Lou looked at *Irish Rose*'s master who nodded, and Lou yelled, "It's a deal." The old Irishman quietly commented, "Skipper, you better stay aboard here. Looks like you're going aboard a hungry ship. How times have changed—with the British Navy coming to ask an old Irish tramp for a bit o' bread." The cook, Mitchell Paige, was raised in Argentia and was overjoyed to be going home.

With the crew and the bread transferred, the corvette turned for Newfoundland. But on the way, and much to Lou's disgust, the warship wasted a half day bombing for fish with depth charges. Though the fresh food was welcome, Lou would have been just as happy to skip the fish fry and dock a half day earlier.

Arriving in Argentia, Lou was "ordered" to debrief an Admiralty officers' panel on the sinking of *Wawaloam*. The officers simply wouldn't believe that the Germans had underwater listening gear. They didn't have it in the last war, so how could they have it now? The panel argued the point for hours while grilling Lou repeatedly about the same details. Lou was as impatient as ever, and perhaps even more so, as a worried Pat was waiting for him in St. John's.

Not having a reputation for concealing his personal feelings, Lou finally had enough and abruptly stood up and said, "You're all idiots and you're going to lose us this war." He then turned and stormed out of the room. He immediately found a local man willing to rent his car, so Lou could drive the crew across the peninsula to St. John's.

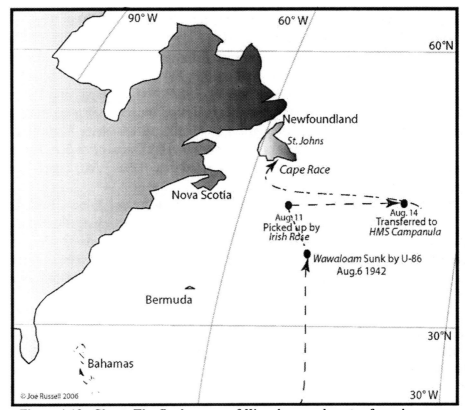

Figure 4-13. Chart: The final voyage of *Wawaloam* and route of survivors.

Lou chugged the grimy Model-A Ford onto the grounds and under the porte-cochere of the British-proper Newfoundland Hotel. Lou and the rest of the crew were wearing the same clothes they wore when they abandoned *Wawaloam*. Lou was a fashion statement in sea boots, red plaid jacket, and a pair of bull's-wool-and-oakum pants. To the horror of the concierge, the captain, crew, and Butch sauntered into the grand salon of the hotel and made themselves right at home. Lou had a seabag slung over his shoulder and looked around for the front desk. Butch, having had no access to trees for some time, made a bee line for a huge potted palm and relieved himself for what seemed like hours. "He murdered an areca palm, if I recall," Lou reminisced in later years.

The stricken hotel manager ran from behind the front desk and squealed, "He can't do that—he can't do that!" While staring directly into the eyes of the manager, in that old familiar voice that brooked only one response, Lou slowly answered, "Leave him alone, he's a survivor." The manager looked at Lou, looked at 80-pound Butch who was still poisoning the plant, looked back at Lou, swallowed, and quickly replied, "Oh…oh, that's different. That'll be all right then."

Lou threw his seabag at the base of the front desk and asked the clerk for Mrs. Kenedy. The clerk looked up and said, "Oh my, she's been waiting for you for over a week!" The reunion was as would be expected, and Pat and Lou weren't seen socially until two days later. Not wanting to risk the lingering death of another parlor palm, however, Lou was seen from time to time taking Butch down the fire escape for a walk. Once or twice, Pat and Brian were seen playing in the lobby. Other than that, they were incommunicado.

When the couple resurfaced, the problem of the crew had to be solved. Lou and the mate were the only ones who had thought of retrieving their papers from the schooner. The rest had left their passports, their very identities, aboard *Wawaloam*. Through the Dutch Consulate and the local Home Office, Lou arranged for passports to be reissued to the crew. The mate, Peter Jones, was from Saba which was Dutch; the rest were from British colonies.

En masse, the crew descended upon a local photographer and had their passport mug-shots taken. Newfoundland didn't have a significant black population and the photographer failed to take into consideration certain exposure factors. After three days cooling their heels, the pictures were delivered. They looked like Rorschach tests—just black blobs with no definition. Realizing his technical error, the photographer re-snapped them, and another three days passed before acceptable photos were returned.

A few days later, Pat, Lou, and Brian waved goodbye from the wharf as the black crewmen boarded a schooner for Barbados. Lou didn't know when, but he promised to call them back up from the Caribbean to sail on his next schooner. As the outbound schooner was pulled out of St. John's Harbour, the couple, with their little boy in tow, began their trip back to the white house at Conquerall Bank. After they arrived, Lou felt uneasy in the house and couldn't figure out why. Two days later, Pat solved the riddle: It just wasn't the same without *Wawaloam* in the front yard.

So ends this day.

Figure 5-1.

The ship: *Sea Fox*
Year of Launching: 1888
Rig: Schooner
Official #: 118216
Builder: Harlan & Hollingsworth,
    Wilmington, Delaware

Material: 7/16-inch Swedish iron plate
Length between perpendiculars: 115 feet
Beam: 23 feet 11 inches
Draft: 12 feet
Displacement: 100 tons

Chapter 5   *Sea Fox* (Redux)

It is now 1943, and Sea Fox *was about to be offered to the U.S. Navy as a coastal patrol ship. A small engine had been installed, so she was now officially an auxiliary schooner. Other than that, she was the same as when Lou sold her. She was in Easton, Maryland.*

* * *

Captain Lou Kenedy was, for all intents and purposes, land-bound. With the sinking of *Wawaloam*, he was ensconced at the Conquerall Bank house with no prospects. He even thought about going into farming. The mental picture of Lou behind a plow draws a smile from anyone who knew him and a belly laugh from anyone who crewed for him. In March, 1943, it was still colder than hell, and with no seafaring future, Lou was contemplating using ol' Dobbin's ass as a compass. Then a letter arrived that saved him from this awful fate. The owner of his beautiful iron *Sea Fox* wrote him to say that he was going to let the Navy take her over unless someone else stepped forward to buy her. She was anchored at Easton, Maryland, the same town where 60 years earlier, Captain Gus Rice, Lou's first skipper on the *Amanda F. Lewis*, marched a naked gunboat crew down Main Street in protest of the old oystering laws.

Lou and Peter Jones immediately took berths on a coal droger that was returning to New York in ballast. They jumped ship at City Island and hopped a freight train for Baltimore. They didn't want *Sea Fox*'s owner to know they had made the trip first as deckhands and then as hobos, so he grabbed a cab to the Baltimore train station where they finally met. The owner drove them in his car the rest of the way to Easton. Lou and the owner came to terms, and Lou again owned *Sea Fox*.

Other than the installation of a small engine and the rebuilding of her yacht interior, she was the same vessel, topmasts and all. Lou was anxious to get *Sea Fox* anchored in front of the Conquerall Bank house and immediately made plans to depart. The harbor at Easton was barely deep enough to float her and the tide was out. A classic Kenedy event was in the offing.

Lou cranked up the engine and put it in reverse. The prop turned six or seven times, a deep clunk shook *Sea Fox,* and the engine stopped cold. It was obvious that there was something wrapped around the prop. In the Caribbean, Lou would have been overboard instantly to handle the problem. This was March in Maryland, however, and the ice had just cleared the anchorage; the water was bitter cold. Lou, never indecisive, hesitated this time.

One of the onlookers on the dock pulled his head over the gunwale and said, "If you're man enough, I might have an answer to this problem." Lou's blood instantly boiled "What do you mean, 'If I'm man enough?'" he retorted. "Of course I'm man enough, what the hell are you talking about?" The stranger said, "I have a diving helmet and it might let you stay down long enough to clear the problem." "Get it," Lou ordered, still irritated over the "man enough" remark.

An hour passed, and the stranger arrived back at *Sea Fox* with a huge brass and copper helmet and a pump with lines to supply air. It was piled haphazardly in the back of a black Model-A pickup truck. Lou tried to lift the hat out of the truck but couldn't; it was really heavy. It took another hour for them to hook up the contraption. Two men lowered the helmet over Lou's head. He had taken off his trousers but left an undershirt on and he was already shivering. Peter Jones and a helpful onlooker began pumping the compressor; another two held a line attached to the helmet. There was no dinghy ladder on the wharf so Lou gave the thumbs up and jumped feet first into the icy water. The helmet was amazingly heavy and immediately pulled Lou's head down to the muddy bottom, while his feet floated straight up. It was as if the helmet were magnetized, drawn to the mud. He couldn't right himself because his hands and arms simply sank into the greasy muck when he tried to push himself up. Air bubbled around his neck and out of the helmet faster than the pump crew could replace it. Lou held his breath but he was running out of time.

When the tether didn't pay out, the shore crew figured something was wrong; then came a tug on the line. The two men hauled on it so hard that they pulled Lou upright and the helmet off his head. The hat flew out of water without Lou. He finally surfaced, gasping for air on the other side of *Sea Fox*. As soon as his head broke the surface, he started swearing a string of expletives that didn't stop until he climbed up *Sea Fox*'s boarding ladder, crossed the deck, and returned to the wharf. Shivering from the intense cold, he was covered from head to toe in bottom mud, a black ooze. Peter Jones started to laugh and said, "Cap, look!" He put his huge black arm next to Lou's sludge covered forearm to compare the color. Peter laughed harder but Lou, covered in the goo, didn't think it was funny and continued cursing everything and everyone.

The skipper found five links of three-inch chain on the dirt next to the dock. He ordered Peter to get some small stuff, and he tied the chain to his right leg with a slip knot as a weight to keep his feet down. He was in a hurry to get the job done because it was cold. "It's cold as a sonofabitch. If I don't get the job done this time, I'll never go back in, so let's get a move on."

He donned the brass hat yet again but this time he sat on the wharf before jumping in. His feet hit the mud first and he was able to gain a bit of stability. The visibility was only six inches or less and most of the job had to be done by feel. He found an anchor chain wound twice around the prop; it took him some time to unwrap it. Meanwhile, on the wharf, Peter and the pumpers were getting worried and started pumping faster and faster. More and more bubbles were rising from the stern of *Sea Fox*.

With one arm, Lou picked up some of the chain and with the other jerked the rope attached to the hat. He slipped the knot holding the links to his ankle and up he came.

"Anyway we hauled up the chain and we found a nice anchor on the end of it and we recovered that anyway. Then I went aboard and drank half a bottle of rum to warm up and that was the end of that story."

In later years, Lou often recounted this story. But the reason it stuck in his mind was not because of the numbing cold or the fact that he almost drowned, but rather because he got some free chain and an anchor out of the deal.

He and Peter sailed *Sea Fox* up to what is now Snyder's Shipyard in Dayspring, across the LaHave from Conquerall Bank. It was still Leary's in those days. There was so much work at the yard, Lou had to hire his own men to do the refit that would once again transform *Sea Fox* from a yacht to a commercial carrier. It took a couple of months, but by summer they had her stripped and ready to go.

Sea Fox's first charter came from P. J. Porter, a shipping agent in Halifax. She was to take a team of divers up to Île Brion to salvage a cargo of aluminum and copper ingots. This was 1943 and the war was still raging. A freighter loaded with the ingots had lost power in the Gulf of St. Lawrence and broken in half on the rocky shores of this little island north of the Magdalens.

Lou, Peter, and a crew from Lunenburg sailed the schooner up to Halifax to pick up the divers and their equipment. In Halifax, the salvage company put an accountant aboard to ensure the accuracy of the salvage proceeds. This gentleman was not an outdoorsman in any sense of the word and thus immediately caught Lou's attention. Lou Kenedy rarely let an opportunity go by to humbug an incompetent or a landlubber. Rarely did these unfortunate targets deserve this attention. But to allow easy prey—like this miserable accountant—to get away scot-free was not part of Lou's nature.

Trying to be helpful, the ever seasick bean counter noticed that the brass-clad compass balls needed polishing and offered to do the job. Lou obliged and stuck a can of brass polish and some rags in his hand said, "Help yourself."

At the time *Sea Fox* was feeling her way through a pea soup fog just off Île Brion, the mate came forward and said, "Cap, you ain't gonna believe what dat sissy's done, you woan believe it."

"I went back and here he was sitting on the rail and he'd unscrewed one of the magnets on the compass and he had it between his knees and he was shining it—having taken it off the binnacle. Well I blew my stack over that and said I was going back to Halifax and get the ship swung* —you know—lots of threats like that. But I knew how to put it back properly, although I scared the life out of him and made everybody laugh. So from then on he was a little bit out of tune with the goings on."

But this was just the start of the bookkeeper's troubles.

The wreck they were salvaging went on the beach in one piece, but the ice had sheared off the weakened bottom. The superstructure and half the hull were high and dry. The bottom, holding the aluminum and copper ingots, had fallen into several fathoms of water. When the salvage operation got underway, the team got one day of good weather and salvaged a significant portion of the bars. The second day, a nor'wester blew in, and *Sea Fox* sailed around the island for protection. After being anchored there for several days, good weather returned and another day or two of salvage work proceeded before the weather closed in again. This cycle continued for a month.

The bookkeeper brought along a black suitcase. He called it a "portmanteau." On the spot, Lou decided that longstanding maritime tradition dictated that a black suitcase aboard ship was bad luck. Further, any owner of a black suitcase would himself be a Jonah. The fact the luggage was called a portmanteau desecrated this "tradition" even further.

Lou finally told the tallyman that his black suitcase was as bad as having a woman or a minister aboard, and its color was the cause of the bad weather. The entire expedition would be a loss unless he went below immediately and painted the suitcase white. The accountant blanched and informed the skipper that the suitcase was purchased in Montreal as a present from his mother. It was very expensive custom luggage. He wasn't going to paint it, period. Lou explained that it didn't matter to him, he'd get paid anyway. But the salvage company wasn't going to be happy with the loss that would be caused entirely by the color of his suitcase. The bookkeeper held fast: no painting. To Lou, the very facts that the suitcase was expensive but also a present from his

---

* Swung: Correcting compass error by compensating for magnetic effects of the ship structure. The ship must be rotated ("swung") through 360° in a location where headings are known. Magnets on each side of the compass are adjusted so the compass reads reliably at all headings.

Mommy made the young man and his portmanteau an irresistible object of attention. It was like throwing raw tuna to a shark.

There was only one radio receiver on *Sea Fox*. It was kept in Lou's quarters, aft, and he was the only one allowed to use it. After five more cycles of alternating days of work and nasty nor'westers, Lou heard weather reports that indicated a stationary high pressure area was descending on the Gulf of St. Lawrence. This promised a week or more of excellent weather. Wasting no time, Lou jumped down to the paint locker, grabbed some dinghy paint and did the deed. The accountant found out about it when he spotted his newly painted luggage hanging from the starboard flag halyard, and he was raging mad.

"I said, 'Well that's what it costs to get the job done.' And sure enough by morning we had a beautiful day and we had a whole week of absolutely beautiful weather and we did a successful job of loading the ship right to capacity with the stuff. And all the crew said, boy that old man sure did a good job painting that suitcase, it just made the whole trip a success."

* * *

For the rest of the year, *Sea Fox* ran successfully in the Canadian cabotage system from Quebec to northern Newfoundland. Seal oil was shipped from St. Anthony's for Montreal; beer loaded for Newfoundland.

After a couple of trips hauling beer, Lou refused beer shipments bound for Newfoundland, because the customs officers and the stevedores were in cahoots and would drink beer while unloading the cargo. One time he found 259 empty bottles in the hold after the stevedores left. That was the record and the last straw.

On a trip to Quebec in 1943, Lou spotted an old steam barque, *City Of New York*. Inquiring as to her fate, he was told the U.S. Government owned her and was considering refitting her as an Arctic patrol ship. *City of New York* was Admiral Byrd's flagship for his Antarctic expeditions and was built like a tank without an inch of hog or a rotted plank. He asked a ship broker in Quebec to find out the particulars on the *City* and let him know if she became available.

A month later in Lunenburg, while loading fish and lumber for the West Indies, Lou was called by the agent and the deal was struck; $1,000 for the *City Of New York*, the whole works: ship, equipment, and rigging. Lou arranged for her to be laid up in Quebec for the winter and took off for Bridgetown.

* * *

Lou had decided to run the German blockade. This didn't make Pat happy, but he was confident he could run the blockade safely, for two reasons. First, *Sea Fox*'s small size made her a puny prize, and second, Lou absolutely refused to run the engine before reaching port, which made detection by U-boats unlikely.

The weather was bad all the way to Barbados, and upon arrival, he found that freights were up—way up. Lou immediately signed a cargo of barreled rum for the British military based on Bermuda. *Sea Fox* could carry 500 barrels of rum, and the freight was $25 per barrel. This was an enormous amount of money to pay for what Lou thought of as a pleasant tropical cruise. Before he left Barbados, the Mount Gay distillery asked him to bring all the empty barrels he could carry back from Bermuda, which had been left there from previous shipments. The war halted the supply of Canadian shooks, and without barrels, there was no rum industry. Lou agreed to haul back as many empties as he could find on Bermuda. The price: $10 per barrel.

The trip to Bermuda was idyllic, and unloading took only a day. Lou knew that if the Bermuda base didn't return barrels, they wouldn't get any rum in the future. So it was no surprise when, after unloading, the quartermaster requested that the skipper come to his office. Sitting at the military gray metal desk, the supply sergeant asked Lou to load barrels to take back to Mount Gay. "Sure," said Lou, "what's the freight?" The quartermaster expected him to take the barrels back at no cost, since there was no other cargo for him to take off the island.

Nonplussed, the Army man sputtered, "Uh…five bucks a barrel?" Lou, pretending incredulity, said, "For Christ's sake, I got 25 bucks for bringing 'em here." "But they were full," the soldier yelled. "Makes no never-mind to me, full or empty, takes up the same space." "That's bullshit!" retorted the quartermaster. That remark increased Lou's feigned anger and he spat, "The deal's off then," and turned toward the door. The military man stuttered a few "buts" and "you can'ts" then pleaded with Lou to return to the bargaining table. After a few minutes of heated negotiation, the crew got busy loading 500 empty rum barrels aboard *Sea Fox* for the return trip. The freight: $20 apiece. (Not including, of course, the $10 per barrel that Mount Gay would be paying.)

It was 1944 and Captain Kenedy just received $27,000 for an eight week cruise in warm water. Beyond this fat fee, Lou's real joy was the coup of getting $5 a barrel more for bringing back empties than he got for delivering the full ones. Add to that a couple of hundred gallons of Eclipse Rum that leaked out of the barrels into his private stock. Including ship maintenance, his overhead was less than $500. In one trip he bought the ship and banked a bundle. Life was good.

"Well after a few trips, the Sea Fox *was not only the fastest schooner down there but now she had a small engine in her besides. Freights were high and all the local schooners were doing very well, though some of them had been lost to submarines. So there were not as many as there were before, so that increased the value of the remaining ones. There were several captains there that wanted to buy her, so finally I sold it to the best situation and that was my last connection with the* Sea Fox.

"She continued in the trade down there for some years, and in the 1960s, she had refrigeration put in her and she was carrying meat and frozen goods from Venezuela to the Islands. While laying in Caracas at the wharf, a steamer drifted or backed into her and crushed her out of shape. It didn't sink her but squeezed her all out of shape, so she was put on the beach because she was un-repairable. You can't bend an iron ship back into shape again. She was 80 years old and her plates were in beautiful condition and it was a shame. Anyway, she was broken up then somewhere in the late 1960s."

To get home, Lou, Peter, and Butch signed aboard an old tramp steamer, *Chomedy*, Lou as an AB. This slow Hog Island steamer would never risk running the blockade alone, so she sailed from Bridgetown to Port of Spain to join a convoy. From there she sailed to Guantanamo to join a larger convoy for New York. *Chomedy* finally landed the trio in St. John's where Lou bought train tickets for Halifax.

The conductor wouldn't allow Butch in the passenger compartment. "I'll give you a bottle of rum if you'll let him ride up here," Lou offered, to no avail. No matter how blatantly Lou bribed him or how threatening he became, the conductor wouldn't yield. Butch was consigned to the baggage car.

The train pulled out, and Lou and Peter wadded up their pea jackets as pillows and tried to get some sleep. After an hour, the conductor tapped Lou on the shoulder. "Uh…mister, mister, I have some bad news for you." Irritated at being awakened, Lou said, "What the hell are you yakking about?" "Your dog jumped off the train." "Jesus H. Christ! How in the hell did that happen?" demanded Lou. The trainman replied, "The door was open for ventilation and he jumped out and we don't know exactly when he left; we didn't see it." "Well stop this piece of shit so I can find my dog, you idiot," Lou yelled. His anger was building.

The conductor explained that they couldn't stop the train, and Lou was beside himself. The train was in the middle of the woods and just inching along up a 20-mile grade. Lou realized that if the dog jumped here, he'd be lost forever in the forest, impossible to find.

Peter tried to cheer Lou up, without success. Losing Butch, the survivor, was devastating.

"While I was feeling miserable and thinking of what to do, the conductor came back and tapped me on the shoulder. 'Hey mister, I got good news for you; the dog's jumped back aboard.' And he had just gone off the train, run along awhile, had a couple of leaks, and jumped back on the train. That's hard to believe but that's what he did. The train never did go very fast; it took forever to get to Port-aux-Basques."

So ends this day.

Figure 6-1.

The ship: *City of New York* (ex-*Samson*)
Year of Launching: 1885
Rig: Barque converted to Tern Schooner by
  L. Kenedy
Builder: K. Larsen at Logebergskaret,
  Arendal, Norway
Engine: 200 hp steam, converted by LK to
  Atlas diesel

Material: Greenheart, spruce & oak,
  bottom 44 inches thick
Length between perpendiculars: 170
  feet
Beam: 31 feet
Draft: 14 feet light/20 feet loaded
Displacement: 515 tons

Chapter 6   *City of New York*

City of New York *(ex-Samson) was built as an arctic sealer. In the late nineteenth century, along with* Pollux, *she founded the Atlantic sealing industry. The thickness of her hull below the waterline was almost incomprehensible at 44 inches. The frames were of the finest oak and were so close together that they nearly touched. The topsides were 34 inches thick to withstand the pressure of the ice if she was ever caught in an arctic winter. Using even the most modern engineering techniques, it would be difficult to judge the ultimate strength of her hull. As a sealer, she needed that massive bow to ride up and crush her way through sheets of arctic ice floes.*

The 170-foot steam barque* *was owned by August Fosse of Trondheim, Norway. February 9, 1912 found* Samson *clearing out of Tonsberg where she had taken on coal and provisions for an extended sealing voyage. She was under the command of C.L. Ring with Hendrik Naess as mate. After an unsuccessful hunt near the Orkneys,* Samson *sailed for the sealing grounds off Newfoundland and Labrador. The seal herds teemed within Canadian territorial waters, and Captain Ring didn't hesitate to poach seals wherever he found them.*

For nearly a month the crew of Samson *loaded 3,000 bloody, frozen harp seal pelts and 100 barrels of seal oil aboard the barque. There wasn't a legal pelt aboard; they had all been taken on the coast of Labrador. By the first of April, 1912, she wasn't even close to capacity, but the herds had thinned so Captain Ring gave up and sailed northeast for the Denmark Straits in search of klappmyss.†*

As Samson *departed the Maritimes, Captain Ring expected icebergs, and as it became colder, he ordered the water temperature monitored on an hourly basis. When the temperature reached 0° C., he ordered readings every half hour.*

By 11:00 p.m. on the 14th of April, Samson *approached 41° N 50° W; it was flat calm, and thick floe ice covered some of the surface, punctuated by icebergs. The captain rang down for dead slow, and the mate was ordered to keep steerageway only to hold their position against the current.*

The mate, Naess, saw a ship's steaming lights and port running light to the north. This was the freighter Californian *westbound for Boston out of Liverpool, and she was also running dead slow as she had also just reached the edge of the ice pack.*

The 447-foot Californian *was under the command of Captain Stanley Lord. His third officer, Mr. Groves, reported running lights to the south, and Captain Lord recorded that they were from a small steamer. As he watched, the smaller ship slowly turned north and showed her port running light.*

Aboard Samson, *Naess called for Captain Ring to come topside. They were carrying poached pelts, and the mate wanted some guidance. The captain saw the* Californian's *lights and ordered* Samson's *running lights extinguished. "New course, NE by E," ordered the captain. The course was repeated by the*

---

* Three-masted sailing ship, with the foremast and mainmast equipped with square-rigged sails. The mizzen has a fore-and-aft rig.

† A variety of seal found in coastal waters of Greenland and arctic Europe.

helmsman. The captain rang down for one-half ahead and Samson *skulked into the darkness.*

At 11:40 Mr. Groves of the Californian *reported the smaller steamer had turned her lights off. At eight bells, Groves was relieved by Second Officer Stone and Apprentice Seaman Gibson. At 12:45 a.m., Stone saw rockets to the south from a large steamer and immediately informed the captain, who was sleeping below. The captain ignored the incident and didn't order* Californian *to investigate the rockets. This inaction would be Lord's undoing.*

Later, Samson*'s mate, Naess, described the night:*

"I was on duty that evening, but I sat with the captain and drank a rum toddy and smoked an evening pipe. Just before midnight I went on deck, waiting to be relieved. While I was walking there, I noticed two big stars in the sky far away to the south. These stars were very low; I told the watch on the bridge, go up the mast and see what it could be. I thought it might have been American seal hunters. The watchman on the bridge shouted that it was not stars, but lanterns. And he told us that he saw a lot of lights. Then suddenly some rockets appeared. Then suddenly all lights went out, and it became dark."*

Samson *didn't try to investigate the flares for fear of prosecution for poaching seals and just wanted to get the hell out of an area that seemed chock-a-block with marine traffic. By dawn,* Samson *was far from the scene and saw nothing.*

The barque's captain and crew forgot about the incident and went about their business sealing in the Denmark Straights. Months later, Samson *was slammed by a huge chunk of ice during a heavy gale. She sought shelter in Iceland, and there the Norwegian consul informed them of the sinking of* Titanic. *According to the mate's logs,* Samson *was within 10 miles of the ill-fated liner as her passengers were fighting for their lives.*

Captain Lord, however, reported that Samson *was between* Californian *and* Titanic, *making* Samson *even closer to the liner than* Californian, *perhaps as close as three or four miles. Captain Ring was never called before any investigative body, but Captain Lord of the* Californian *was hauled in front of the Wreck Commissioner's Court, the official inquiry panel requested by the British Board of Trade. This court was headed by the Right Honorable Lord Mersey, Judge and Wreck Commissioner, who was assisted by a panel of Assessors. Lord Mersey voiced the sentiment of the Court when he wrote:*

---

* Quoted from http://home.earthlink.net/~dnitzer/5Otherships/Samson.html.

These circumstances convince me that the ship seen by the *Californian* was the *Titanic* and if so, according to Captain Lord, the two vessels were about five miles apart at the time of the disaster....When she first saw the rockets, the *Californian* could have pushed through the ice to the open water without any serious risk and so have come to the assistance of the *Titanic*. Had she done so, she might have saved many if not all of the lives that were lost.[*]

His inaction during the Titanic *catastrophe relegated Captain Stanley Lord to a life in command of drogers and near-derelicts. This controversial history is the basis for* Samson *being identified as the famous "Third Ship" at the sinking of* Titanic.

* * *

Sir Ernest Shackleton was beaten. In 1911, Roald Amundsen and then in 1912, Robert Falcon Scott reached the South Pole before him. No consolation for Shackleton, Robert Scott froze to death while returning to his base camp. So Shackleton, looking for a new challenge, came up with the idea of being the first to cross the Antarctic continent.

It was one of the most successful failures in history. He mounted an expedition for the Antarctic. Almost immediately upon his arrival in January, 1915, his ship, Endurance, *was frozen tight in the Weddell Sea ice. The men huddled aboard her until the pressure of the ice crushed her and she sank in November. The antarctic summer was upon them and men were imprisoned on an iceberg that broke loose and floated aimlessly around the Southern Ocean. There were 28 men on the berg with only three small ship's boats as a way home.*

In April, Shackleton calculated that out of sheer luck, they were within 100 miles of Elephant Island, which is 670 miles southeast of Cape Horn. They took off in the small boats and made landfall on April 15. Leaving 22 men on Elephant Island to while away their hours eating penguins and seals, Shackleton and five others sailed a 22-foot jolly boat named James Caird *800 miles to South Georgia Island. This has gone down in history as one of the two greatest rescue sails of all time. The only comparable voyage was William Bligh's 3,000-mile odyssey to East Timor following the* Bounty *mutiny.*

---

[*] "British Wreck Commissioner's Inquiry, Report on the Loss of the *Titanic* (s.s.), Circumstances in Connection with S.S. *Californian*," July 30th, 1912. (ending paragraph)

Fifteen days later they reached South Georgia and beached the boat at King Haakon's Bay. Leaving three of the six crewmen behind, Shackleton and two others became the first men to cross the rugged mountains and glaciers of South Georgia Island. Perhaps it wasn't as notable as crossing the Antarctic continent on foot, but, by God, it was a first.

From a mountaintop overlooking the whaling station at Stromness, he saw a three-masted ship anchored in the harbor. She was Samson, *loading whale products. Her crew was ashore. The three men slid most of the way down the mountain on their butts and then walked into the station. Sir Ernest's first words were, "My name is Shackleton."* Samson's *crew were shocked, then overjoyed to see him safe and sound. They immediately offered to stage a celebration in honor of his deliverance.*

He respectfully declined the celebration on the grounds that there were still men in harm's way at King Haakon's Bay and on Elephant Island. Within hours of their arrival, Samson *sailed to pick up the three men left at King Haakon's Bay and then carried Shackleton and the five men to Chile, where he mounted two unsuccessful attempts to rescue the rest of the expedition. Finally, on August 30, 1916, the remaining 22 men on Elephant Island were rescued by Shackleton aboard the Chilean tugboat* Yelcho. *A raucous party ensued where Shackleton's men toasted* Samson *and her crew for their part in the escape from a frozen death.*

* * *

Captain Roald Amundsen, the famous Arctic explorer, had sailed Samson *on several of his Arctic expeditions near Spitzbergen and was familiar with her strength as an ice ship. She was similar to his famous research ship,* Fram. *In 1927, as Admiral Richard Byrd was preparing for his first expedition to the Antarctic, Amundsen recommended Byrd purchase* Samson *as his flagship.*

Byrd took Amundsen's advice. But on her way to New York from Tramso, Norway, heavy weather caused the steam engine mounts to loosen, nearly causing a boiler explosion. She continued to the U.S. under reduced power and arrived in New York three weeks later. Byrd was livid; she was in terrible shape and had to be hauled to replace a significant number of rotted planks; the rigging had to be replaced and the engine rebuilt. By the time Byrd cleared New York for points south, he had dumped over $160,000 into the newly renamed City of New York. *This was a staggering amount of money for 1927, especially since the money had been collected in nickels and dimes from children in all parts of the nation.*

Though she was the most important ship in the fleet, the City *was only one of a flotilla of support craft that delivered the tons of expedition supplies to*

Dunedin, New Zealand. Once in Dunedin, she was reloaded with a more diverse cargo in the event she was the only ship that could reach the Bay of Whales on Antarctica. She would carry all the vital equipment and supplies necessary for a skeleton scientific team to spend one year on the ice. On December 2, 1928 at 6:00 a.m., City of New York *and the 800-ton steamer* Eleanor Bolling *cleared Dunedin southbound. There were 29 men aboard the* City *and 54 aboard the* Bolling.

The winds were fluky, and when the City *couldn't keep up with the larger steamer, the* Bolling *took her in tow. After hand-transferring 90 tons of bagged coal from the* Bolling *to the* City, *the barque was towed to the edge of the Ross Ice Shelf by the whaler* C.A. Larson. *Once at the shelf, she crushed her way through the ice and arrived alone under sail in the Bay of Whales on December 28, 1928. She was loaded with a disassembled Ford Tri-Motor, 1,200 gallons of gas for the airplane, 75 tons of coal, 54 men, 80 dogs, two prefabricated buildings, and food for 15 months.*

The floe ice was continually moving and breaking off. The City *couldn't get a permanent grip anywhere on the ice. In search of a suitable anchorage, Byrd ordered her east toward Edward VII Land, but to no avail. Leaving Byrd and the expedition behind with plenty of provisions, on February 22, the* City *finally gave up her search for a safe harbor and sailed for New Zealand, chopping deck ice all the way.*

The Ford Tri-Motor, named the Floyd Bennett *after the pilot who flew Byrd over the North Pole, was assembled and eventually made the historic over-flight of the South Pole, making Byrd the first man to fly over both poles.*

A year later, January 6, 1930, the City *left Dunedin to pick up the expedition members at the Bay of Whales. She was nearly sunk by the sheer weight of accumulated ice during another prolonged gale, but the* City *reached the explorers after 12 days crunching ice and three mid-ocean recoalings from the* Bolling *and the whaler* Kosmos.

Admiral Byrd and City of New York *arrived safely in Dunedin on March 10, 1930. To great fanfare, the* City *triumphantly sailed into New York harbor on June 18, 1930.*

It isn't clear why Byrd didn't use the City *on his second trip to Antarctica in 1933, since she was available and owned by the government. Instead he bought an old whaler,* Bear, *from the city of Oakland, California. He refurbished her and named her* Bear of Oakland. *The* Bear *was another barque, built in 1874 in Greenock, Scotland and only a little larger than the* City *but 11 years older.*

For several years, the City *was sailed around and displayed as a celebrity along the U.S. east coast. After her trip into the Great Lakes for the Chicago World's Fair in 1934, she was ordered laid up in the St. Lawrence River near Montreal, where she was anchored for over 10 years.*

* * *

Back from the Caribbean on May 2, 1944, Lou checked in with Pat at Conquerall Bank and said hello to his daughter, Patsy, and six-year-old son, Brian. Anxious to get to the job of overhauling *City of New York*, he left almost immediately for Montreal. When he arrived, he arranged for a tug that was already en route to Port Hawkesbury to take her in tow. Since the tug was going there anyway, Lou was able to negotiate a very low tow rate—of course. During the trip, Captain Kenedy was the only one aboard the *City*. He lived in what was left of the torn-out guts of the ship. On deck he had to hop from deck beam to deck beam, as the planking was rotted. When he arrived in Port Hawkesbury, another tug, *Foundation Franklin*, towed her down to Leary's Yard in Dayspring, across the river from his home in Conquerall Bank.

Before leaving Quebec, Lou had arranged with Leary's to take on the job of rebuilding the barque. But while he was gone, Mel Leary died, leaving Lou without a shipyard to perform the extensive work needed to bring the *City* up to Kenedy standards. Teddy Snyder was Leary's foreman and knew exactly what work was required. Lou and Teddy got together and worked out a formula where Teddy would buy the yard from Mrs. Leary. From that time on, the yard has been called Snyder's Shipyard and has become an institution in the Maritimes.

"So that [continued operation of the yard] *was what I wanted. It would be good for him to get started because it would be steady work for six months because it was a big job.*

"Now she was an unusual vessel for Nova Scotia because she was an old barque and she was built for the ice. She had 14 inches of planking in three layers and every one was caulked and trunneled* and the outside layer of four inches or almost five inches was greenheart. Everyone knows what greenheart is—it's a terrible wood. You can't cut it with a chisel hardly or anything and it dulls all the tools you use on it. She was 18.5-feet deep in the hold, which is very deep for a vessel like that. When she was finished, she drew 14 feet light, which is a big draft and loaded, she'd draw 20 feet, which is something for a schooner.

"The ship had to be all re-decked and re-planked. The poop deck was good but it didn't have any hatches in it; she had a flush poop deck. We put skylights and a companionway made of all the teak that I had removed

---

* Pegged in place. The term "trunnel" is derived from "tree (i.e. wooden) nail."

from the Sea Fox *two years before when I changed her over for trading. So I had saved these things and they just came in perfect for* City of New York. *We put hatches in her and a new deckhouse forward with galley, fo'c's'le, engine room, winches, and deck machinery—all made by the*

Lunenburg Foundry—and a fo'c's'le head. We went in the woods and cut a bowsprit. We got a spruce tree that was nearly 4 feet thick and when we cut it, it had 157 rings in it, indicating 157 years old, from the late 1700s. It was an original tree [virgin timber] *and we dragged it out of the woods with oxen, about 40 feet of it. I think 40 feet was what we wanted and it squared 22 inches about 18 feet from the butt, which is what we required for the piece of wood the way her heads were formed.*

"We had about 18 men working there for months laying new deck and building a beautiful large cabin, with a prime companionway—mahogany posts and brass rails and all that. She was a tween-deck vessel."

Figure 6-2. Captain Lou aboard *City of New York,* **1947.**

When the interior was essentially finished, Lou had her towed to Lunenburg. Her spar timbers had arrived via railroad from British Columbia. Just as he had done with *Wawaloam*, Lou hand-shaped the spars ashore while onlookers gathered to watch him, using a curve-handled broad axe, adze, and drawknife. This was a time-consuming process, but to Lou it was the right way; it was his way; it was the only way. And yes, it was the inexpensive way.

Every aspect of the refitting of the *City* was done in Bristol fashion. She was rigged as a tern schooner rather than her original barque configuration. The barque's square-rigged sails were impractical; they would have required a larger crew and increased the difficulty of sail handling.

Once the masts and spars were prepared, she was towed to the Smith & Rhuland dry dock where she was caulked and painted. Back in the water, the masts were stepped using the steam crane at the yard. Then the booms, gaffs, and rigging were fitted and sails bent.

Before the refit began, Lou sent back to the Caribbean for his *Wawaloam* crew.

"When we started this job, I sent back to the West Indies and got my same men and the same mate, old Peter [Jones], *and he did all the*

rigging. Everybody said we'd have a hell of a job rigging a three-mast schooner because there was nobody around who wanted to take it on. Well, I said, my mate can do it and he did. He had already rigged the Wawaloam *and this time he rigged the* City of New York. *She was a heavier, bigger vessel, and needed heavy rigging and gear. But he did a magnificent job and she was a sharp and well done vessel."*

The *City*'s hull wasn't the only part of the ship that was heavily built. The masts were 24 inches in diameter and up to 90 feet long. The topmasts were 12 inches in diameter and soared another 56 feet above the cross trees. Her mizzen boom was 68 feet long and her jib boom stretched 48 feet. Everything was in perfect proportion. But she was heavy and round-bilged and when fully loaded—especially with bulk cargos like salt—she rolled uncontrollably. The roll was so bad that after the first trip hauling salt from the Turks, Lou put her on the hard and installed two bilge keels[*] 70 feet long and 18 inches deep. This solved the problem instantly.

"It stopped the rolling to a great extent and made her a much more livable vessel. She was one ship you could get in the worse kind of gales and you had nothing to worry about. You could go down and play cards off watch and not worry about leaking or anything."

* * *

A young Walter Boudreau had recently survived the sinking of the barkentine *Angelus* and was still shaken by the loss of life when he signed articles aboard *City of New York* in late 1944. *Angelus* had been bound for Nova Scotia, loaded with Barbados rum and molasses, and was sunk by a U-boat 200 miles north of Bermuda. Boudreau was one of only two survivors out of a crew of nine.

Aboard the *City*, his responsibilities included assignment as the foretop-man, which required him to climb the foremast ratlines to control the foretops'l. Controlling this elevated sail was complicated, and it had to be done frequently, whenever the *City* tacked or jibed.

Walter Boudreau sailed on only two trips aboard the *City,* but he was impressed with Lou. His son passed down the following quotation in his book *The Man Who Loved Schooners:*

Many, including myself, thought that Captain Louis Kennedy [sic] was a bit of a rogue and could be a hard man. But we were living the

---

[*] Auxiliary keels on the ship's bottom, outside of and parallel to the main keel, to provide stability against rolling.

last of the true days of sail and this way of life demanded tough men. During my years at sea I met many sailormen, but Captain [Kenedy] was perhaps the finest seaman I ever had the honor of sailing with. I admired his strength and determination and this is borne out by the fact that I named my first born son, Louis, after him. *

* * *

Figure 6-3. Brian and ship's dog Gotlik.

In late 1944 the war in the Atlantic was winding down. So once the bilge keels were installed, it was safe and comfortable for Lou to take the family along with him. Brian was seven years old, and Patsy was one. Brian's school obligations made it impossible for him to be year-round crew. For Brian, the worst event of every year was when he left the ship to return to the French boarding school in Nova Scotia.

This was the beginning of 10 years of growth for the Kenedy clan. The family grew—another daughter, Gabrielle, was born during the *City* era; the bank accounts grew; and Lou Kenedy's Olympian confidence in his original decision to follow the sea soared yet higher—not that Lou Kenedy's confidence ever needed bolstering.

The family settled into a routine that included nine months of boarding school for Brian and summers aboard the schooner. Lou's trips without the family could take up to three months, and homecomings were a special time. As each return to the family neared, Pat began to bustle about and the kids didn't sleep well and became a bit unruly. But as soon as the skipper walked through the door, all was right with the world. He knelt, and his kids ran to his arms, squealing with delight.

Lou's daughters were his princesses; they could do no wrong. When he got home, he turned his attention to spoiling them. Lou's normally colorful language, sprinkled with well-known expletives, was transformed into uncharacteristic gentility when he was with his girls. Brian, on the other hand,

---

* Boudreau, Robert Louis, *The Man Who Loved Schooners*. St. Michaels, Maryland, 2000, Tiller Publishing, p. 39. (Used by permission of publisher.)

was expected to be as tough as his father and was treated as a man, a seaman, very early in life.

At the same age that a young Lou Kenedy was sailing away carefree summers aboard *Tilky*, Brian Kenedy signed articles aboard the *City* at 50 cents a week. He was nine years old. He was expected to stand all normal watches and slept in the fo'c's'le. When he was 11, he was raised to $1.50 per week and at 17, just before enlisting in the Navy, he was making $125 per month.

Though it was hard work for Brian and even the girls, it was also a lot of fun, especially when Lou wanted to tease the onlookers.

Once while unloading lumber in Yarmouth, Patsy, around five years old, wanted to help Brian who was working in earnest to get finished. Brian wanted to go to a football game and resented having to work that day. He had a long face and struggled while swinging the gaff loaded with lumber from the hold to the dock. It was quite a process, but the gaff was empty when Patsy pulled a line to bring it back over the hold. She had no trouble, even as a little girl.

Tourists wandered by—two dapper couples—and they watched the kids working the cargo. They watched for about a half hour, talking among themselves and getting worked up a bit. Finally, one of the men asked, "Captain, are those your children?" Lou answered, "Yeah. Those are my kids, all right." The couples went back into a huddle, and after awhile one of the women said, "Gosh, they're working awful hard, aren't they?"

Lou replied, "Around here when they drop the bottle, they gotta grab a rope." They went off shaking their heads and talking among themselves, mumbling about child labor and slavery and abuse, just loud enough for Lou to hear them and smile. As soon as the couples were out of sight, Lou motioned for Brian to take off for the football game.

During Lou's 10 years aboard the *City,* innumerable milk runs were made down to Barbados. Again, it was lumber down and molasses for Newfoundland or salt from Turks on the return trip. And, of course, bootleg rum was always an extra income source. She would carry 850 tons without complaining. However, because of her age, the maritime authorities set her Plimsoll mark at three feet three inches from the waterways. At this height, only 750 tons could be loaded. But Lou took care of this problem:

"...but I carved a new Plimsoll about two feet down or two feet three inches, and for three years we'd have that painted on. Then every three years she'd have to be inspected, so we'd paint the true one on and paint the other one out. In that way we were able to carry an extra 100

tons or so of cargo, which didn't bother her at all. This goes to show there was always some way to get around things."

As heavy as she was, the *City* was a good sailer. She was deep so leeway wasn't a factor, and her weight always carried her around on her new tack. On one trip out of Barbados for Nassau, with a full load of sugar and 1,000 barrels of rum, she averaged just over eight knots. Seven days from Barbados to Nassau is excellent time. There were some motor freighters that couldn't equal that record.

That particular trip was exceptional for another reason.

Figure 6-4. An enormous load of Nova Scotia lumber for Boston. Photo by L. H. Whitacre, Jr., *Quincy Patriot Ledger*. (Used by permission.)

When loaded, *City of New York* drew too much water to enter the inner careenage at Bridgetown, Barbados. As a result, she had to anchor out with the steamers, and be discharged and loaded by lighters. Just after the war, the new Labour government in England encouraged their island colonies to organize the maritime trades. The stevedores were one of the first unions to organize and had signed a contract with the steamer operators in which their ships would be unloaded by union labor only. Schooners were exempt from this contract.

City of New York, however, though she had no engine, anchored out for loading, and the unions claimed she was under the same contractual obligations as steamers, because she wasn't inside the careenage.

All his life, Lou Kenedy carried a resolute dislike and distrust of unions. This new union rule on loading was an outrage to him. He had no choice but to accept the union labor, or the sugar and rum wouldn't be loaded. So he relented, and 22 stevedores swarmed over the ship. This was twice the number needed to load the *City,* and the sheer number of workers slowed the loading. And, of course, they didn't work up to Lou's level of energy. At 1600, the stevedores began leaving but indicated they would finish the loading if Lou would pay overtime. He reluctantly agreed. The longshoremen wasted the hour stumbling around, and at 1700 left the ship without discharging the last sugar lighter. They said they would return in the morning to finish.

Another union rule was each man would be paid a minimum of one-half day. Even though there was less than an hour's work to do, if they waited until morning, all 22 men would get a half-day's wage. That did it. Lou took matters into his own hands.

First, he and his five-man crew discharged the remaining lighter in less than a half hour. He then went to town and found his agent and informed him he didn't need any stevedores for the next day. A thousand barrels of rum were delivered to the dock the next morning, and, as requested, no stevedores arrived. The *City's* crew loaded the barrels into lighters run by non-union workers and ferried them out to the schooner. Lou's crew loaded them aboard the *City,* then Lou returned to the town to arrange for the delivery of 1,000 cases of rum for the next morning.

This time, the Mount Gay agent hesitated to deliver the cases to the wharf. The stevedores had found out Lou loaded his own ship and threatened the lighter operators if they helped load the *City.* "Skipper, the lighter captains won't take the cases. They're afraid the dock workers will beat them up," said the agent. "Screw them," said Lou, "just have the rum on the dock in the morning."

The next morning, Lou towed his two dories to the wharf with his yawl boat. The rum was there waiting, and his crew started loading. A group of 20 union members were drinking and playing dominoes at tables set up in the shade of a warehouse when one of them spotted the *City*'s crew loading the boats. The domino game was suspended as the union men began yelling and screaming expletives and warnings at Lou. With sticks and canes in their hands, they moved menacingly towards Lou's crew and the remaining stack of rum cases. One man waved a cricket bat over his head.

Sheffield Gumbs, an AB aboard the *City,* was an enormous and powerful Aruban who under most circumstances was a gentle teddy bear. At six feet three inches, he weighed in at well over 350 pounds—an imposing figure. When he spotted the crowd moving toward them, he felt trapped between the mob and the water, and inexplicably, his normally languid personality disappeared. Without warning, Sheffield—called "Pancho" by his friends—stretched out his arms and alone rushed the oncoming mob, screaming over and over, "I mash you, I mash you!" at the top of his lungs. Pancho had his shirt off and his bare chest reemphasized his size and power.

Lou, usually the first to confront these situations, was taken by surprise. But he finally sprang into action and followed Pancho into the anticipated fray. The other four crewmen got the hint and ran behind Lou holding rum bottles by the neck to use on the roughnecks.

The notable part of this incident is that nothing happened. The mob was so taken aback by Pancho's ferocity and the headlong charge by Lou and the crew that they stopped in their tracks. They looked at each other for a moment, and before the *City*'s crew could reach them, they ran in 20 different directions. Pancho, Lou, and four other crewmen had chased a mob of 20 strong longshoremen off their own dock.

Returning to the loading, Pancho was shaking and apologized to Lou for losing his temper. Lou laughed and told him that it was the right thing to do, and he only wished he had thought of it first. Then, to everyone's surprise, he told Pancho to divide a case of rum between the crewmembers.

Loading the 1,000 cases of bottled rum took three trips in the yawl boat, towing the dories. Once the loading was finished, Lou's agent arrived in a bum boat. He told Lou the authorities wanted to see him ashore. "If they want to see me, let them see me aboard my ship. That's OK with me." The harbormaster and customs officials had no intention of going out to the ship, but when Lou went ashore to clear for Newfoundland, he was met with a phalanx of English government officials.

For reasons unknown to this day, Lou disliked the English just as much as he disliked unions. When the officials confronted him ashore in Bridgetown, he wasn't in any mood to tolerate their demands. They offered to compromise on the fees that should have been paid to the stevedores.

"...*Well, he said, 'There was an agreement between the steamers and the people ashore that they would all load them.' 'Well,' I said, 'there may be an agreement between the steamers but you don't see Lou Kenedy's name signed anywhere. I run my own ship my way and that's the way it's going to be and schooners were not subject to this around the islands.' But they said, 'Well she loads out in the bay. She's got to be under the same as the steamers.' I said, 'No way.' So they said, 'We will make a compromise with you. You pay for the stevedores as if they had worked and then there won't be any problems.'*

"*I said, 'I'll make a compromise—it'll be a frosty Friday in hell when I compromise with you. I won't give you a red cent. How's that?' 'Oh then we won't let you clear.' 'How are you going to stop me? What law is there not to clear? I don't give a good crap if I get clearance or not. I'll go without it.' So I had no problem getting clear.*

"*Those fellows were standing there sucking their thumbs as far as I was concerned. We took off and everything went fine; it was a great trip.*"

* * *

On the 20th of December, 1945, the *City* was beating toward Lunenburg with its load of salt and rum. At the latitude of Hatteras, they came into a strong sou'west gale, so strong that in the same region a U.S. Navy cruiser had her deckhouse stove in, killing 30 Navy sailors, and an oiler broke in half near the same latitude as the *City*. Lou threw out a drogue and ran under bare poles to wait out the storm.

By late in the day of the 20th, they were able to set some sail. But some of the sails began ripping seams. From the captain's log:

... reefed the main but 10 hrs later it let go again along the reef line, shipping heavy seas, back in a force 8 gale, from SW with heavy seas. Thereafter had confused seas, force 3-4 winds, snow, cold, fog...

A young sailor from Lunenburg was standing his watch on the forward end of the poop deck because the sea state was too fierce to stand fo'c's'le-head watches. While he stood there keeping a sharp eye on the stormy seas, a sea gull landed on the top of his head.

"...something which I had never seen before, and he reached up and took it by the feet and held it and we tried to feed it and keep it as a pet but it didn't like that and eventually flew away. But I never saw a forerunner like that and the crew all said to him, 'Boy, that's bad luck for you.'"

That evening, the storm blew up creating 40-foot seas. Two seamen were on watch on the forward part of the poop. They were pacing back and forth as well as they could on the rolling ship. She was riding fine until she rolled to weather just as one of the 40-footers broke over the poop. Skylights were smashed; the yawl boat was torn from her gripes and flipped upside down in her davits. The entire crew was topside because of the storm and immediately turned to, picking up the wreckage. Only after a half hour of hard work did Lou realized there were two men missing.

"...a young fellow making his first trip to sea from the Bridgewater area and a colored boy, who had been with me for quite a few years. I wouldn't say a boy—he's now a man. He started off as a boy and he was studying navigation by a correspondence course. I was helping him with it over the years and he was a very fine young fellow; and so was the other one. And it was a terrible thing to think that we had lost these two men on a dark night like that without knowing it. Of course, there was nothing we could have done in a storm like that for them; but if we had known they had gone over, we could have thrown lines astern. They might have grabbed hold of them and we could have pulled them back. We didn't know it until we'd missed them."

The lost Bridgewater native was the young man upon whose head the sea gull landed. The other was Reginald Reid, the Bajan stowaway aboard *Abundance* on Lou's first trip up from Barbados to Nova Scotia.

Lou's log entry of the trip is succinct:

SHIP'S LOG
SCHOONER City of New York FROM: Turks TOWARDS: Halifax
DATE: 20th day of December 1945
REMARKS: Lat 36'55" Long 68'17." Have trysail on main, hove to, helm hard down. Boarded amidships by heavy sea, washed two men overboard & lost. Stern boat washed out of its skids, poop ladder lost, one cabin skylight opened & flooded cabins, even washed dory thwarts into cabin, which is all that is left of dory, which was broken in half in

an earlier sea. Couldn't do anything for the men. Only one hand pump working as forward pump threw its chain, governor on pump engine broke. Wind WNW force 10.

2200: Got pumping engine going & pumped out. Heavy W & N gale & desperate seas.

2400: Still hove to....

0500: Polaris bearing 40°7". Heavy NW gale snow & sleet. Heavy confused swell & vessel rolling & tossing violently. How long O Lord?

So ends this day.

As the City arrived in Lunenburg, Lou raised a Canadian flag from the starboard flag halyard. He held it at half mast for a week in honor of the lost men. Lou was tired and took some time off before his next trip.

* * *

The log of August 26 and 27, 1947 read:

Eugene Augustine falls from masthead to deck, breaking staysail bull rope on the way, unconscious for awhile but no bones broken or cuts & apparently no internal injuries, but severe shock etc. Doc took him to hospital for rest & observation. Cook AWOL & no supper. Aug 27. Eugene improving OK, cook in jail for drunkenness. Paid his fine & returned to vessel at 1030 hours. Gordon Seymour has gonorrhea & syphilis & went to hospital on Thursday for circumcision & wages stopped till he returns for work, etc.

So ends this day

Apart from the nonchalance of the forgoing log entry, the significance is that Lou was first and foremost concerned about the damage to the bull rope, then he deigned to mention the injuries to poor Eugene. Next he laments the lack of supper so he bails the cook out of jail—the bail was not a gift but a loan against wages. Lord only knows what eventually happened to poor Gordon Seymour, but he didn't get paid a minute of sick leave.

* * *

Lou had always smuggled rum from the West Indies to Nova Scotia. Everyone knew it, but the skipper was never caught at it. With the purchase of the *City*, his bootlegging activities increased substantially. She was so big, it was almost impossible for the customs agents to search every nook and cranny. But generally, Lou put the rum in plain sight.

On the *City*'s first trip up from Barbados, Lou brought back 13 five-gallon kegs of rum as gifts for the crew who had toiled so long on her refit. At that time, whoever reported contraband was entitled to a reward equaling 25 percent of the value of the goods. Someone in Barbados apparently reported the sale of the 13 kegs. While Lou was unloading salt for Willoughby Ritcey, in Riverport:

"All of a sudden, while we had been discharging salt for a day or two, down from Halifax came a crew of Mounties; there must have been about five of them. Four men and a head fellow over them and it was February and the wife was aboard and she was knitting a lot at that time. I said to the wife, 'You get your heavy clothes on, get on deck and sit on one of those vegetable lockers and start knitting.' And the mate ... I said, 'Let's open the spanker and dry it.' So we spread the spanker all over the deck. In the meantime, of course, we had started discharging salt. Four of the men came down that were all dressed up and had long steel rods they were pushing through the salt.

"Only a stupid person would bury it in the salt; that was so stupid because eventually the salt had to come out and anybody would just stand there and watch the rum get uncovered; he'd get caught, for Christ's sake. It wasn't the way I smuggled rum. So anyway, then they rooted around up in the forepeak, all kinds of timbers up there reinforcing her from the ice and all types of cubbyholes and places to crawl around, and the same way aft. And the head officer said, 'Cap, we know you got 13 kegs of rum.' Evidently somebody in Barbados had declared it to them, so they'd get the reward for any fines incurred. The head Mountie said, 'It's a 25 percent reward for stuff like that, you know that?'

"I said, 'Gosh, if you can find any, just give me one and you can have all the rest. I just need one.' And he said, 'Oh no, no. I know you got it. Just declare it and it will be alright. You just seal it up and that's the end of it.' 'No—no—I got nothing to declare.' And the wife was sitting on top of this box with about six kegs under her and she's sewing away—in February—on deck and knitting. Anyway finally he says, 'Boy there's more cubbyholes on this ship than I could ever look through; I can't find anything.' I said, 'I told you there's nothing.' So we're all satisfied and that's the way those 13 kegs got by—ha, ha, ha, ha. That was knitting the way to rum."

* * *

Usually, before officially arriving in Canadian waters and discharging the cargo and crew, Lou and the mate would go on a midnight foray near his home on the LaHave River:

"I had my usual quota of small five-gallon kegs of rum. On the way in from Barbados, I stopped at the LaHave Islands at night. It was a Saturday, we couldn't do anything if we did go to Halifax. And we went ashore, myself and the mate, while the crew was sleeping. Nobody knew what was going on and we took about 10 or 12 kegs of rum and we dug a hole in the sand on one of the LaHave Islands and buried them. Covered them over and left them to recover at a later date. They were perfectly safe there."

The rum in these kegs was frequently bottled for friends under Captain Lou's private label known as *"Skunk Squirt."*

Figure 6-5. **Private labels for high class rum.**

"So anyway we did have aboard the boat a bottle of vender's rum—old 'Black Diamond.' Vender's rum was cheap rum that was bought from the distillers, rebottled under a different label and watered down almost like grog. Anyway we had this $4 bottle of terrible tasting stuff, not fit to drink. But we had that aboard anyway and I often wondered what I was going to do with it when I had so much good rum; what was I going to do with this bottle of vender's stuff?

"Well, we started discharging molasses in Halifax on Monday and that day, or the next one, the head stevedore came to me. He says, 'Cap, I know you've come from the West Indies; you got to have some rum aboard; everybody has rum aboard coming from the West Indies.' I said, 'I haven't got any.' He said, 'I don't believe you.' 'Well,' I said, 'I don't!' 'Well, the boys are dry and they would like to have a drink and we'll buy it from you.'

"I said, 'Well, I tell you what I've got. I've got a bottle of vender's stuff, if they want that. It's not very good but it's vender's stuff and I'll let you have it for $5.' I gave him the bottle. He says, 'Oh boy, oh boy, now we're going to have a good drink.' So down he goes in the hold and after a while, he came up and he says, 'Boy oh boy, that vender's stuff—

that bottle never saw the vender's. You just put that label on there and it was a vender bottle.' 'Oh no,' I said, 'that was vender's stuff.' 'Oh,' he says, 'not that—that was the real McCoy. Those boys sure liked that.' And I said, 'I'm glad they liked it' and evidently there's a lot in the head that makes you think what you think."

As is true today, in the waning days of pure sail, crew members aboard vessels departing for foreign ports could buy liquor in bond very cheaply. A five-gallon keg of excellent rum only cost $18. Kegs were sealed into a liquor locker with wax and ribbon seals to ensure they were not opened before leaving port.

The kegs were carefully crafted of unfinished white oak staves. Lou emptied the rum by knocking one hoop loose, and drilling a hole under the hoop line. Once a keg was empty, he replaced the hoop, then sanded, sealed, and oiled or varnished them. The end product was very attractive. Pat would make cushions and they were used as seats and small tables all over the ship. He also gave them away as gifts.

Standard procedure for unloading a cargo of rum at a port was to load it on railroad cars under the watchful eyes of the customs official. Ever vigilant to find an inexperienced official, Lou once lifted one of these little kegs off a railroad car, threw it in his jalopy, and took it back to the *City*. A customs official was right behind him to reseal the keg up properly in the liquor locker. When Lou boarded, he found Teddy Snyder below sitting on one of his keg seats reading a book. "Teddy, get your ass off the seat. Quick!" Lou demanded. Teddy stood, "What for?" he asked. Quickly, Lou replaced the empty keg seat with the full keg he had just brought from the train. "Sit down," Lou ordered. Moments later the customs officer arrived to seal the liquor aboard.

"The customs officer said, 'Where do you seal up your stuff?' I said, 'Right over there. There's a seal, some liquor in there now sealed up.' So we busted the seal and I was struggling with the keg as if it was heavy. I carried it and he says, 'Can you carry it alone?' And I said, 'Oh yes, I can carry it by myself, don't worry.' I was hoping I wouldn't hit anything because the echo of the empty keg would give me away! Boom. Because it was empty. So anyway, I put the empty keg in the locker, customs officer sealed it all up very solemnly; I signed a lot of papers. We drove him back to Bridgewater, came back and I said, 'Now boys, knock one of those hoops off. We'll bore a hole.' And we had a good little party there with rum that was never sealed up."

* * *

During one trip up from Barbados before an engine was fitted, the winds simply wouldn't cooperate, and the voyage up to Turks to load salt took almost three weeks. Unknown to Lou before leaving Barbados, an alcoholic crewman had secretly sold most of the beef and pork to buy booze in Bridgetown, and when they arrived at Turks, the meat barrels were almost empty.

Kenedy went ashore at Turks to victual the ship. The prices of pickled beef and pork were high, and Lou, true to form, refused to pay what he thought was an exorbitant price. He figured he could make it to Lunenburg on the food they had. He told the Kittitian cook, Neville, they'd just have to make do with what was left and try to catch fish on the way up.

Neville was a marvelous cook and served aboard the *City* for most of the 10-year Kenedy tenure. But Neville couldn't read. After three more weeks of virtual calm, the meat barrels were empty. They hooked a few fish but because the *City* was barely drifting, they couldn't troll fast enough to attract the big pelagic fish such as dolphin and swordfish.

One morning Neville brought out huge plates of corned beef hash and gravy. The crew was overjoyed. Over the weeks, oatmeal and Cream o' Wheat with tinned milk had worn thin. After the meal, the skipper said, "Neville, I thought we were out of Spam and canned corned beef." Neville answered, "Cap, I foun' a whole box o' dem in de win'lass room. Have a big picture of a dog on dem." The entire crew had just happily gobbled down the last of the Dr. Ballard's dog food reserved for Butch, the survivor. Lou said, later, "It wasn't bad, either."

* * *

The next summer, Brian signed articles aboard the *City* for a voyage up to Bonavista, Newfoundland to deliver a load of creosoted timbers for the new municipal dock. These enormous pilings were unloaded with the foremast gaff with help from the donkey engine. After they were pulled out of the hold, they were plunked down in the water. A small launch pushed a raft of them ashore. The days were long, and by evening the men were tired and just wanted to eat and relax. But the skipper had other ideas.

The Newfoundlanders were inveterate lobstermen, and the harbor in Bonavista was dotted with close to 50 pots. One evening, Lou summoned Brian and the mate, Pentz, to his cabin. They were both exhausted. Lou said, "Hey, you two go out there in a dory and pick up some pots so's we can have a lobster dinner." Pentz, not wanting to do anything but rest, said, "Jaysus,

Skipper, you can't just go pull up a man's pots, we could get shot, for Christ's sake." Lou had an answer to every problem and replied, "Here's what you do. Every pot that you pull that has lobsters, put a bottle of rum in it." Pentz and Brian pulled five pots that contained 25 lobsters and put a bottle of Mount Gay in each pot.

Brian recalled:

> *"The next morning when we got up, lo and behold, there were lobster buoys for as far as the eye could see. When we got ashore we were told that during the night some traps had caught bottles of rum and the whole village had set pots to try their luck."*

* * *

Figure 6-6. Bath time at sea for Patsy and Pat, in a puncheon.

On July 10, 1902, the seven-masted schooner *Thomas W. Lawson* was launched from the Fore River Ship and Engine Building Company in Quincy, Massachusetts. She was the largest schooner ever built. At 369 feet long with a 50-foot beam, she drew 35 feet and carried 4,900 tons of cargo. Her 25 sails spanned 43,000 square feet and weighed 18 tons. While on her first transatlantic voyage in 1907, she was sunk off the Scilly Islands, with the loss of 13 of her crew.

These data are of little interest to today's children but to Lou Kenedy's kids, knowing the details of the *Lawson* was roughly equivalent to knowing the names of the Beatles during the 1960s.

A controversy that has followed the *Lawson* since her launch is the naming of each of the seven masts and their attendant sails. The American sailing community simply named them after the days of the week starting with Monday as the foremast. On the other hand, her first skipper, Captain Arthur L. Crowley, called them Fore, Main, Mizzen, Number four, Number five, Number six, and Spanker. However, throughout the Maritimes, it has always been the right of the workmen on a new vessel to name the unique aspects of a ship. At the time of the launch, the workmen at Fore River named them Fore, Main, Mizzen, Middle, Spanker, Jigger, and Driver. These became the acknowledged names throughout New England and Canada.

In the fall of 1948, the *City* arrived in Yarmouth, Nova Scotia with 1,000 puncheons of molasses. The trip began in the summer, so the family was aboard. Lou was well known on the Yarmouth waterfront. One afternoon he hoisted five-year-old Patsy on his shoulders and walked up the wharf to Big John's, a small pub where sailors had congregated for years. Patsy's mom encouraged her to go with Lou to the pub, because having a princess as chaperone ensured an early and sober return.

Patsy ducked as they passed through the doorway. Inside it was dark. After coming out of the bright sunlight, Patsy couldn't see anything for a minute or so. But soon the little girl's eyes adjusted to the darkness, and she squinted each time the door opened. Her eyes widened when she saw the walls were covered with pictures of famous schooners and full-rigged ships; glass floats hung in nets from the ceiling and more nets with cork floats draped the walls. Bare hanging light bulbs were the only illumination, one above each of six wooden tables placed under the nets. The room smelled of tobacco and stale beer. To Patsy, it was a place that represented all she thought her father stood for: tough ships and tougher men who braved the sea.

As he lifted Patsy down from his shoulders, she noticed a picture hung between the mirrors on the mahogany back-bar. Pointing to it she squealed, "Look, Daddy, it's the *LAWSON*!" The bartender was new and didn't know Lou. He smiled and said, "She's a smart little booger, ain't she?" Lou replied, "You bet she is," and ordered a beer. He really didn't like the barkeep calling his princess a "booger," but he let it pass. The bartender then turned to the tiny blonde and said, "I'll tell you what I'll do. You tell me the names of the masts on the *Lawson* and I'll give you the picture." Instantly, and as one word, the towhead spat out, ForeMainMizzenMiddleSpankerJiggerDriver."

The bartender fell dead silent for a moment, looked embarrassed, and said, "Well, you got me," and turned to take care of a customer. Lou sat down and began talking with friends and Patsy played with her Coca-Cola. After a half an hour or so, Lou was ready to leave, and he noticed the picture was still hanging behind the bar. He got the barkeep's attention and pointed to it. The bartender said, "I was only kiddin' and I didn't think she'd know the answer, and anyway, Big John would kill me if I gave his picture away."

Without hesitation, Lou Kenedy's right hand shot across the bar and hooked the bartender by the throat, his thumb pushing on his Adam's apple.

He pulled him nose to nose and whispered, "Give—the—kid—the—picture." Behind him, a drunken AB yelled to Lou, "Why don't you screw with me, you dumb bastard?" Lou heard a bottle break and a chair fall over.

The bar was silent except the sound of the swinging door closing behind some of the more timid patrons as they scurried out. Lou didn't even look behind him. Patsy hid in the nook between her Dad's legs and the bar, holding on to his pants. Hearing the racket, the owner, John MacLeod, strode in from a back room. MacLeod was an old Nova Scotian dory fisherman who was even more physically imposing than Lou. Though he owned the pub, he never took a drink and was respected throughout the harbor.

"What the hell's going on here, Lou?" John bellowed. "Tell the guy behind me to sit down or I'll break this son of a bitch's neck, then I'll break his," Lou demanded. The bartender tried to signal the drunk to go away.

Pointing to the drunken sailor gripping the neck of a broken beer bottle, John yelled, "You! Get out!" The sailor hesitated, so John moved toward him: the drunk waved the broken bottle at the pub owner. MacLeod instantly rushed the drunk. He had at least five inches of reach on the sailor. He grabbed the arm holding the bottle with his left hand and quickly smacked the sailor twice on the jaw with his right fist. Pop, pop. The drunk folded at the waist and dropped to the floor. John motioned for the downed sailor's partner to get him out of the bar, and he was dragged into the bright sunlight of the street.

Wiping his hands on his shirt, the bar owner turned his attention to Lou who still had a grip on the bartender's neck. "Now, what's the problem here, Lou?" "Your pansy bartender lost a bet and now he won't pay." "Pay the man, Ali!" ordered MacLeod. The bartender, Alasdair Bell, still in the grip of Lou's right hand, couldn't speak and just rasped, "O.K." Lou let go and the man rubbed his neck, took the picture of the *Lawson* off the wall, and handed it to Patsy. Surprised, MacLeod asked, "What the hell is this?"

Without hesitation, Patsy looked straight up at John and rattled off the story. "He said he'd give me the picture if I could name the masts then he wouldn't give me the picture and my Daddy made him do it." Then, as an encore and without prompting, she repeated, "ForeMainMizzenMiddleSpankerJiggerDriver. Let's go Daddy." Then she skipped, blonde hair a-bouncing, out of the bar with the photo of the *Lawson* held to her chest with both hands. Lou shrugged and John MacLeod started laughing. Lou could still hear him laughing when he and Patsy were a block away. That picture of the schooner *Thomas W. Lawson* hangs in Patsy Kenedy Bolling's home to this day.

Figure 6-7. *Thomas W. Lawson*, the only seven-masted schooner ever built. This is the photo that five-year-old Patsy won.

* * *

During summers, many of the voyages of the *City* were made under charter to the U.S. Government. A series of radar stations was being built across northern Canada and Alaska to warn of possible approaching Russian bombers. The first phase of this was called the "Pinetree Line," later replaced by the DEW (Distant Early Warning) Line. The government required that the *City* have an engine and against Lou's better judgment, he sent to War Assets in the States, and a monster four cylinder Atlas Diesel engine was soon delivered by railroad flat car.

Figure 6-8. Twenty-seven-ton Atlas Diesel engine coming aboard at Lunenburg.

"...it was a big, heavy thing and arrived at the railway wharf in Lunenburg. We used the old crane and unloaded it from a flatcar. It weighed 27 tons. After the City *came off the ways at Lunenburg, we returned to Dayspring where we set it up and lined it up. Of*

course, before we left Lunenburg, Teddy Snyder got the old shaft log cleaned out and a new stern bearing installed through the Atlantic Bridge Company, who designed the equipment. The Lunenburg Foundry made the tanks for the fuel and all the equipment. So we had an engine and we gave her a tryout. She would steam 8.5 knots light in our travels and it was very satisfactory. It was a big four-cylinder engine that did about 350 revs and 350 horsepower."

Unknown at the time and without fanfare, the installation of this engine marked the end of sail-only cargo transportation out of North American ports.

Before setting off on Pinetree Line expeditions, Lou also decided to add one more layer of green-heart sheathing to the bottom of the *City*. Instead of an expensive haulout, Lou careened the 170-foot ship on the shore next to Snyder's and did the work himself, with the help of his crew.

On one of the early Pinetree Line charters delivering aviation gasoline to Baffin Island, Pat was left behind in Conquerall Bank, as she was due to give birth at any time. Once anchored off of Labrador, the headquarters for the expedition, Lou asked the officer in command whether he could get a message relayed from his wife when the baby was born. The

Figure 6-9. *City of New York* **careened at Snyder's Shipyard before sailing for the Arctic. The large white "waterline" on the bow is the first four forward planks of additional greenheart lumber being installed. Eventually, the entire bottom was sheathed—again.**

officer said that he could get in deep trouble if he received and passed on civilian messages. He was allowed to process official business only.

Lou said, "But, Jeezus, I want to know about the baby." The officer thought for a moment and said, "When we receive the message from Halifax, we'll figure out a way to get it to you."

Several weeks later, while supporting a construction team further north, a launch came along side the *City*. A radioman was aboard and said he had an urgent but strange message for the captain. He came aboard and found Lou having lunch in his cabin. "What is it?" asked Lou. The radioman said, "I have a message that says it's for you but I don't think it's for you, it must have been misrouted." Looking up from his soup, Kenedy reiterated, "What is it?" "It makes no sense but here goes: *The submarine is launched; it has no periscope.*" Lou's second daughter, Gabrielle, was born.

The Pinetree Line trips were difficult as winter set in, and the technicians from the Air Force were all landlubbers.

"...nearly every day we'd tow a dory ashore to a stream... fill the dory nearly full with fresh water and tow her out slowly to the ship and pump it out into our tanks. But after some period of time in the fall, when everything started to freeze, it got harder and harder because the water was running under the ice in the streams. We had to chop holes and all to get our buckets down to get water and then it would freeze in the dories and at the last of it, it was really a very hard job to do."

* * *

As the 1950s rolled in, the profitability of the traditional trade route from the Maritimes to the Caribbean dried up. Motorized vessels were faster, more efficient, and less dependent on fair winds to keep schedules. This reduced Lou and the *City* to taking advantage of Canadian cabotage and government charters. But even the preferential treatment of Canadian-based vessels by the government couldn't make up for the cost increases due to the new-found power of the maritime unions. The showdown between the unions and Captain Kenedy finally came at Halifax in 1951 while loading 6,000 55-gallon drums of avgas for the Canadian Air Force based above the Arctic Circle.

Several of the Caribbean islanders who had been with Lou on *Wawaloam* were convinced by some local union members that they weren't getting enough money for a dangerous and frigid trip to the Arctic. The union guys told them they should strike prior to leaving port if they didn't get more money.

The fuel was loaded, and Lou had cleared customs. As he was walking down the steps of the customs house, he was confronted by a group of union workers who told him to go to the union hall for instructions on how to treat his new union crewmembers.

"I told them to go to hell, climbed into my shore boat, and steamed back to the City.*"*

Figure 6-10. Gabrielle Kenedy peeks from a butterfly hatch.

When he arrived, the only ones aboard were the mate, the engineer, the second engineer, and the cook.

"They said, 'The boys—they've gone in the dory and they've deserted ship, and they took the dory.' Well I said, 'They can go back to Anguilla as far as I'm concerned. I don't give a goddamn, but they're not going in MY dory!' So we jumped in the boat and we went back across the harbour and here I saw the fellows rowing and I grabbed the painter of the dory and started towing her back to the ship. One of the sailors got out his sheath knife and, Christ, he didn't say anything but he started going at my wrist, which was holding the bow of the dory at that time and I took this tiller extension, which was removable—it was an oak or a birch stick, and I whacked him across the wrist and broke his wrist. He dropped the knife and started howling."

Another group of union members on the dock jumped into a motor skiff and caught up with Lou towing the dory full of crewmembers. They crashed into the dory and the islanders tumbled into the other craft. Lou had his dory back.

Upon his return to the *City* there was a union skiff alongside and two union organizers were standing on the deck. "Captain Kenedy? We can talk to you here. This is what we want." Lou dove below and the union men thought he was trying to run from them and followed him to his cabin. This was a tactical error as the only reason Lou went below was to retrieve the now infamous .45 caliber revolver—the same one that Windy Mason used to capture the police barracks in Bridgetown.

"Now nobody goes in a three-mast Master's cabin unless they are invited. That's sure. And I went to my drawer to get my .45 and turned around and they said, 'We got you here now where we can talk to you.' And I said, 'You're damn right. The way I talk is over the barrel of a gun, you sons o' bitches. And lay down!'

"And they said, 'Oh God, I haven't seen anything like this since the War.' I said, 'In the War you were digging potatoes; you were bums over in Poland.' They lay on the deck and I had leather boots on and I kicked them a few good ones in the ribs and I said, 'Get going, boys, before I drill holes through you.' And I must say they went pretty fast; they followed my orders and they got up on deck and I said, 'Take all the crew with you. If you think you can do better for them than me, you look after them.'"

Lou called his wife in Conquerall Bank and had her call Guy and Fred Earle in Carbonear, Newfoundland. They were instructed to have three or four seaman waiting. The five men handled the 170-foot tern all the way to Carbonear without a problem, and the rest of the voyage was uneventful.

The newly unionized Caribbean islanders were picked up by immigration and jailed until passage could be arranged back to Barbados. They slept in the paint locker for the whole trip home. Years later, Lou still received letters from the men asking to be taken back as crew. He never answered their letters. His almost manic hatred for unions never flagged.

Lou's last trip on the *City* was another union fiasco, even bigger than the previous one. At the time, he was looking to sell the schooner. He was in Sheet Harbour, Nova Scotia, loading lumber. It was the end of the day, and Lou was below in his cabin having a drink, discussing the loading techniques with the lumber supplier. There was a racket topside; the shop steward for the Sheet Harbour Pulp Wood Union burst into the cabin uninvited. "Who's the captain here?" he demanded. "I am!" Lou answered. "Now who the hell are you coming in like that without being invited?" The union man replied, "I represent the Sheet Harbour Pulp Wood Union." The schooners were never expected to comply with union contracts, so Lou simply replied, "Screw off."

Still threatening, the steward said, "I'll give you a piece of advice: Don't try to load this ship or somebody will get a broken leg." As we know by now, Lou was never afraid of a fight and said, "Now I'm going to give *you* a piece of advice. You get your ass up on deck as fast as you can and keep going or I'll break your goddamn back."

The lumber supplier was frightened and said, "Now you've ruined it. We won't be able to load; we won't get our men; nobody will work. They'll all be afraid to work." Lou's response was, "Well, I'm not using those guys—those union guys. Not me. I'll take care of it."

Again that afternoon Lou called Pat at home and asked her to hunt up his logging buddy, Blake Taylor. He was somewhere in the backwoods near Caledonia. Lou instructed her, "Get that old fellow Blake; get him to bring his men. Tell them there's a racket down here and be prepared for a fight." At two in the morning, Blake and his lumberjacks arrived amid much rattling and banging. They had rumbled down in a jeep, and somebody had sat on the only shotgun and broken the stock. Lou told him, "Don't worry about that. I got plenty of arms here, no problem." They sat in the cabin, popped a keg of Mount Gay, and planned for the next day.

Up early, Lou had his coffee, and by 0600, trucks full of union men began arriving. The skipper could see their cigarettes glowing in the darkness as they surrounded the wharf.

As it dawned, Blake's men started to load the lumber. They had slung one load aboard and were slinging the second load when the burliest of the union members tried to grab a piece of chain away from one of Blake's Lunenburgers. He was a little guy but had plenty of guts to confront the union gorilla who grabbed his chain. "No son of a bitch from Sheet Harbour is going to take my fookin' chain!"

"So then the ugly guy went to grab it again and I was in a strategic position up on the poop right abeam of him; and I hauled out my .45 and I said, 'That's my chain. You put your hands on that chain, you won't have any hands.' And there was a deadly silence. And I said, 'Go ahead. Don't keep me waiting.' I said, 'Either grab it or don't grab it.' He kept following the chain with his hands as the little Lunenburger swung it, but he wasn't touching it. My gun was sighted right on his hands. Then, all of a sudden, he turned to the crowd and his voice cracked and he kind of squealed, 'He ain't got a license for that gun.' I says, 'Go ahead and sing that song some more mister. I sure like it.'"

The day before, Lou had gone to the tiny police station that two Mounties called headquarters to discuss the impending fracas. Only one of the Mounties was available and came down to the *City* just after Lou threatened the gorilla. The union men were demanding Lou's immediate arrest for threatening, but the Mountie was on Lou's side and told them to leave the dock.

Grumbling, they dispersed but only to call in John Sullivan, the union leader who happened to be in Halifax at the time. The story goes that the local union had to guarantee Sullivan $300 to come down to get the *City* loaded by union workers. Sullivan and his entourage arrived en masse; the leader strolled down the dock and stopped next to the gang plank.

"Who the hell are you?" Lou lied. "You don't know who I am?" said Sullivan. "Don't know; don't give a shit," answered the skipper who turned to continue supervising the loading.

But Sullivan thought he had a bargaining chip. He thought that because the name of the schooner was *City of New York*, its business was centered in New York. In fact, Lou seldom carried loads to the larger ports, because they were served by motorized vessels. "Listen," said Sullivan, "if you don't cooperate here, you'll never be able to offload in New York, that's a promise." "A promise?" Lou asked. "I'm dead serious," said the labor man. "Then it's a deal," said Lou, "Here it is: You get your fat ass off my dock and I'll never offload in New York."

After a couple more rounds of similar repartee, Sullivan gave up and walked away shaking his head. When he got back to the crowd of union members, an argument arose because some of them didn't quite understand that John Sullivan would get his $300 whether or not he was successful negotiating with the captain of *City of New York*.

What the union leader also didn't know was that Captain Kenedy had at that time made an offer on *Vema*, another even larger schooner grounded on a Staten Island mud flat where she was slated for destruction. He was planning to sell the *City*, and whoever bought her would be the one with the union problems, not Lou Kenedy.

In the 10 years that Lou owned the *City*, he was never offered a dime for her. But, amazingly, on November 14, 1952, two telegrams reached Lou. One was out of the blue from a group that wanted to buy the *City* to put her into the Prince Edward Island-San Juan, Puerto Rico potato trade. The other was from the owners of *Vema* accepting his offer to buy her. He affirmed both wires and within hours Captain Kenedy had changed commands.

The *City*, however, was not so lucky. After a year of work, the group that purchased her had her towed from Lunenburg to Yarmouth for refit. But on December 30, 1953, she broke her tow line, caught fire, and sank on Chebogue Ledge outside Yarmouth Harbour. Her bleached bones eventually washed up on the shore nearby.

So ends this day.

Figure 6-11. Shortly after Lou sold the *City*, she burned and sank off Yarmouth, Nova Scotia. Photo by Bob Brooks of Yarmouth. (Used by permission.)

Figure 7-1.

The ship: *Vema (ex-Hussar)*
Year of Launching: 1923
Rig: Tern Schooner (yacht)
Builder: Burmeister Wain Shipyard,
    Copenhagen
Engine: Burmeister Wain Diesel, 800
    horsepower

Material: Riveted nickel steel
Length overall: 202 feet 6 inches
Beam: 33 feet 2 inches
Draft: 15 feet 1 inch
Displacement: 533 tons

Chapter 7   *Vema*

The fourth of five yachts named Hussar *built by the investment banker,*
E.F. Hutton, this particular Hussar *was an opulently-appointed yacht replete*

with gold bathroom fixtures and marble fireplaces. She was equipped with a grand piano and stained-glass skylights.

Before World War II, this Hussar *was bought by shipping magnate George Unger Vetlesen, and re-christened* Vema, *a name derived from the first two letters of his family name and the first two of his wife's name, Maude.* Vema *was very fast; under Vetlesen's ownership, she made a few remarkable voyages including one 10-day, eight-hour trip from New York to the Lizard.* This was a record for a auxiliary yacht. In 1928, she was only three hours behind* Atlantic *in the King of Spain race from Santander, Spain to New York, in spite of dragging a 90-inch prop.*

Vema *was never involved with scientific research before Captain Kenedy purchased her in 1952, but the Vetlesen family name is now renowned for a foundation that supports oceanographic research and awards the prestigious Vetlesen Prize in the earth sciences.*

During World War II, Vema *was converted into a navigation training ship. Her rich guest accommodations were stripped and replaced by 40 pipe bunks. After the war she was used as a dormitory for students at Kings Point Marine Academy. She was then abandoned at Staten Island to be broken up and sold as scrap.*

* * *

When Captain Kenedy arrived at Staten Island to take possession of *Vema*, he brought his wife and kids down from Lunenburg along with Walter Pryde as engineer, Clarence Pentz as the mate, and Ed Sabin as cook's assistant and AB. Pat did the cooking. His big Newfoundland husky, Gotlik, was also in the entourage.

The first problem was the ferocious guard dog that had been put aboard by the scrap yard. The huge but undernourished German shepherd with only one eye had been thrown food at intervals. His only drinking water came from rain that accumulated in a few bowls that were scattered on deck. The dog's incessant bark was punctuated by low, ominous growls. The barks were answered by Gotlik's howling. The scene was annoyingly noisy.

The dockmaster met Lou on the wharf next to *Vema* with a rifle and said that there was no way anyone could board the vessel as long as the dog was alive and that he would shoot the shepherd for him. Lou was instantly outraged. The accusations that Lou was kinder to his dogs than to his crews is not without foundation. One of the numerous trip-wires of Lou's volatile

---

* Lizard Point, the southernmost point in England, in southwestern Cornwall.

temper was animal abuse, especially to dogs, hence: "If you touch that dog, I'll take the rifle and shove it up your ass!"

The dockmaster was taken aback by Lou's signature bluntness and said, "Suit yourself, but you'll never get aboard while that dog is alive."

"Bullshit," said Lou and climbed down to the deck. The guard dog held his ground, and Lou stayed perfectly still. The dog approached growling and barking; Gotlik was nearly frantic on the dock. After a three-minute standoff, the big shepherd stopped barking and moved within five feet of Lou. Lou never moved but he started talking to the dog in a low voice. In another three minutes, the dog was within striking distance and was growling and baring his teeth. Lou continued whispering, "Everything is all right."

Ten minutes after Lou confronted the dog, the old half-blind pooch was letting Lou rub his ears, and the event was over. The dockmaster walked away shaking his head. "I'll be damned. No one's been able to get near that dog in a year and a half." Lou called the dog "Walter" after Walter Schug, the U-boat skipper who sank *Wawaloam* years earlier, and he was a loyal family pet for two years before he died of old age. He and Gotlik were wary of each other for a few weeks but reconciled to each other's existence and eventually became inseparable.

Getting down to the task at hand, Lou was a bit depressed at the amount of work to be done. The deck was encrusted with dried dog feces, since no one had ever cleaned up after the pooch. They simply tossed food to him and left him to his own devices. The scuppers were four inches deep in the filth, and the only way to clean it was with flat shovels, brooms, and bucket upon bucket of salt water drawn from the estuary.

Walter Pryde finally got one generator running, and the crew was able to use *Vema*'s beautiful electric winches to help move her out of the hole in the mud in which she sat. The main engine wasn't running. To extract *Vema*, at each high tide a hawser was run from a bollard on the wharf aft of the counter to one of the winches, and she was pulled backward a boat length toward the end of the dock. After 200 feet, she would suck herself back into the black New York goo, and as the tide ebbed, she would dig another hole in the mud. Each high tide, she was pulled back another 200 feet. After several fleets, she was finally free from the muck, and a tug was ordered to tow her to City Island.

There the first chore was painting the topsides. She was a quilt work of red lead splotches, and "we weren't going to bring her back to Nova Scotia looking like that." So Lou and the mate went over the side in a dinghy and slapped a coat of white paint on her hull from waterline to gunwale. This was no mean feat on a 200-foot schooner.

After painting, the crew got busy aloft. Due to the size of the spars, the running rigging used enormous blocks, most of which had been removed and stored below. They were so heavy, they had to be run up the steel masts with halyards. After the blocks were shackled aloft, new halyards were run for two heads'ls and the three lowers (fore, main, and mizzen). Each of the lowers had outhauls for the booms and gaffs, in addition to throat and peak halyards.

"...but we didn't splice the ends—just tied them off that first day. But to do that, all those blocks had to be rigged and there was a pile of line used in one day, I tell you.

"The next day or so we spliced the new line and whipped the ends. The vessel was starting to take shape and the crew got busy bending on the canvas. The job was made more difficult by the countless old, brittle hoops. The masts were a full two feet in diameter, so the hoops were huge. After two days of dragging canvas up and down the decks, raising and lowering the sails to ensure the hoops were not sticking, the sails were finally where they belonged.

"We didn't bend the mizzen. She had a big trysail so we bent that because it was wintertime anyway."

Figure 7-2. *Vema's* figurehead.

Meanwhile, Pat was below cooking on a kerosene pressure stove with a tiny, rudimentary oven that sat on top of the burners. Amazingly, she produced a smorgasbord of pies, pastries, roasts, and casseroles in the pitiful little oven, and the crew was well fed. The main galley stove and equipment used steam from a boiler in the engine room, but the boiler didn't work. Lou waited to have it overhauled in Nova Scotia, where the repair would be less expensive.

Everything was ready for the engineless trip to Nova Scotia on Friday, January 15, 1953. But Lou Kenedy NEVER began a trip on a Friday. This superstition, among others, was adhered to scrupulously throughout his life. It extended even to automobile and airplane trips. So it wasn't until Saturday, the 16th of January, that *Vema* was towed out of her berth. She flew down Long Island Sound with a stiff breeze off the port quarter.

In addition to poop deck steering, *Vema* had a bridge forward of the foremast. It was a wonderful steering station, with great visibility. But on this first trip up to Dayspring for the refit, the bridge steering wasn't rigged. When *Vema* reached the mouth of the LaHave, the wind turned favorable, and Lou was able to sail the huge yacht through the winter ice to within 100 feet of Teddy Snyder's wharf. He dropped an anchor and warped her to the dock.

"And then, boy, we could get to work and fix everything up. So Teddy Snyder took over and the Atlantic Bridge took over in the engine room and went to work on the engines and got them organized and got the furnace going. The first day we started the engine was quite an event. It certainly ran beautifully—quiet, like a big steam engine. The real puzzle to us, she had a 90-inch propeller that had adjustable pitch or a feathering propeller, and it had an electric motor on it to make it work. We didn't know anything about that and how it would work; they pressed the buttons and the first thing it was running and the next thing the propeller was cutting in ahead or astern, whichever way we wanted."

While Teddy's crews were methodically repairing systems, Lou arranged a charter with Doc Ewing of Columbia University's Lamont Geological Observatory. It was to be a research cruise into the Caribbean and the Gulf of Mexico. The ship was certainly equipped for such an expedition. The galley was 60-feet long, and the 40 pipe-rack bunks supplied plenty of room for the scientists.

The crew's quarters, located appropriately in the fo'c's'le, were original and sported 10 mahogany bunks, each replete with reading lamps, rails, and lee cloths[*] in case of nasty seas. Amidships, the original mess room was straddled by individual cabins for each of two engineers, the bosun, and the mate. For Pat and Lou, there was an opulent captain's cabin with a varnished mahogany floor graced with marble inserts, a bathtub, and built-in bedroom suite including a settee. Lou summarized later, "It was very nice accommodations."

By the middle of March, *Vema* took on two railroad tank cars of fuel and set sail for New York to pick up the research scientists. They arrived the day before Good Friday, 1953; Lou's agent reported to the charter party that *Vema* had arrived as scheduled. The scientists couldn't get any work done on the

---

[*] Fabric panels that may be fastened at the side of a bunk to prevent the bunk occupant from falling out when the vessel is heeled over.

Good Friday weekend so, as usual, the inevitable demurrage fight ensued. And, as usual, Lou got his money.

"And I told them that the charter said—like all charters—that it starts when the ship reports ready for service. Well they said they didn't want to pay for her over the weekend because they couldn't work on her. Well, I says their work was none of my business; that was their business. And needless to say, I got my money; I insisted on that."

On Monday, *Vema* was towed over to Todd's Shipyard in Hoboken, and over the next two weeks, an enormous amount of scientific gear was rigged. A monstrous winch was installed amidships with over three miles of two-inch cable to be used for taking core samples of the bottom at the various study areas.

Once the refit was done, 35 scientists and engineers boarded *Vema,* and she set sail for San Juan, where more equipment was installed. They rendezvoused with the 140-foot ketch *Atlantis*, a research vessel out of Woods Hole Oceanographic Institution (WHOI). The two vessels were slated to "buddy-boat" during the expedition. After a month working around Puerto Rico and the Bahamas, *Vema* was heading back south when the beautiful Burmeister Wain diesel cracked a head and was shut down. But the ships were in the trade winds by this time, and the loss of the engine was of no consequence.

"...we operated just as fast and just as good as Atlantis *was doing under power. So everything went along very well. We went into Guantanamo Bay, Cuba, and they were changing some personnel, I guess. We tried to have the head repaired but they couldn't do it in the Navy machine shops there. So we continued under sail."*

Gotlik the husky was very fast. He was fascinated with birds and when ashore would catch seagulls and even snipes; he could grab them right out of the air and hold them in his big soft mouth. Prancing over to Lou, he always proudly displayed them as his contribution to the family. Lou would take the bird and say, "Good dog" and then let the bird go, none the worse for wear.

Figure 7-3. Agile ship's dog Gotlik climbed ladders like a monkey and captured tropical birds for the expedition biologist.

As part of the expedition, a zoologist aboard *Atlantis* was charged with capturing tropical birds and recording their physical characteristics. But he didn't have much luck catching them. As a matter of fact, he never caught a single bird. Gotlik, on the other hand, would spend his evenings—especially along the Mexican coast—catching an assortment of tropical birds that lit aboard *Vema*. He grabbed parrots and herons and other unique specimens—exactly what the *Atlantis* zoologist wanted to see. Virtually every morning, Lou would radio *Atlantis* and say, "We got a big bird here. Anyone interested?"

"So they'd launch a boat and come over and get the bird so we were the retrievers of the birds. He wanted to buy the dog so he'd have a means of getting these rare tropical things. But, of course, he wasn't for sale, at any price."

* * *

The expedition came to an end in Galveston in June of 1953 where the scientists left *Vema* and she was ordered to New York. The damaged engine still couldn't be used, but she made the trip from Galveston to Miami in seven days—against the prevailing winds and seas. This is a remarkable voyage. The as-the-crow-flies distance is about 870 nautical miles, but *Vema* tacked against the weather which essentially doubled the distance. Traveling 1700 miles in seven days makes an average speed of over 10 knots. The trip up from Miami, however, was slow, 14 days. But when *Vema* arrived at New York, she had a bone in her teeth and entered the harbor under full sail doing 13 knots. She was met in the Narrows by the 170-foot Belgian training brigantine *Mercator,* also under full sail outbound for Europe. They passed within feet of each other. A newspaper helicopter overhead photographed this scene, once common, but now rare—two tall ships passing each other with all canvas set.

News boats followed *Vema* as she held full sail all the way to Lower Manhattan, where she was met by tugs that towed her back to Todd's Shipyard in Hoboken. Believing Columbia University had instructed Todd's to remove the equipment installed in February, Lou thought *Vema* would be laid up there for several weeks before returning to Conquerall Bank. Instead, he was met by the financial officer of Lamont Geological Observatory. On the spot, a deal was struck to buy *Vema* from Lou.

"Lamont Geological Observatory of Columbia University—the scientific part—were interested because they had been involved in this trip we made down south, and they wanted to buy the vessel. So we made arrangements that were satisfactory to both me and them. Anyway

they bought her. Also we had the engine repaired. Todd's was able to do it. It was impossible to get any parts for this engine because she'd been built in 1923 and the patterns of the parts had been either lost or destroyed. They weren't available anymore, anyway.

"I agreed to stay on as master for one trip and we were going to make a trip around Nova Scotia and Newfoundland and the North Atlantic and back to New York."

Pat was signed as "second cook" and also tended to the two little girls who were by then 6 and 10 years old. Brian signed articles as bosun, and three of his school chums signed on as ordinary seamen. It was quite a reunion when they all traveled to New York to board *Vema*.

"But I had the same mate and engineers, of course."

During the first expedition down south, Lou had gained a healthy dislike for the scientists. To him, they had no respect for the sea or its traditions, and for Captain Lou Kenedy there was no greater sin. They considered *Vema* nothing more than a piece of equipment and treated Lou as an inconsequential and uneducated technician. In their minds, seamanship was not learned over countless years of lumpy seas and lost ships but rather was a skill that could be mastered by sheer intellect. And since they fancied themselves intellectuals, they believed they could, through simple, geometric logic, master the elements of navigation and ship operation instantly.

It was July, 1953 when *Vema* left New York for Cabot Straits in a dense fog. At noon on the third day of steaming, never having seen the sun, Lou suddenly announced, "Here we are. Just the latitude and longitude you wanted."

"And they said, 'That's all right captain, just keep on going.' I said, 'O.K.' Vema continued steaming until midnight when he informed them: 'I gotta turn around and go somewhere else because we're going to run into Newfoundland.' And they said, yes, they thought the same thing. So I said, 'Where will we go?' They said, 'Go back to where you were at noon.'"

At 1100 the next morning, Vema arrived back at the location of the noon position, still thick-a-fog. The scientists had no clue as to Vema's position and believed that Lou was also lost.

"...but I told them they were pretty near where they wanted to be. And at noon, the sun came out and I got a latitude sight. After 1300, I started working longitude sights and it came out that after four days

steaming, we were three miles out of position; and three miles, we did that in 20 minutes and we were in the right spot. And after that they never questioned what I said about where we were."

There was certain scientific equipment aboard *Vema* that had to be streamed aft, and the technicians asked Lou to give them an hour's warning before stopping so they had the time to retrieve the gear. If the schooner hove to or changed course before retrieval, the streaming gear would tangle.

While steaming southeast of Cape Race, Lou had been monitoring stateside weather broadcasts, and the glass was falling precipitously. Though at this time weather reporting wasn't what it is today, it was clear to Lou that a hurricane was working its way up the American east coast. Lou called the chief of the scientific expedition and told him to haul in his equipment as a hurricane was fast approaching. The scientist was ecstatic. "Oh, that's great. We want to go right into the center of this hurricane and see what they're like. Nobody's told us what the center of a hurricane is like." Lou immediately turned to the mate and instructed him to lower a lifeboat outfitted with grub and water. The scientist asked, "What's that for?"

"I said, 'It's for you to get in and go to the center of the hurricane, I'm staying here! My job is to take you out and get you back safe, not to drown you and drown me, too.' So anyway that settled that.

"Throughout the powerful storm, Vema was hove to under heavy fore stays'l and trys'l. And they stood and we took—I want to say we took a beating because she lay too beautifully. But I have movies of it and the seas were higher than my eyes at the bridge which were 28 feet above the water and those crests were quite a bit higher than my eye—

they were probably in the 30-foot range. My wife wouldn't come on deck. I kept telling her to come on deck and have a look and she wouldn't. She stayed in the galley and was baking bread. That took her mind off the thing but she had to hang on, I tell you. Anyway everything went along."

One of the final straws for Lou's rocky relationship with

Figure 7-4. A moment of incompetence by a technician led to a broken mizzen boom and gaff.

the scientists was when, without asking, one of the techs let go the mizzen sheet because a quarter tackle was in his way. The 72-foot boom was in a gallows but *Vema* was rolling, and it just jumped out off the crutch and started swinging. The 56-foot gaff followed the boom to the starboard shrouds and they both broke, dumping tons of rig into the Atlantic.

Lou went overboard and attached a heavy throat halyard to it and they hoisted the mess aboard. They cut the sail off the gaff and boom and after several hours of back-breaking work, got the mess untangled. Lou was seething and at that moment decided not to sign for another stint aboard *Vema*.

"So anyway I couldn't take those scientists. So I got off and we went home and the Vema *continued on working for them but they gradually learned. I think Captain Kohler took her and he had more patience than I. He taught them, and also they learned through their mistakes, I guess, that they couldn't run a vessel like a truck. He got along with them and he trained them right. He had many very successful years with the vessel. She was some ship.*

"She was the last three-master out of Nova Scotia. City of New York *was the last one for carrying cargo but* Vema *was the last big vessel doing scientific work out of here. By the way, the* City of New York *was the last sailing vessel to carry lumber out of Nova Scotia. It was the last sailing vessel to carry salt to Lunenburg. She was the last sailing vessel to carry molasses to Newfoundland. And* Wawaloam, *the one before, was the last to carry molasses to Moncton, New Brunswick. Molasses used to be carried to Moncton all the time, but she was the last one to go up the Peticodiac River. So they weren't the first to do things but they were the last, we'll say."*

Vema is now chartering in the Caribbean under the name *Mandalay*. She is a pitiful caricature of the ship she once was. A deckhouse that resembles a motel has been built from stem to stern and tiny sails are rigged like an amusement park ride. The sails give the illusion of sailing to landlubbers.

So ends this day.

Figure 8-1. *Alpha* **rounding Hog Island Light.**[*]

The ship: *Alpha*
Year of Launching: 1919
Rig: Ketch
Builder: Unknown, Waterhezen, Holland
Engine: Dorman six cylinder 125 BHP direct
    drive (1:1 ratio engine to propeller)

Material: Iron
Length overall: 80 feet
Beam: 18 feet
Draft: 6 feet 6 inches
Displacement: 86 tons

[*] Photo by Jarvis Darville. (Used by permission.)

> *"It's a mantle piece!"*
> *"You're not going to make us go to sea in that little thing, are you?"*
> *"It might roll over; it's so small, you know."*
> *"Why don't you go out for a while before we go on a trip with you."*
>
> Comments of Pat and the Kenedy girls when they first laid eyes on the "tiny" 80-foot *Alpha*.

Chapter 8   *Alpha*

Through maritime jungle drums, Lou had heard an 80-foot iron ketch was for sale and lying at City Island, New York. He was curious but wasn't sure what the hell he would do with her. In the spring of 1954 the captain and 16-year-old Brian caught a train down from Bridgewater to survey *Alpha*. They borrowed a rowboat from a fisherman at the dock and rowed out to the ketch. She dripped rust, but the hull seemed sound. Her teak deck was a mess and the rigging was a total loss, but the Dorman diesel was in good condition as was the embarrassingly opulent interior.

"But she could be had for a song. So I sang that song and I got her."

Lou was unsure of what he would do with *Alpha* but figured if nothing else, he'd fix her up and sail her around for a while just for fun, then resell her for a profit.

The purchase of *Alpha* represented a sea change in the life of each member of the Kenedy family. *Alpha* saw them move to tropical climes, Brian grow and leave for a life of his own, and the girls mature into vibrant young women. But the *Alpha* era took a primitive, deep psychological toll on Pat. Of course, throughout the turmoil to come, Lou was unmoved and seemingly unaware of the family storms on the horizon.

This first voyage of *Alpha* was no different from Lou's other luckless first voyages. It was April, and with Brian as the only crew, they spent a couple of days jury-rigging *Alpha* to make the trip up to the LaHave. The rigging and sails, however, were in miserable shape. By the time the ketch reached Martha's Vineyard, a three-day nor'easter set in, and the sails were shredded. After three days of sewing, they set off again only to reach Cape Sable with the heads'l and mizzen again in tatters. But no worries: the old slow-turning Dorman diesel ran like a watch—a guttural, pulse-pounding watch—until all the fuel in the main tank drained through an undetected hole and into the bilge. Then it stopped, dead. And, of course, the secondary tank had only few gallons in it, but it got them close to Liverpool. *Alpha* sailed into the port under the main, and Brian dropped the hook. The boy rowed ashore and lugged back a couple of jerry cans of diesel, just enough to get the Dorman primed and *Alpha* over to a proper fuel dock where the one sound tank was filled.

A few days later, the ketch sputtered up the LaHave and tied up to Teddy Snyder's in Dayspring, where work was started in earnest. They painted and varnished, overhauled the engine and generator, and turned *Alpha* around fast for the summer charter season. When all was bright and shiny, Lou had the opportunity to do a thorough survey.

Alpha sported two sets of davits, one on each side amidships, supporting two 16-foot shore boats. One of these boats was Lou's pride and joy, and in the near future, a small blonde would take over as its sole skipper.

The little boat was entirely built of mahogany, and—

"...had a beautiful little English one-cylinder [Stuart-Turner] *engine in it, which ran as smooth as glass. You'd think it was a V-8. It had a handle on it that you just pushed one way to go ahead and one way to go astern. In between, a clutch disengaged the engine from the prop. It was very, very handy and the farther you pushed it, the faster it went. So for total control, it was just that one little handle. I owned her for many years."*

Alpha's interior was nothing less than a huge piece of fine mahogany furniture. The full length of the wide, varnished companionway was carpeted with a Persian runner. The companionway ran fore and aft; the doors of the three guest cabins were ornately carved. Each cabin had its private head and shower. The bunks, actually double beds, were beautifully sculpted and varnished. Writing desks were built in below polished bronze ports large enough to offer romantic, diffused light and an outside view.

The heads were 1920s era, gleaming brass Wilcox-Crittenden boomers with pump handles that reached chest level. With that much leverage, they could suck the chrome off a trailer hitch. The free-standing vitreous lavies boasted polished brass hot and cold water valves; the white porcelain handles were inscribed *Heiß* and *Kaltes* in blue script.

That summer Lou chartered to the carriage trade around the Maritimes and New England, with Brian signed as an AB and Ted Bligh as cook. Those chartering the *Alpha* were invariably wealthy, and some were famous. It was a happy time for Brian that he recollects fondly to this day. *Alpha* soon left for Maine and finally ended up in Oyster Bay, Long Island, where they picked up the family and friends of a very successful clothing manufacturer. The rag man's wife was in a cast as she had fallen off a horse and broken her arm. As soon as the charter party boarded, Lou cast off for the Connecticut River.

"Now there was a report of a big hurricane off of Hatteras and all the weather reports were very emphatic that it was going to go east-southeast of Nantucket and offshore. It would make unsettled weather but there would be no threat. Well, of course, like all hurricanes, you have to see it to believe it; take it with a grain of salt what the weather people have to say, especially in those days before they had so many electronic gadgets to help them."

As *Alpha* headed through Long Island Sound, the breeze piped up from the east-northeast and continued to build. As the storm reached a moderate gale, Lou realized *Alpha* would not reach the Connecticut River during daylight hours. He decided to find a safe harbor to avoid the storm that was closing in on *Alpha*. Duck Island Roads was the nearest protection available.

Near New Haven, Duck Island Roads was nothing more than an open road with a minimally-protective island off shore. But in the 1910s a granite rock breakwater 400 yards long was built west to east that used Duck Island as its eastern terminus. Another 200-yard breakwater was built from the island due north creating a "V" that gave protection from southerly and easterly seas. The roadstead was far from a secure anchorage in a brewing hurricane, but when *Alpha* arrived, it was full of yachts seeking refuge. Lou found a good spot to drop the hook and got busy preparing *Alpha* for the storm.

Figure 8-2. Beautiful main saloon. Note carving on cabinet panels.

The hurricane was "Carol." She caused major damage on the East Coast in August of 1954, with sustained winds of over 125 miles per hour. Pennsylvania, New York, and New England suffered $4.2 billion in flood damage alone, most caused by the torrential rains that came after the storm passed.

Aboard *Alpha*, the crew brought the dinghies inboard, lowered them to the deck and lashed them down with gripes. They took down the awnings and stowed all loose gear.

"The charterers came and asked me what's going on, and 'Where are we going tomorrow?' 'Where are we going tomorrow?' I answered. 'We'll be lucky if we can just stay here.' And he says, 'Oh, the radio says that this hurricane is going to go way offshore.' I said, 'I'll believe it when I see it.' I said, 'I'm preparing for the worst.' And he says, 'What can we do to help?' 'Well,' I said, 'just relax, you're in good hands. I'll do the best I can for you.' So we had a pleasant supper and all, and by morning it was really shrieking."

After dinner, the two big anchors were checked and another 50 feet of chain was payed out, putting the total length of the rode at 180 feet. Since the water was only 10 to 12 feet deep, the scope, at close to 20 to one, should have been adequate. By this time, the breakwater was awash and the top of the granite rip-rap was only occasionally visible through the exploding surf. Wind-powered waves were rolling freely over the top, making the anchorage untenable for the smaller yachts.

At 0900, it was as still dark as dusk and the yachts disappeared, one by one, into the mist and driving rain. They were pushed toward the western breakwater which was largely invisible due to intermittent downpours and scudding sea foam. The roar increased.

At 1000, *Alpha* began to drag her anchors. The wind roared at over 80 miles an hour, and the din made it impossible to communicate on deck. As *Alpha* bore down on the granite boulders, Lou saw all the other yachts had gone aground and were, one by one, breaking up.

"We'd see the boats hit the rocks and start to smash up and the people jump out of them and run along over these rocks to the little island, Duck Island, which had a house on it, a small, one-story bungalow. And there were some trees on it and the people must have all gone there and congregated and finally there were no more boats left in the harbor."

The charterers were huddled below in the deckhouse and every so often Lou swung down to check the barometer. Every time he tapped the face, the black needle dropped lower. After several hours, *Alpha* had dragged to within a few yards of the western breakwater, and each time the stern rose and crashed down, Lou thought the rudder would splinter against the rocks and spell the end of the ketch. His biggest worry was how to get the charterer's wife off *Alpha* with a broken arm. Once aground, the crew and passengers would have to mount the deckhouse or climb the rigging, then jump to the rocks as the surge brought them closer. But Lou saw no possible way to get the lady ashore safely. He could barely disguise his concern over his position and saw that his charges were becoming more and more afraid.

While *Alpha* rolled heavily in the surf toward the rocks, Lou swung below for a last barometer check before preparing to abandon ship. He tapped. No movement. He tapped again, and still the needle didn't move. He said, "Good." The glass had fallen to 28.4 inches. And back on deck, the wind had already abated and breaks in the clouds were showing. He quickly called the crew aft and in his captain's voice, ordered the anchors weighed and cranked up the diesel. There was no powered windlass aboard the ketch and all halyards and anchor chains were hauled by hand.

At this point all became calm. Lou knew *Alpha* was in the eye of Carol.

"And we hove those anchors up in a few minutes, and we steamed across the harbor to the other side where I figured the wind would come from the nor'west or the west. And sure enough, as soon as we got the anchors down, it started to blow from the west. Now this became clear weather, no rain; and it cleared off—but blow!! My God almighty, it blew, can't tell you how hard, and the water started washing through the channel.

"There was an opening on both sides of this harbor and it blew a current right through. It must have been running four or five knots, and boats started floating by that had broken from their moorings further up the coast. One of them we caught hold of with a line on and got it around its mast. We grabbed the mast as it went by. But the line soon chafed on the forestay and nothing we could do about it. And it took off and we'd see it go down on the breakwater. This is the northern breakwater from Duck Island which was higher. There it hit the rocks and in a few minutes there was nothing left. The masts came down and the boat smashed to kindling wood. At least a dozen boats did that. There was a mass of wreckage because porches, roofs, bits of houses, outhouses, and all the rest were floating by; great swirls of them. And

down against this shore was a mass of broken timber, planks, oars, wreckage of all kinds."

When the wind finally abated, *Alpha* was the only survivor in the road. All the other boats had either been swept out to sea or smashed to flotsam on the breakwater. Lou launched the big lifeboat, and he and Brian rowed it over to Duck Island where the survivors of the wrecked yachts were still huddling in the shack. They were in bad psychological shape but physically fine. Lou brought all 15 of them out to *Alpha* and fed them bacon and eggs and milk, juice, and water—lots of water. Within a few hours, a coast guard plane circled overhead and contacted Lou on the radio he had installed in Dayspring. A few hours later, a police boat arrived and took the refugees ashore.

The next day, in a dead calm, *Alpha* steamed out to Martha's Vineyard. On the way she passed rafts of floating wreckage that reminded Lou of the acres of vegetation that drift in the Sargasso Sea.

The full power and effect of the storm was not evident until *Alpha* reached Edgartown on the Vineyard.

"The next day we got to Martha's Vineyard. We went in there and looked for the yacht club and here was just a roof standing on pillars. The lower part of the yacht club was washed right out, right through. The sea had made a clean sweep and just the pillars held the roof. And the piano was out in the street, washed there; and the street was full of boats and wreckage."

Alpha then motored across Vineyard Sound to check on the condition of Woods Hole and the 140-foot ketch, *Atlantis*, the "buddy-boat" that accompanied *Vema* on her first expedition. Along with several 70- to 90-foot schooners, *Atlantis* was on her side, well up the beach and stove in.

"There was nothing left. That hurricane did tremendous damage in New England and in Boston. It blew a lot of roofs off and damaged church steeples and so on. I don't know how many people were lost but it was plenty."

The next day, *Alpha* left for Nantucket still passing tons of wreckage. A few miles out, Brian spotted a swamped boat a couple of hundred yards to starboard. There was a stiff southerly breeze blowing, but Lou ordered *Alpha* stopped anyway. The boat was bailed out and lifted aboard. It was a brand new, steel, double-ended lifeboat. As they cleaned the grass and debris from the boat, the name "Agnes Norton" appeared. The name was welded on each side of the bow. *Agnes Norton* was a purse seine trawler that was sunk by hurricane Carol with the loss of all aboard. Lou kept the boat as a tender and lifeboat for *Alpha* during the entire time he owned her.

Pat was not aboard during this time, and Brian was unaware of the real reason why his Mom stayed home with his new sister, Rosemary, who joined the family in the summer of 1954. He thought it was solely because the little girl was sickly, suffering from Celiac gluten intolerance. Pat was home because of the stress of little Rosie's birth and ill-health but also because of deep depression caused by the lifestyle change occasioned by Lou's long absences. Pat withdrew from the family and entered a period of dark reflection. Lou, not known for his sensitivity, or for that matter, tolerance of the illnesses of others, simply ignored the problems and continued chartering *Alpha* while Pat stayed in Conquerall Bank and withdrew further into her own shadowy world.

* * *

In the fall, the charter season ended, and Brian returned to Bridgewater High. After the exciting summers with his Dad, going back to school was always difficult.

With the kids in school in Bridgewater, Lou accepted a charter as a supply ship for a research expedition to the Caribbean. Lou's decision to work for the Navy was another point of depression for Pat. He would be gone for six or eight months, leaving her alone with the kids. During the schooner days, his absences were much shorter; he could make a round trip from the LaHave to Bridgetown in as little as eight weeks.

Lou was overjoyed because at the stroke of a pen, he justified the decision to buy *Alpha*. Although the summer's charters had been fun, short, and marginally profitable, they were not up to the financial standards of Lou's previous commands. The Navy charter, on the other hand, would last about six months, and the income would pay Lou back for the entire investment in the ketch, including the refit, and leave a fat profit in his pocket. As soon as the charter agreement was consummated, three crew members signed articles including Walter Pryde, the engineer on *Vema*.

But the prospect of a prolonged separation desolated Pat. She had presumed that the charters around Nova Scotia and the Northeast would go on for a few years. This would keep Lou nearby to help out with the kids and the house on the LaHave and be a husband. But if Lou knew anything of his wife's looming psychological crises, he did not show it.

Others in Conquerall Bank and Dayspring, however, were fully aware of Pat's mental state. Isabel Marcus, the wife of the doctor who delivered Rosemary, spoke succinctly to Lou about the problem and offered to find a solution so that Pat could sign aboard *Alpha* as assistant cook. Lou shrugged and said, "Why not?" But when told of the plan, Pat immediately rejected it because Rosie was chronically ill and there was no one to care for her. Isabel knew of a retired nurse in Conquerall Bank (known to the family only as Nurse Corkum) who might be willing to take care of little Rosie while Pat was gone. Ethel Kaizer, Walter Prydes's mom, would take the older children so they could continue school.

Realizing the curative value of a cruise to the Caribbean without the kids, Isabel insisted on handling all the details with Nurse Corkum, and a deal was struck. Pat signed articles as assistant cook, and in October of 1954, *Alpha* skirted hurricane Hazel and arrived in San Juan on the first of November.

The Navy engineers and technicians climbed aboard at Isla Grande, and Lou immediately set sail for Antigua, which would act as the supply base for the mission. The assignment revolved around the secret testing of the nascent Loran navigation system. The engineers planned to set up a station that in conjunction with other stations around the Caribbean would communicate with aircraft that regularly flew over the region. Positions would be charted electronically much faster and to a degree of accuracy that was, by an order of magnitude, more precise than celestial navigation or even radio direction finders.

After stops in St. Lucia and St. Vincent to load equipment and stores, *Alpha* returned to Antigua before setting sail for the object of the expedition, a little Venezuelan guano speck known as Isla Aves (Bird Island). A 24-hour run from Antigua to the southeast—about 150 miles—found *Alpha* in the tiny lee of an islet only 400 yards long by 100 yards wide at its widest part and only 14 feet high. Even from the crosstrees, it could only be seen from a couple of miles away, so accurate navigation was vital. Ironically, an expedition that was organized to test Loran couldn't use it, as it was still unavailable. Navigation was 90 percent celestial, with a bit of help from radio direction finders that were not particularly accurate at the distances involved. But, of course, Captain Kenedy always arrived on time.

"This island was called Bird Island, as I said. There are periods in the year that the birds lay their eggs, and they come by the hundreds of thousands. The whole island, they say, is solid birds. If you'd walk among them, they're all around your feet and everything and nests everywhere. They're all sea birds, of course, and all around were fish.

And the fish were so plentiful—fish called walleyes. We could stand up to knee depth and as the waves in the surf would turn, they'd be in the water as thick as raisins in raisin bread. We could harpoon them standing right there. That's how we could get our dinner anytime we wanted—fresh fish. Also, at anchor where we were, you could fish right off the side of the ship and catch all kinds of tropical fish. It was a very prolific place."

Isla Aves, shaped like a new moon, offered little protection from the prevailing swells. Once, the seas broke over the entire island and work had to be halted and the engineers moved back aboard *Alpha* to await calmer seas. But the real problem was landing men and materiel through the surf to the beach camp. Several times the Navy men tried to surf the equipment-laden dinghy onto the beach with disastrous results. Instruments, generators, and other gear were lost and legs and arms were broken. Lou had to make emergency trips back to Antigua to tend to the injured. The inexperienced Navy engineers allowed the dinghy to get sideways to the breakers or let the boat get out of control while surfing. The resultant capsizes and pitchpoles were predictable.

Lou returned from Antigua, and after watching several dinghy loads of newly-delivered equipment wind up in the briny, he took control. He rowed the dinghy from *Alpha* to just outside the surf line and dropped an anchor. The bow faced the swell and the dinghy bobbed comfortably, stern to the beach. Lou then payed out the anchor line until the stern was close enough to the sand for the men to safely offload the equipment. The dinghy's flared bow kept the cargo high and dry. Problem solved.

But Pat Kenedy was still mired in her own private prison, and she saw no window of escape. She spoke seldom and went to bed alone, troubled and morose. When not carrying out her duties aboard *Alpha*, she would walk the beach for hours until needed back aboard.

During one of these lonely times on the island, an ugly brown and white gannet swooped down within a few feet of her and snagged a wiggling piece of flotsam off the sand. Upon closer inspection, she saw that the beach was crawling with silver dollar-sized green creatures, flipping down the beach toward the surf like tiny men in clown shoes. Then, another bird dove in for lunch, and Pat, trying to scare it off, fell on her butt. She felt movement under her and jumped up to find two baby turtles struggling to free themselves from the packed sand. She lifted them out of the imprint she had made and being careful not to step on any of the other babies on the beach, carried the two miniature leatherbacks down to the water. Laying them shell-up a few feet from the water's edge, they scurried instinctively toward the surf and disappeared under an incoming wave. They reappeared for a moment as the wave receded only to disappear for good when the next wave rolled in.

Undisturbed as it was, the islet was a significant sea turtle hatchery. Hundreds of mother leatherbacks, green turtles, and loggerheads returned annually to lay their eggs in the soft sand and scrub above the shingle beach.

Pat turned when she heard a commotion behind her. There were a dozen birds fighting over newly hatched babies struggling to dig themselves out of their sand nests. Pat ran toward the birds, screaming at them to leave the babies alone. She scared the birds off and sat there in the burning Caribbean sun for hours as the turtles scrambled for the relative safety of the surf. Twice she wanted to return to *Alpha* but as soon as she was a few yards down the beach, the birds would resume their feeding frenzy, so she ran back to protect her wards. Between sorties, she sat in the sand with her face cupped in her hands. Beach sand and hair were stuck to her face by tears and sweat. She wept, stopping only to scream and jump up to scare the marauding birds. Tears rolled, but her turtles lived.

Not showing up for work was a major *faux pas* aboard Lou Kenedy's ships. At dusk, Lou missed his cook's assistant. He went ashore to find Pat sitting near an open fire in the engineer's camp. The birds had called it a day, and the babies didn't need her protection until daybreak. Lou asked her what the hell she was doing there. As she turned to Lou, her eyes reflected the sparks from the camp fire. She was, for the first time in months, truly angry; angry at Lou, angry at the turns her life had taken, and especially angry at the birds that ate her baby turtles. Lou saw, for the only time in their life together, the wrath of God in Pat's eyes. He began ordering her back to the boat to get dinner ready but stopped short when she looked up at him. He realized something was truly different, metaphysically different. Pat was not the cook, the mother, the housekeeper; she was not the sailor nor the ever-suffering wife but rather the savior of baby turtles, and there was nothing more important than that. Lou somehow knew not to push. He turned around and sloshed out to the dinghy anchored just out of the surf line and rowed back to *Alpha*.

Later in the evening, Lou returned to the beach to bring Pat a blanket. He handed it to her and returned to the dinghy. Neither said a word. One of the engineers accompanied Lou back to *Alpha*. Pat spent the night ashore by the fire.

Karl Klausner, the scientist who accompanied Lou back to the ketch, spent the better part of that evening and a bottle of Mount Gay sitting on the settee, forward of the mizzen, asking Lou about the sea and his life. After an hour or so, Karl gently mentioned that he thought Pat seemed upset about something. Lou reacted instantly in his usual style and threatened to beat the crap out of Karl if he didn't "shut the hell up." It was none of his business. In spite of the threat, Karl persisted and explained that his wife had acted similarly after the birth of their second child. Lou calmed as Karl compared his wife's symptoms to what he observed in Pat. As the conversation continued, Lou seemed amazed there was such a syndrome and other women reacted the same as Pat to birth and changes in lifestyle. In fact, he was amazed anyone would be sensitive enough to note the similarities in behavior between two particular women. This was unplowed ground for Lou Kenedy.

At dawn, Pat was still asleep near the pile of burnt-out driftwood. The cool morning trade winds were only a whisper. Lou returned carrying an armful of gunny sacks and plopped them down on the sand. She awoke with a start. Lou told her she'd "save a hell of a lot more turtles" if she carried them to the surf in bags. He turned and again walked back to the shore boat.

For the better part of a month, Pat hauled baby turtles from their nesting holes down to the surf. When one batch of babies was safely in the water, a few days would pass and another batch would break the surface of the sand and struggle into the sunlight. During that month, she carried thousands of the little animals to relative safety. Most of an entire generation of Isla Aves sea turtles owes its existence to Pat Kenedy. She returned to *Alpha* periodically to clean up but stayed ashore during two resupply trips to Antigua. By the time Lou returned from the second trip, the turtles had all been hatched and carried to the surf. She could no longer help the babies, and she returned to *Alpha*. There was no discussion of her time on the island but the day she returned, she smiled at Lou and said simply, "It's time to start cooking." Her personal crisis was over, and she now longed to get back to her kids in Nova Scotia.

When the charter was finished, *Alpha* hauled the equipment and personnel to San Juan. Lou said goodbye to Dr. Klausner and put Pat on a plane back home before proceeding to the Bahamas.

Alpha was then chartered to Dr. Sam Shepard, a now well-known Cleveland, Ohio, osteopathic physician. Long before his trial and ultimate posthumous exoneration, Lou squired him and some yachtie friends around the Bahamas for a month.

* * *

The next project for *Alpha* was as the main set for *Flame of the Island,* a "B" movie starring Yvonne DeCarlo and Howard Duff. With a thin plot about a scheming woman trying to horn in on the establishment of an island casino, it featured a young James Arness as the heavy. Ida Lupino was also on the set as she was, in real life, married to Howard Duff.

Alpha was a major prop in the film and was the "set" for scores of scenes. Lou called it a "sea-going western," and not surprisingly, he was unimpressed with the producers. He didn't trust them, and the charter contract included prepayment clauses. The charter was to begin on March 3, 1955, and as always, Lou and *Alpha* were on station at the appointed time. The movie crew was ensconced at a luxury hotel in Nassau, and Lou strode into the lobby looking for the studio rep. The assistant producer was having breakfast in a dining room, and Lou walked up and said, "We're ready."

The studio man, overly tan with slicked-back blonde hair and wearing a tie, was reading a paper that he deigned to lower only long enough to tell Lou that it would be a week before filming started, because some equipment hadn't arrived. "Come back in a week," said the studio man, and he kept reading the paper. Lou said, "That's OK by me, but today is payday." "But we don't need you yet," said the assistant producer. "Just come back in a week," and he returned to reading his paper. Lou snatched the paper out of the twerp's hands and with the tie, pulled the man nose to nose. This is classic Lou Kenedy. The man could hardly breathe—much less speak—as Lou explained demurrage to him and instructed him to find the cash and pay him for the first week. Lou released the man, and he choked, got up, and ran away. Within five minutes, a young woman, an assistant to the assistant producer, came down with the first week's charter fee in cash. She gave it to Lou, and the captain returned to *Alpha* and cooled his heels for a week.

The first day of shooting began with two limousines full of actors, producers, and directors, as well as two truck loads of equipment and crew members arriving on the dock. Once it was all loaded aboard *Alpha*, the assistant producer smiled as if nothing in the past had ever occurred, and said, "OK, Cap, we're ready to go." Lou just looked at him, shook his head, and said,

> "'Yeah, you're all ready to go but I'm not.' He said, 'Why not?' I said, 'Well you know, it's a funny thing. It's payday again and I don't work very good without my pay.' And they said, 'Oh, don't worry about that. We have barrels of gold or whatever.' It was up in the hotel. And I said, 'Well that's no good to me. It's not aboard here. I need it down here.' I said, 'The best thing you could do is get in your 16-passenger Cadillac and go up and get some of that gold and bring it down to me, then I'll work real good.'

"So after that, me and the head fellow got along well. He said, 'You should join our organization. You're a real good businessman.' They appreciate being put upon, and they'll walk all over you if you get soft, but that didn't happen."

Back during the hurricane off Duck Island in Connecticut, a thick glass port had been cracked. The cracked glass was over an inch thick so the pane didn't fall out, but it looked shabby and would have been expensive to fix. During the movie shoot, Lou saw an opportunity to get it replaced for nothing.

For one scene, Ed Sabin, the cook aboard *Alpha*, was to toss canisters off the bow that were to explode alongside the boat simulating an attack by armed thugs. Lou positioned the boat so the sun shone on the port side, and the cameras were set up. As soon as Ed had thrown a half dozen canisters, Lou yelled, "Stop! You broke my port light." The director looked at the cracked glass, apologized, and told Lou to get it fixed and have the repair bill sent to him at the hotel. Shooting of *The Flame of the Islands* continued and finally wrapped at the end of March, 1955.

* * *

Though Lou had been to and through the Bahamas many times, the shallow draft of *Alpha* allowed him to discover many coves and anchorages.

"We explored all kinds of shallow water, places that I had never seen, because the Alpha *drew only six and a half feet of water although she was a large vessel. But all through the Bahamas, most of the harbours are only six or eight feet deep, 10 feet max. So she was an ideal boat for that, considering her size.*

"In the Bahamas, in this type of cruising, going from island to island, you see all beautiful beaches, nobody living on them, deserted islands covered with scrub trees, palm trees. You can go fishing and lobstering (they call them crawfish down there). Anything you want, just go and get it with a mask and spear. It was really a different way of life for all of us, and we surely enjoyed that. At the end of winter, we came north again with the Alpha.*"*

After the winter in the Bahamas, *Alpha* slogged for 20 days northward against contrary weather before entering the LaHave. It was one of Lou's slowest trips north, ending when he pulled the ketch directly into Snyder's for a refit. Iron vessels tend to foul faster than wooden ones, and *Alpha* was no exception; she was a veritable traveling ecosystem, her hull thick with marine life. A haulout at Smith & Rhuland solved the problem quickly.

Lou had spent the trip up from the Exumas developing a plan. He wanted to move the family—lock, stock, and barrel—down to the Bahamas. The first and most formidable obstacle to this plan was Pat. Her life revolved around Lunenburg and Dayspring with the kids settled in school, and she was still a bit psychologically tender, having only recently worked out her issues on the beach at Isla Aves.

To add to the overall dissonance, Lou was met in Conquerall Bank with Brian's decision to join the Navy. Lou agreed with the idea, but the strong, red-haired 18-year-old had become an expert sailor and a real asset to Lou's crew during the summers. It was the loss of crew as well as a son. And of course, Brian's departure wouldn't help Pat's state of mind. So Lou bided his time, and after a quick facelift at Teddy's and a haulout, *Alpha* slid back in the water to fulfill a summer's worth of charters in the Maritimes and New England.

Now Patsy stepped up to the plate and informed her father that she wanted to crew for the summer charter season on the New England coast. Lou wasn't sure, but she argued that she had been on many trips aboard *Vema* and that he needed her now that Brian was signing off.

"And my young daughter, Patsy, she was 12; she was 11 then but she turned 12 during the summer. She said she wanted to go along and I said, 'Well it would be a long time.' She'd been on trips before with her mother and all, but this would just be with a bunch of men and just me."

The little tow-head looked up at her father with her signature frown and stated almost as one word, "A girl has to leave home sometime and it might as well be now." How could a father resist?

Having total confidence in Lou to care for her oldest daughter, Pat was willing to let Patsy go, and Lou was proud to have the person who turned out to be his natural successor sign articles as an AB.

"I took her along because it was good company for me and she was a great girl to be with and she was very attentive and would listen and learn anything about ships that was possible."

A pea-soup fog shrouded the channel when *Alpha* motored out of Lunenburg Harbour for points south. Ed Sabin was cook and deckhand; Lou, of course, was skipper, engineer, and mate; Brian was boatswain; and Patsy was the only AB. As the ketch steamed seaward, Lou put Patsy at the wheel and said, "Hold her southeast by east, one half east." Patsy replied, "Southeast by east, one half east, sir." Lou left the helm for a moment but quickly returned. He was sure that after a year ashore the girl couldn't possibly remember how to box the compass. He tested her, "Are you sure you remember the points of the compass?" "Daddyeeeeee! Of course and don't ask foolish questions." After that, Lou never doubted her abilities, and she became a valuable part of the crew during what was to Patsy a magical summer of chartering out of Essex, Connecticut.

First, they sailed to New London where Brian, for the last time, signed off articles from a Lou Kenedy ship and enlisted in the United States Navy. Brian spent an exemplary 10 years in the Navy which he followed up with a successful business career, finally retiring in Florida.

At summer's end, *Alpha* returned to Dayspring. Lou's experiences in the Bahamas had convinced him he should move the family south to Nassau. He was backed up in this decision by Rosie's doctor who thought she might not "make it" if she stayed in northern climes. With urging from two directions, Pat acceded to Lou's wishes.

Alpha put in at Teddy's to begin a major refit. The captain went out into the woods and picked a tree for the new mizzen; a farmer and his team of horses pulled it to Snyder's where it was shaped appropriately. Lou made up new standing rigging.

A blacksmith made new chain-plates, and Teddy's men built the mizzen boom. In Lunenburg, Boomdie Hebb stitched a new suit of sails; Dauphinee made new lignum vitae-shelled blocks. The new mizzen was stepped 10 feet further forward than before and was so high that it was hard to tell if *Alpha* was a ketch or a schooner. The hull was painted, engine rebuilt, and varnish redone.

The family quickly leased out their Conquerall Bank house and moved all their gear aboard *Alpha*. The whole family, except for Brian, was aboard, along with Ed Sabin to help in the galley. Ed was still using the ancient Aga stove that burned soft coal.

* * *

Rosie, still a toddler, enjoyed roaming at night. One evening on the trip south, when she was responsible for watching Rosie, Patsy took a cat nap in the deck house. Rosie decided to join Patsy in her bunk, but there was no room. Instead, she snuggled up under the settee in a pile of soft, cuddly life vests and went sound asleep. When Patsy went on watch, she started looking for Rosie, with no success. Patsy woke the family, and the search began in earnest. After hours of looking in every conceivable cranny of *Alpha*, the search was called off. Predictably, Pat became hysterical. Lou, trying to be the strong one, said that turning back would be fruitless, like looking for a needle in a haystack. The family was destroyed as the magnitude of the tragedy sank in. Gabrielle was in tears. The thought of the terror that the little girl must have known when she fell overboard was too much to bear. Pat wept in her cabin as Patsy and Lou continued to run the boat.

About an hour later, Rosie crawled out of her cocoon, rubbing her eyes and wondering why everyone was crying. The reaction was predictably emotional as floods of happy tears and hugs overwhelmed the little girl. From that time on, Rosie wasn't allowed out of her mom's cabin at night, or out of her sight on board a ship for years. Whenever Rosie and Patsy slept together, their big toes were linked with a carefully-tied string.

After the presumed tragedy, *Alpha* proceeded slowly south, arriving in the Bahamas in time to enroll the girls in Xavier College in Nassau. Lou ensconced the family in a two-bedroom cottage on Lightbourne Lane while he pursued charters of every conceivable type.

* * *

The first charter after moving the family to the Bahamas consisted of a retired Army colonel and his brood on a two-week tour of the Bahamas. One night while *Alpha* was tied alongside the government dock at Dunmore Town on Harbour Island, Lou awoke at two in the morning to the sound of six or seven 20-somethings throwing a party on the dock. Lou, not wanting to have his charter party awakened, got up, dressed—which means he put on a pair of shorts and a T-shirt—and approached the group of barely clad young men and women. Still sleepy, he began the conversation out of character when he politely asked them to take the party to a deserted beach, as there were people sleeping aboard the boat. This cooperative attitude was unusual; we all know by now that confrontation was Lou's normal *modus operandi*.

The group agreed to leave, and Lou returned to *Alpha*. He took off his shorts and T-shirt and snuggled back into his bunk, congratulating himself on defusing a possibly raucous situation. But a half an hour passed, and there was no reduction in the racket outside.

Lou dressed, again. He now reverted to his standard method of handling delicate situations. He marched down the dock yelling "Get the hell out of here." He was only that polite because he thought that his charter party might overhear him.

Only now did Lou notice that a local tough was the organizer of the party. Socks Curry was a roustabout on the Harbour Island docks, and the islanders were afraid of him. His reputation for starting and finishing fights was well known in the area. Even the fishermen at Spanish Wells gave Socks a wide berth. He was young, powerful, and a bully.

Socks, who stood four inches taller than Lou, strode chin to nose with the captain and launched a tirade, interspersed with expletives, about his own proud culture and his inalienable right to be on "his" dock at any time, as well as the fact that he was a native and Lou, by God, wasn't!

Then Lou, weary of the one-way conversation, coldcocked him. The punch came out of nowhere, an uppercut to the jaw that staggered the young Bahamian. Socks stumbled backwards 20 feet before he fell. When he hit the dock, his head snapped back, and it was hard to tell whether the resulting crack was the sound of Socks' head or the concrete that it smashed. Socks' bicycle was also on the pier, so for good measure and to insure Socks was completely enraged, Lou picked it up with both hands and chucked it into the drink. Socks was dazed as he got to his feet and weaved back to a friend's car parked at the foot of the dock.

For a moment, Lou thought the confrontation was over, but without warning, Socks charged him wielding a tire iron. By then Ed Sabin, the cook, awakened by the fracas, climbed over *Alpha*'s gunwale carrying Lou's old Colt 45. He ran toward Lou yelling, "Take this, for Christ's sake, Skipper! Don't let him kill you."

"And I said, 'No way!' So when he came this time, I whaled him across the side of the face with the pistol. That was a big .45 Colt and that laid him out. So he got up after a bit and ran like hell."

Actually, he ran like hell to the local police station which was only a block away. In a few minutes, a very polite constable ambled down the dock and told Lou that Socks had filed a complaint against him, and he should come to the station to answer the allegations and file a counter complaint. It was two in the morning and Lou was tired and told the officer he would be there first thing in the morning. The constable politely insisted and finally convinced Lou it would be better to get the formalities over with that night while events were still clear in everyone's mind. Lou reluctantly agreed and followed the fellow to the station.

As they walked into the station, Lou saw Socks writing while hunkered over an old oak desk on the far wall. No other constables were visible. That's because the other officer was behind the door poised to jump, subdue, and incarcerate Lou as he entered the building. The plan worked—in a manner of speaking. They did manage to get Lou into a cell but only after he beat the slop out of the two arresting officers, ripped off their jackets, and broke both of their noses by pulling their heads down and kneeing them in the face. Blood was everywhere.

"But I was madder than a boil and you don't get a Lunenburg guy in that kind of condition without being riled up."

The cells were in a separate room, out of sight of the constables, and the jail was laid up with coral blocks. The window bars were horizontal, not vertical. The beach sand used for the mortar was salty, which made it weak. Though the walls were a foot thick, the mortar had little intrinsic strength, and the bars were held in mainly by the weight of the coral blocks above them. The bunk was built with two-by-four stringers and braces, so the captain pulled it apart. He used the long stringers to build a scaffold that spanned the cell from the sill of the window on the solid steel door to the outside window sill. Bouncing as he straddled the scaffold, Lou, using a smaller piece of lumber, began prying the window bars against each other.

The officers heard the noise but couldn't get in his cell because the scaffolding was braced against the door and the sill. They made a hell of a racket trying to enter, to no avail.

The one-inch-diameter bars were of malleable iron and bent easily. After a minute or so, the mortar holding the bars began spalling, then crumbling. A few minutes more and the bars were so deformed and displaced that there was enough room for Lou to squeeze head-first out the window. He fell to the ground, lucky not to have landed on his head, and ran around to the front door of the constabulary. He poked his head in to check the situation. By then, the two officers were able to get into Lou's cell, because he was no longer holding down the bracing scaffold. Lou crept quietly to the cell door, poked his head in and calmly said to the startled policemen, "Boys, I'll see you in the morning" and closed the door, locking the men inside.

The officers, afraid of falling head-first out the window, stayed in the cell until they were discovered at 8:00 the next morning.

While the two now-released policemen told their story to their lieutenant, Lou was already at the nearby courthouse ready to defend himself. The captain of the station expected to see *Alpha* long gone and was surprised to find a jovial Lou Kenedy at court, demanding justice.

The charges against him were assault against Socks Curry, resisting arrest, escaping from custody, and destroying Crown property.

When called upon to testify, Socks whimpered and whined about being pistol whipped and finally began crying. Lou gushed, "Boy, that's the kind of wail I like to hear. He's crying now." Before the judge could gavel him out of order, the courtroom broke into laughter.

Socks Curry was a known thug, so the assault charge was dismissed. In fact, the magistrate fined Socks £25 for trying to use the tire iron against Lou. The charges against Lou for resisting arrest and escaping from custody were dismissed, because he had been arrested illegally; there was no charge against him when the officers wrestled him into the cell.

But the last charge was serious and inescapable. Lou had to pay his debt to society for destroying Crown property. He was found guilty of destroying several of Her Majesty's brass buttons that adorned the coats of the arresting officers. As the magistrate pronounced sentence upon the captain he said,

"One does not, with impunity, destroy or disrespect the Queen's buttons. Only at one's peril is Crown property defaced within my jurisdiction. Captain Kenedy, you are found guilty and hereby fined £25 and in addition, you are sternly admonished to think twice before again maliciously removing the Queen's buttons."

That would be the end of the story if the old colonel aboard *Alpha* had not written a

Figure 8-3. Charterers enjoying a swim on Sandy Cay. Photo by Jarvis Darville. (Used by permission.)

doggerel poem: "Captain Lou at Dunmore Town." This enhanced version of the adventure was somehow delivered to the hands of Lou's friend, Burl Ives, who set it to music and sang it for the entertainment of the island crowd. Burl and Lou were best of buddies along the Nassau waterfront. Many remember the frequent sight of 300-pound Burl Ives riding on the back of Lou's Lambretta scooter while Lou steered them to the next pub down the road. Incidentally, in later years, Lou and Socks Curry became friends.

* * *

In 1950, before the Duvalier family laid complete waste to Haiti (a state of affairs yet to be rectified), the government of President Dumarais Estimé was overthrown by and run under the liberal hand of General Paul Eugene Magloire, "Bon Papa." This era was often called "Haiti's Golden Age of Peace." During this time, glitterati from all corners of the world jetted to the island nation for R & R; among them were Irving Berlin, Truman Capote, and

Noel Coward. Magloire was supported by U.S. President Eisenhower, who once hosted a lavish state dinner in his honor.

At the time, Haiti was plagued by a caste system based on skin shade; the lighter the skin, the higher the class. Magloire had been installed in office by the wealthy Mulattos who were unhappy with the previous president's habit of bringing the lower classes into the political mainstream.

Though Magloire was a dark-skinned, middle-class Haitian, he was tolerated, enjoyed his new-found wealth, and entertained lavishly. He was also known as *Kanson Fé*, Iron Pants, and was a perfect spokesman for the Mulattos' selfish lifestyle and thinly-veiled racism.

However, by 1956, because of problems—damage caused by 1954's Hurricane Hazel, the pilfering of relief funds, plummeting coffee prices, and generally increased repression—his formerly-loyal Army cronies turned against Magloire and his regime.

During the spring of 1956, *Alpha* was chartered for an entire month by a wealthy Canadian, Colonel Andrew Olin, and his family of six. They brought 24 bags of luggage, and to support their passionate drinking regimen, they loaded 20 cases of booze and 40 cases of bottled soft drinks. Rum and Coke was one of the colonel's favorites.

Clearing out of Nassau, with Pat and Ed Sabin aboard, *Alpha* began an idyllic cruise through the Exuma Cays, over to Great Inagua, and then to Haiti. Then they stopped at Gonaïves, on the Gulf of Gonaïves, where the family befriended a gregarious Haitian doctor who led them on tours throughout the northern parts of Haiti.

The Olins were fascinated by the doctor's guided visit to Henri Christophe's castle, San Souci, and his fortress, Citadelle Laferrière, near Cap Haitien. Christophe, a black American revolutionary war veteran from Grenada who fought the British near Savannah, Georgia, became the president and then king of Haiti after fighting another revolution against the French.

On the last day with the kind medic, the Olins returned from an afternoon trip around Gonaïves, commenting that the people on the street seemed standoffish and suspicious. Lou thought nothing of it, and the next morning, *Alpha* continued to Port-au-Prince.

In the capital, the charterers and crew were adopted by a taxi driver called "T-Bone." No mulatto, his black skin proved his pure-African heritage. T-Bone drove a dilapidated, early 1930's vintage Chevy. He spoke good English and was a fountain of knowledge about Haiti and its history. He also had his fingers on the pulse of Port-au-Prince politics.

For two days, T-Bone squired the crew and charterers around the capital while delivering non-stop commentary on everything and everyone from the architecture of the city to the name of the bartender at the local *salon de pastis.*

On the morning of the third day in Port-au-Prince, the *Alpha* group was shoehorned into T-Bone's car for a tour of the city and to do some souvenir shopping. Several blocks from the wharf, T-Bone turned a corner and jammed on the brakes to avoid plowing into a wall of humanity.

Civil strife had broken out, and people had taken to the streets. It was the beginning of a revolution. Colonel Olin quizzed T-Bone on the events and immediately ordered the car back to *Alpha.* His family loaded two bags with the bare necessities and had T-Bone rush them to the airport.

"The Olins became very upset and flew off to Jamaica. They decided to end their trip there and they flew off, but they didn't take all their luggage with them. They left it with me. They only took two bags and left me with 20! There, I'm stuck with them. But anyway they paid for the whole month so we were all right as far as finances went."

With Captain Lou's financial priorities firmly focused, the crew went out to have some fun. The raging revolution caused a gasoline shortage that was solved by Lou contributing outboard motor, pre-mixed gasoline for T-Bone to use in his car. The only problem was Lou's British Seagull outboards required twice as much oil as U.S. outboards. As they traveled around the city, T-Bone's car laid down a smoke screen rivaled only by certain military operations.

T-Bone showed them all the sights, most of which included violence, gunfire, and bloodshed. One afternoon, T-Bone ran down the pier and excitedly asked Pat and Lou to get in the car.

"...one day they started closing up the shops and one thing and another. It was all kinds of unrest. I don't know what was going on for sure because we were on the dock but T-Bone says, come quick, come quick, the dictator (I think his name was Magloire) he's gonna resign and come up and we'll hear all about it. So we went up and as we were going up these big cars with men with feathers in their hats and outriders, motorcyclists with machine guns, and the cars would have flags on them and the fellows would have big peacock feathers. It looked like a comic opera; but anyway it wasn't very comic. We got to the palace and everybody was trying to crowd in as close as they could to hear the speeches but there were marines there with fixed bayonets and

they poked my wife in the stern to discourage her from going any further."

Lou had schlepped along a portable radio so that they—or rather T-Bone—could keep abreast of the happenings.

"...but they were talking in French; and although we knew some French, we couldn't follow it very well because they didn't speak French as clearly as French is supposed to be spoken, heh."

"Le Bon Papa" gave a rousing speech that was apparently approved unanimously by the crowd, because when he finished, an earsplitting cheer went up from the throng. Lou asked T-Bone why the joyful reaction, and the taxi driver flashed a grin while shouting Magloire had just quit. And as those words left T-Bone's mouth, the mood of the crowd abruptly changed. The 1,000 or more people that were only a moment before loudly praising the decision of the president to resign were now groaning and booing.

"...what did he say now? T-Bone said he quit as president but he's going to be the commander of the army. And I said, well that's a hell of a lot better job than being president. You can get something done anyway."

The next day, the outcry over Magloire's plans to become the head of the army made it impossible for him to stay in the country. T-Bone explained the situation, and Lou sprang into action. He figured Magloire would need a way off the island, and he might have a captive charter right in front of his nose. So Lou instructed T-Bone to take him to the presidential palace, which was really a country estate. He talked his way in and ended up face-to-face and speaking pidgin French to Magloire's brother. Lou offered to take the dictator off the island for a fee. The brother thanked Lou but said they had an airplane ready to take them to the U.S. the next morning, but if something happened to the plane, they would come down to the dock and board *Alpha* for a getaway.

Magloire's entourage flew out of Haiti and got clean away the next morning; *Alpha* was not needed. At that point, Lou took fiscal advantage of some of the provisions his departed charter left behind.

"Evidently the Coca-Cola factories in Port-au-Prince couldn't get bottles. I knew that they were out of them so we finally made a deal. In the Bahamas, we were getting a shilling an empty bottle. Well, a shilling was more or less 25 cents and, in those days, that was some price for a bottle. Although I do understand even at that time that they cost nearly

10 cents each to make; but we got two and a half times what Coca-Cola had to pay for them. But in Haiti, we got $1 a bottle. So we did pretty well. We sold the whole works. I wasn't going to be cluttered up with a whole bunch of empty bottles."

En route to Nassau, Lou learned that no one had any details of the Haitian situation. The education he got from T-Bone held him in good stead as several stateside radio and TV stations used Lou as their only source of information on the coup in Haiti.

"So then we took off and went back to Nassau and, strangely enough, as we learned on the ship-to-shore radio, there was no news coming out of Haiti. Nobody in the States knew what was going on at all. Evidently there were very good weather conditions [for radio transmission] because I called up the Nassau marine operator to make a call and the operator asked me to find out what was going on in Haiti. She put me on to a newspaper there and I gave them the whole story and they were able to read me good and get everything correct. And then she said that we better call Miami, so I called Miami and I was able to get them good; and I gave them the whole story. That was the first story that came out of Haiti about the revolution."

Figure 8-4. Lou's youngest, Rosie, aboard *Alpha*.

(Paul Magloire, soldier and politician, died July 12, 2001 after returning to Haiti to advise post-Duvalier governments.)

* * *

Over the next few years, *Alpha* and Lou became known as *the* premier Bahamas-based crewed charter vessel and captain, respectively. Charterers included the British Governor of the Bahamas, and *Alpha* was the most sought-after spectator boat for the annual Out-Island Regatta at Georgetown. However, by 1958, two items were in dire need of attention. First, *Alpha* required a major refit, and Patsy, at 15, had reached the age where all Kenedy children are shipped off to boarding school. In August, the entire family boarded *Alpha* for an uneventful, 10-day, nonstop trip to Nova Scotia to put the ketch on the ways at Smith & Rhuland in Lunenberg to tend to her bottom and enroll Patsy in Mount St. Vincent Academy in Halifax.

Afterwards, *Alpha* put in at Teddy's in early September 1958 to begin another refit. The usual tasks were performed: the engine was rebuilt, bright-work was varnished, topsides were painted, the interior was given a face-lift, and new settee cushions were uphol-stered. Finally, the forepeak was cleaned, relined with galvanized sheet metal, and filled

Figure 8-5. Assisted by daughter Gabrielle, Lou siphons rum from a barrel into coke bottles, while Rosie watches.

with soft coal. The forepeak was the coal bunker for the old Aga stove that still puffed away in the galley.

By the time *Alpha* was ready, the beautiful old house at Conquerall Bank had sold. The refit had taken a whole month, a lifetime to Lou Kenedy.

Finally, on September 20, 1958, crewed by Pat, Lou, Ed Sabin as cook, Gabrielle, and Rosie, *Alpha* cleared for Nassau, entering U.S. Customs at Newport, Rhode Island. They took in some America's Cup races, then proceeded down the coast to Norfolk, Virginia, to enter the Intracoastal Waterway for the trip south.

In early October *Alpha*'s arrival at Morehead City, North Carolina was marked by nine-year-old Gabrielle dropping Lou's wallet overboard. Except for $20 that Pat had in her purse, the family was temporarily broke. Their money was in a bank in Lunenburg, and their letter of credit was made out to a bank in the Bahamas. Lou continued down the Intracoastal Waterway, and using AAA roadmaps, miraculously reached St. Augustine without running aground. There, a Good Samaritan overheard the girls complaining about not being able to afford to see Marineland. He loaned Lou $100. The girls got to see Marineland, the move to the Bahamas went forward as scheduled, and life continued in the cottage on Lightbourne Lane.

* * *

Allan's Cay, a small islet in the Exumas, had a tiny anchorage that *Alpha*, under most circumstances, could not enter due to overcrowding. It was perfect for smaller vessels, but *Alpha* at 80 feet long had to anchor across the entrance of the bay. The anchorage was open to the west, but typically May saw the northeast trades take over and made the cove a well-protected refuge.

One afternoon during a charter in May of 1959, Lou dropped the hook at his normal position at Allen's Cay and dinghied the charter party ashore for snorkeling and a picnic. That night the glass began to drop and a drizzle closed in. There was not a whisper of breeze, and the anchor chain hung straight down,

Then, with no warning, the wind began to howl, a ball of wind from the west. The American naval station on Eleuthera, based on information radioed by a research buoy, announced later it blew up to 87 knots. It was an intense gale—a mini-hurricane—that blew up from nowhere. *Alpha* was blown forward as if the engine were driving her and overran her anchor chain, which slipped the cathead. Once her bow slewed west, the stern was less than 50 yards from the shore. As the anchor flipped on the bottom, she got sideways, and just as Lou dropped the other anchor, she hit and started pounding on the coral-sand shelf. The pounding awoke the charterers, and they rushed on deck to help.

If *Alpha* had stayed where she had first grounded, it would have been an easy task to pull her off and refloat her during a high tide. But a six-foot storm surge flowed in from the west and set *Alpha* up on the beach. The surge was so severe that the low portions of Allen's Cay were underwater.

In an hour, the storm was over, and *Alpha* was hard aground. Even at high tide her prop was still out of the water; at low tide she was high and dry. She was heeled over on her starboard side parallel to the beach with her masts at a 22 degree angle pointing east and with her bow to the north.

The smaller boats in the bay fared no better; all were high and dry, but some larger yachts remained afloat. The wind had ripped hatch covers off and even shredded sails that had been gasketed to their booms. The damage to *Alpha* was minimal. She sat on a hard, flat coral ledge—like a concrete road—with no coral heads or rocks to penetrate her hull, so the hull was intact. She was an iron vessel, but even so, any lumpy rocks could have punched a hole in her, but there was no damage, nothing.

The charterers were graciously accepted aboard one of the other boats still afloat in the harbor. At daybreak, Lou radioed friends in Nassau. Within 24 hours they arrived en masse, five boat-loads of buddies, wives, and equipment. Food, beer, ice (always ice), shovels, air compressors, diving equipment, picks, and heavy hawsers were all brought to bear on the project.

On the second day after grounding, they got started in earnest by removing all of *Alpha*'s loose lead ballast. This was hours of backbreaking work in a hot, breezeless bilge. All other loose items were removed, along with the batteries. They were removed not only because they were heavy but also to stop any acid leakage. The fuel was pumped out and her water tanks were emptied.

At high tide, on the second day, hawsers were attached to the samson post and two powerboats with twin gas V-8's started to pull. After an hour of roaring, all that was accomplished was a lot of noise and sand stirred up from the bottom. *Alpha* didn't budge, not an inch. She didn't even begin to rotate her bow seaward.

Lou got an idea. His experience with the Navy's antisubmarine warfare sounding devices gave him the notion that dynamite might be the answer. When he braced his friends with the idea, they were incredulous. Who in the hell but Lou Kenedy would ever think of blowing his boat off the hard?

Figure 8-6. *Alpha* **blown ashore by freak storm at Allan's Cay, Exumas, 1959.**

"No," Lou explained. "We're gonna dig a canal along her keel and pull her into it."

So Lou and the skipper of one of the power boats sped across the Yellow Bank in the middle of the night to pick up a case of dynamite in Nassau. It

took them 10 hours round trip. At daybreak, the other volunteers, using picks, mauls, and star drills, started burrowing holes in the hard coral three feet apart along the entire length of the keel. The holes were four to five feet away from the hull and as deep as could be dug. None of them was over four feet deep.

Figure 8-7. Friends and crew drilling holes in coral ledge for dynamite.

When the holes were finished, Lou warned everyone to get clear while he wound primer cord to the fuse of one stick of dynamite and dropped it down the first hole, closest to the rudder. He rolled out 50 feet of primer cord and cut it off with his pocket knife. Lou held his Zippo under the end of the primer cord and flicked the steel wheel. The cord lit immediately, and Lou ran like hell up the beach yelling, "Fire in the hole, fire in the hole!" He joined the rest of the salvage crew huddled together behind the only two coconut palms on the beach. In expectation of the blast, like the quiet before a storm, it was deadly still. The only movement on the beach was an old black Allen's Cay iguana that unwittingly waddled around *Alpha*'s stern and became the only casualty of the incident. The poor devil was blown to bits when the first explosion rattled around the tiny anchorage. Bits of coral blew 200 feet in the air and twice that far into the bay.

Before all the pulverized rocks had splashed around the cove, Lou ran down to *Alpha* to find that a perfect crater had been blasted and no visible damage had been suffered by the ketch. He immediately loaded the next hole. He yelled, "Fire in the hole," 22 more times before the coral along *Alpha*'s keel was broken into manageable gravel. Then everyone got busy excavating the *"Alpha* Canal."

Lou's son-in-law put it this way:

"How many yachtsmen do you know who have the expertise or balls to set off a series of dynamite charges under their vessels? Would they blow a hole in the hull that you could drive a VW through or blow the glass out of adjacent yachts? This is a pretty drastic step to take. The only downside of the event was that the bow was loaded with beer and soft drinks, and the dynamite shook the hull so violently that for months thereafter, whenever one was opened, it exploded, causing gales of laughter all around."[*]

When the next high tide arrived, the sails were set—the masts were pointing to weather—spare halyards were run out to the two most powerful motor boats on site, and they started to pull *Alpha* upright. A tremendous groaning and gnashing sound echoed out of the iron hull as she slid down into the trench and flopped over onto her port side. She was almost afloat at this point.

The next tide, fortunately, was a spring tide, and kedge anchors were set along with hawsers to the motor boats. With a great thrashing of engines and screeching of iron on coral, *Alpha* was afloat out of the trench. She bobbed like a duck as she was running very light.

It took two days to get the ballast and batteries back into her and straighten out the mess below. As they got underway for Nassau, Lou discovered the only serious damage done to *Alpha*. The rudder stock had been bent; she would steer well to port, but the rudder would only turn a couple of degrees to starboard. But Lou coaxed her into Nassau where *Alpha* was dry-docked and repaired.

True to form, Lou decided that all the inside lead was unnecessary and *Alpha* would run shallower in the Bahamas without it, so he sold the excess loose lead for almost as much as he paid for the ketch in the beginning.

"...so I more than made up the cost of the whole loss and dry docking with the lead I sold, because lead was bringing a good price at the time. It always does I guess. So that was a disaster that turned out fairly well in the end. There was absolutely no damage done to the hull. She was pretty stout but it was one of those things; when you go to sea you've got to watch for the unforeseen. There was nothing we could have done about it anyway, if we had known it was coming except to have had the engine running and turned her around and faced the wind, but nobody could foresee a west wind at that time of year."

[*] Conversation with author.

* * *

A more lucrative project for *Alpha* came at the behest of the U.S. Navy and its antisubmarine warfare programs (ASW), known at the time as DECCA. Lou's work at Isla Aves had prompted the Navy to recruit *Alpha* with her shallow draft to plot locations throughout the Bahamas for the installation of DECCA equipment. Lou began this work at the time of phenomenal growth in tourism and yachting in the Bahamas. His enthusiasm for chartering was on the wane as he wasn't fond of catering to rich people's whims—especially if he didn't like them.

For the next two years *Alpha* alternated between installing top-secret acoustical gear while crewed by stuffy, single-minded engineers, and the wonderful summers when the Kenedy clan, including Brian, would descend on the ketch. They spent happy days snorkeling, fishing, eating Pat's galley creations, and enjoying each other's company while cruising the islands.

* * *

A couple of Hollywood production companies had used an aging but sound, ex-U.S. Coast Guard patrol boat in filming the "Flipper" movies and TV series. In March of 1962, Lou learned she was for sale. He flew to Fort Lauderdale and negotiated the purchase of *Aquanaut*. He hired Captain John Stafford as *Alpha*'s master to continue the ASW work.

Though the Navy contracts seemed never-ending, Lou knew he should be prepared for them to dry up someday. *Aquanaut* was a better vessel for that ASW work and also for fulfilling the opportunities he foresaw in salvaging and Bahamian government work. The Bahamian government, supported only by import duties, had no vessels of any size, and the illegal importation of goods and humans—mostly Haitians—was rampant. As you will see, there is a certain irony in Lou wanting to help the Bahamian government curtail smuggling, as he was a renowned master in that very art.

Lou never did agree with the way anyone else ran a ship, and John Stafford was no exception. Only a year after buying *Aquanaut*, Lou sold *Alpha*. She was taken to the Virgin Islands and chartered there for several years, but finally the Dutch iron became too thin to replate. She is now a reef attracting fish off the coast of Fort Lauderdale, Florida.

So ends this day.

Figure 9-1.

The ship: *Aquanaut*
Year of Launching: 1941
Rig: Motor Vessel
Builder: Wheeler Shipyard, Brooklyn, NY
Engines: Two GM 8-71 Diesels (Retro-fitted
   from the original Sterling Viking II gasoline
   engines.)

Material: Hull – Wood; Wheelhouse –
   Everdur bronze
Length overall: 83 feet
Beam: 18 feet
Draft: 6 feet 6 inches
Displacement: 76 tons

Chapter 9 *Aquanaut*

"Neptune" was the code name for the naval gunfire support and amphibious assault operations of Operation Overlord, the Normandy invasion. It was Franklin Roosevelt himself who suggested that a squadron of small, fast boats be on hand to rescue sailors and infantrymen who might be wounded or otherwise unable to reach the beaches due to vessel damage or *grounding. This idea of a rescue squadron came late in the planning stages of the invasion, and there was no time to produce a custom vessel for the job.*

Since the Coast Guard was renowned for saving lives at sea, it was only natural that the Chief of Naval Operations, Admiral Ernest King, turned to the Coasties to provide rescue services for the Normandy beachheads.

Off the east coast of the U.S., the so called "matchbox fleet" of 83-foot patrol boats was handling anti-submarine duties. The fleet was given the name because they were built of wood and most had gasoline engines. When new, the vessels were capable of 20.6 knots, but by the time they were loaded down with armaments and radar and sonar, and the engines had endured a couple of hundred hours of wear, the real top speed was degraded to the middle teens.

Admiral King quickly ordered 60 of them* to New York harbor, loaded as deck cargo aboard freighters and shipped off to their base at Poole, England.

Upon arrival in Poole, the 60-vessel squadron was—only for the invasion—named U.S.C.G. Flotilla One, which was in turn split into two 30-boat groups for deployment to Normandy. Coast Guard Commander Alexander Stewart renumbered each vessel from 1 to 60 for easy identification. Flotilla One was responsible for saving over 1500 lives on D-Day.

Aquanaut was the fourth 83-footer built.† The wheelhouse was solid Everdur bronze cast in Boston and shipped via railcar to the Wheeler Shipyard. As the war continued and bronze became scarce, the wheelhouses on later boats were built of plywood (hulls 83436 through 83529).

* * *

By late 1961, Ivan Tors Productions in Fort Lauderdale had finished shooting a feature film called *Flipper*, an eminently-forgettable movie about a boy and his dolphin. It starred Chuck Connors and was released in 1963. (*Flipper* morphed into an equally forgettable TV series shot in Nassau and Miami.) Ivan Tors had also produced the *Sea Hunt* TV series, but was now moving away from the underwater genre and on to even more camp 1960's shtick such as *Gentle Ben* and *Africa—Texas Style!* One of the tools used in Ivan's sea-life films was an 83-foot, ex-Coast Guard patrol vessel named *Aquanaut*. But Ben the bear had little use for such a boat, so Ivan put it on the market in early 1962. Lou heard the vessel was for sale and started negotiations. On March 8, 1962, Lou took possession of *Aquanaut*.

---

* 230 were eventually built.

† Hull #83303 – the series started at #83300.

Periodically, Tors' studio reverted to its sea-story heritage and hired Lou and *Aquanaut* to do some work.

The two 300-horsepower diesel engines pushed her to 14 knots, and she was air-conditioned. An electric winch did the cargo handling as her stern boasted a roomy hold. Her towing bits were heavy duty, and she was perfectly equipped for survey, diving, and police work. The fo'c's'le was large enough to sleep eight, and the galley/messroom was built to accommodate a full crew.

Immediately after Lou purchased her, the U.S. Hydrographic Office chartered *Aquanaut* to survey the Tongue of the Ocean, a mile-deep strip of ocean floor between Andros Island and New Providence. The Navy wanted Lou to continue the work he began on *Alpha,* installing the super-sensitive acoustic detection equipment that became the forerunner of the current anti-submarine warfare systems that detect subs thousands of miles distant. The Tongue of the Ocean has no shallows and is not a regular shipping route. This kept the area quiet enough for the equipment to be effective. The hydrophonic gear was so sensitive it could pick up and track the sound of vessels' propellers as they cruised in and out of European ports.

Lou loved the work; except for the occasional obstreperous scientists, he enjoyed the people, and the efforts were important to the governments involved.

* * *

In early 1964, Hollywood producer Robert Arthur needed a vessel that could pass as a Japanese patrol boat as a prop for his upcoming film, *Father Goose*. The movie was to be filmed in Jamaica and would star Cary Grant and Leslie Caron. Arthur was referred to Ivan Tors, the last owner of *Aquanaut*, who in turn referred him to Lou.

Lou struck a charter deal with the film company, but arriving on time was of the utmost importance. The contract had a capital-lettered clause: "IT IS OF THE ESSENCE OF THIS CONTRACT THAT THE VESSEL BE READY FOR SERVICE ON THE PRESCRIBED DATE AT 8:00 A.M. LOCAL TIME." There were expensive consequences for being late, and of course, Lou had his standard demurrage clauses added. The Hollywood types never figured they would be at fault for delays and happily agreed to Lou's punitive demurrage fees.

With only two other crew members, Lou cleared for Jamaica via the Windward Passage.* *Aquanaut* kept to the east side of the channel as Cuban gun boats were known to harass small commercial vessels in the passage.

---

* The channel between Cuba and Haiti.

Some were actually impounded and the crews jailed before deportation. During the nighttime trip through the Windward Passage, the lights of a vessel were spotted to the west. The ship was adrift and no one aboard *Aquanaut* could read the Morse code signals aimed at them, because they were sent too fast and what was readable was in Spanish. Afraid it was a Cuban gunboat trying to draw them into Cuban waters, Lou turned away and sped from the scene. Lou, to his dismay…

> "… *heard on the news next day that there was a small steamer broken down in the Windward Passage and she was requesting help for a towboat to take her to Miami or somewhere to get her out of trouble. Here we missed a real good payday if we could have picked her up and given her a tow because salvaging—that would have been pretty good. But anyway too much caution worrying about the Cubans and we missed out on a big deal."*

Ever the Samaritan, Lou didn't care one whit about saving the lives and property aboard *Maria Dolores*, the distressed vessel. He only lamented the loss of the "big deal."

Finally arriving at St. Mary's Bay, Jamaica at night, Lou picked his way into the cove and at daylight raised the yellow pratique flag and waited for the health, customs, and immigration officials to arrive.

The bay was lovely. Christopher Columbus wintered in St. Mary's Bay during his second voyage in 1593, and Lou mused as to how the Great Navigator must have gazed upon the same beautiful scene he now enjoyed.

From the deck of *Aquanaut* he saw the movie crew and equipment ashore on the beach and the quay. There were tires on fire and smoke billowing everywhere to simulate a bombing attack. At noon, Lou grew impatient and rowed ashore. He found the film's head man, Ralph Nelson. Ralph brushed him off and told him he wouldn't be needed for two weeks and to park *Aquanaut* out of the way in the southern corner of the bay.

This was fine with Lou as he was on the payroll. But when he strode into the customs house on the beach, he was met with a hostile government official who threatened to jail Lou and his crew and impound *Aquanaut* because he had come ashore before Jamaican officialdom had boarded the vessel and cleared him in. Lou didn't even get angry.

> "And I said, 'How long was I supposed to wait?' And he says, 'Until we come out.' I said, 'Not me. I've come here to you.' He got the big book out and he said that I was liable for this…that…and every other kind of laws. And I said, 'Oh well, I tell you what I want to do. I just

want to call up the head of customs in Kingston and I'll admit to all of this: That I came ashore without being boarded, but I'll also mention to him that I have been in this harbour for 12 hours and you haven't come aboard. I don't know what he'll say to that but that's what I'll tell him.' And then the fellow said, 'Oh, it'll be all right. Everything's O.K. now.' And when I didn't let him pull the bluff over me, why, he backed right down."

It was more than two weeks later that *Aquanaut* was needed. A cannon was mounted on the bow along with a huge Japanese flag that flew from the gaff. *Aquanaut*'s part was small and she was on film for a total time of less than a minute. Her *raison d'etre* was to chase a dinghy and a launch loaded with Cary, Leslie, and some children around the bay.

Figure 9-2. "Japanese" crew for filming of *Father Goose*.

There was no significant Japanese community on Jamaica but most of the nightclubs in Kingston were run by Chinese, so they were enlisted to play the Japanese crew of the "gunboat." The Chinese were dressed in Japanese Navy uniforms, but they were accustomed to working at night and had to wear sunglasses while aboard *Aquanaut* as their eyes were bothered by the intense Caribbean sun. Some of them became seasick before they left the dock. Lou's German first mate, Franz, had to teach them to use the cannon and machine guns. Franz had a thick German accent which was almost unintelligible to the pseudo-Japanese nightclub operators, who themselves had accent problems.

Then it happened; Lou learned that all these extras were getting paid. He was spending all day long on the boat taking directions and not getting an "extra" dime. He leapt into action.

That evening ashore, the captain bought the largest woven palm frond hat he could find. The brim was nearly three feet across. The next day he wore it on the bridge, and the director said bluntly, "Take that thing off." Lou refused, saying "I can't take the sun. I have to wear a hat or I'll get a stroke." "Well, you can't wear that thing," the director replied. The plot became clear when Lou said, "If I take the hat off, I'll be in costume because I'll be dressing the way you want me to."

Disgusted, the director agreed to pay Lou $20 a day as an extra, wearing a T-shirt and Japanese hat. Lou asked him where he would get the T-shirt. "We'll give you one," said the director. "I got very delicate skin and I gotta have a clean shirt every day. You got to give me a new one every day."

"So I wound up at the end of the picture with about 10 or 15 or more T-shirts and about $400 in pay and I used to say to people, 'Do you want to see my $400 straw hat?' And they'd say, 'What!?' I said, 'Yeah, here it is,' and I'd show it. They said, 'Gosh you could buy that for 10 shillings.' I said, 'Yeah. But I got paid $400 for taking it off.' So I called it my $400 straw hat."

The film continued to fall behind schedule. Cary Grant inadvertently wore the wrong color shirt in some later scenes and they had to be reshot. This caused two separate, month-long delays. Lou told the director he couldn't stay because of a prior commitment to the Navy. "But," said Lou to the director (the spider to the fly), "If you pay me time and a half, I'll see if the Navy will let me postpone the mission for them." The director agreed and Lou stayed and flew Pat down to Jamaica to spend time on the set. After the first month, the director said they needed another few days of work. Lou agreed only at a rate of time and a half with a one-month guarantee and the production company had to agree to pay all of Pat's expenses at the hotel. The director was forced to accept Lou's terms, since he couldn't change props in the middle of the movie.

Of course, Lou's pending contract with the Navy was fictional.

When the film was finished, the head of the production company tried to renege on paying Pat's expenses. Lou replied by thanking him for the cannon on the bow of *Aquanaut*. The movie man exploded as Lou explained that it was bolted to the vessel and is thus was now part and parcel of the boat and unless the hotel bills are paid, the weapon will stay aboard. The cannon had been rented from a museum in Miami and if it were lost, the production company would have been charged many times more than the price of Pat's hotel bill. As usual, Lou prevailed, got his money, and in mid-July of 1964, *Aquanaut* returned to the Bahamas hydrographic work along with the occasional rescue.

* * *

In early 1965, the producers of the movie *Thunderball* chartered *Aquanaut* as the main dive boat for the underwater scenes. This time, Lou got along famously with the film crew and even the stars. Of course, payment was prompt.

* * *

Rosie remembers the family times aboard *Aquanaut* as being special:

"On one of these trips, we went to Staniel Cay and our friend there, Joe Hocher, the manager of the Staniel Cay Yacht Club, had just sold some diesel fuel to a Haitian freighter, but the Haitians had no money, so Joe took a horse they had aboard as payment and proceeded to give the horse to me. When Dad found out, he rolled his eyes back, puffed hard on the pipe, and tried to figure out how to get this animal aboard Aquanaut. *It was a great adventure, with the whole island turning out to see this horse, now named "Fury," walking down the dock. Then with several planks from the dock to the boat, we had some very persuasive, energetic men pushing and pulling this poor animal aboard for the trip to Nassau."**

* * *

A recurring project that faced Lou and *Aquanaut* was rescuing Fred Whittier's beautiful 56-foot schooner, *Esperanto*. Fred was an old schoonerman from Gloucester who had sailed aboard the famous *Gertrude L. Thebaud* against *Bluenose*[†] during the well-known and hotly-contested 1930's schooner races. When he retired, he built his dream vessel on Abaco and settled in for a life of leisure. He signed the occasional charter to keep the maintenance kitty filled. *Esperanto* was built along the lines of a coastal trading vessel, not a Grand Banks fishing schooner. She sported a bowsprit and drew only six feet.

"A real fine-looking seagoing vessel. But she had all inside ballast and being pretty lofty rigged and being built a little bit shallow for the Bahamas, she probably would have been better if he had put some outside ballast on her rather than have all the ballast inside. I know that's the truth."

---

* Conversation with author.
[†] See note at the end of Chapter 2, *Adams*.

Esperanto was built of the iron-hard pine found on Abaco. Fred soaked the lumber for over two years. At Will Albury's Yard on Man-o-War Cay, with the help of two friends, he built the magnificent schooner with topmasts and all the accoutrements.

* * *

Here's a note on radio usage in the Bahamas during this time: VHF had just been introduced and didn't have the needed range, as the Bahamas run hundreds of miles north to south. The ubiquitous old AM radios had the range but were outlawed once VHF became widely available. Lou and his sailing buddies in the Bahamas were not about to invest in new radios when they had perfectly good ones aboard. So Lou and his boating friends used AM radios with the old hailing frequency of 2738 kHz and emergency frequency of 2182 kHz. They used pseudonyms for their boats so they couldn't be identified and prosecuted for unlicensed radio usage. Lou's imaginary vessel name was *Alabama,*[*] and Fred Whittier aboard *Esperanto* used the radio call name of *Royal Fortune.*[†]

* * *

In September 1965, a hurricane roared through the Bahamas, passing to the north of Abaco. *Esperanto* easily rode the storm out in a hurricane hole on Man-O-War Cay. When it seemed safe to leave, Fred and *Esperanto* headed

back to Marsh Harbour. But with Fred's luck— there was always a cloud hanging over him—the hurricane reversed course and sought him out. What happened next was an illegal radio conversation:

"*Alabama, Alabama, Alabama, this is Royal Fortune, over.*"

"*Royal Fortune, this is Alabama. What can I do for you? Go ahead.*"

Figure 9-3. *Aquanaut,* **with** *Esperanto* **alongside after refloating the schooner from stranding at Marsh Harbour in September 1965.**

---

[*] *Alabama* was Raphael Semmes famous flagship during the Civil War.

[†] *Royal Fortune* was the name that the pirate Bartholomew Roberts gave to all three of his infamous vessels.

"Roger, Alabama, the schooner's on the hard in the middle of the settlement at Marsh Harbour. The hurricane backed up and hit us hard; it lifted us right into town."

Lou motored down to Marsh Harbour and began the process of coaxing *Esperanto* back into the water. She was damaged, and after *Aquanaut* towed her to Fort Lauderdale, Fred Whittier spent $50,000 and seven months rebuilding her.

On May 2, 1966, on the way back to the Bahamas from rebuilding *Esperanto* in Fort Lauderdale, Fred radioed Lou again. *Esperanto* was sunk at Stirrup Cay and he needed help to raise her and again tow her back to Fort Lauderdale. Lou scared up a crew of locals and loaded pumps and headed for Stirrup Cay in the Berry Islands, 70 miles north-northwest of New Providence.

Figure 9-4. Fred Whittier sorting out his rifles aboard *Esperanto* after her first sinking.

Lou didn't get the full story until he arrived to find her on her starboard side, sunk in 12 feet of water in a nicely protected anchorage close to Stirrup Light. Fred said they were eating supper and the weather was rotten. Lightning flashed with scudding clouds and spritzing rain. Strong wind gusts swung *Esperanto* violently on her anchor.

"Suddenly it sounded like a railroad train going by, Fred said. It was a waterspout. They didn't see it because they were below, but it must have been a waterspout. It tore everything up on deck: sails, awnings, all kinds of things. Lifted things off, dinghy, oars went overboard. And she rolled over with the masts in the water and the water started pouring in the open hatches. The two men got out, grabbed the women by the hair and yanked them out through the hatch. Lucky it worked that way because they would have all drowned if they hadn't acted promptly. And in no time the ship sank."

Figure 9-5. *Esperanto* **sunken at Stirrup Cay, Berry Islands on May 2, 1966.**

It was over as soon as it started. Fortunately, there was another boat, un-scathed, anchored in the bay. With the *Esperanto* survivors sitting on her overturned hull, one of the men swam over to the other boat and brought back a dinghy. They called Lou and spent the night aboard a neighboring yacht, waiting for *Aquanaut* to arrive.

When Lou got to Stirrup Cay, he immediately tied a hawser to *Esperanto* and pulled her almost upright, resting on her keel. Fortunately, the bottom was pure sand, with not a rock to be found. With all 600 horsepower screaming, Lou towed her toward the beach as far as possible without grounding *Aquanaut*. The schooner was now nearly upright in eight feet of water. The deck was still awash, but one hatch was exposed enough to build a cowling to keep the water out during the first few minutes of pumping.

"We put a couple of pumps to her and before you knew it she was afloat again. But you never saw such a mess. The cabin bulkheads were mostly sprung. What a mess with papers, charts, groceries, bunk cloths, equipment, tools, guns—he had a collection of guns, rifles, shotguns, and pistols—everything piled up in heaps. And it was discouraging to look at this mess of expensive equipment, radios and stuff like that, everything piled up in a heap and full of seaweed. Paper—wads of it. He

had quite a collection of books and pamphlets and magazines and, of course, he had charts all the way from South America to Nova Scotia and they were all disintegrated where the sea had been washing in and out. After she was sunk, why there was a surge there and it kept working for a day. It just chewed everything all to pieces.”

Lou towed *Esperanto* back to Fort Lauderdale where Fred spent another "royal fortune" and several more months rebuilding her yet again. The waterspout sank her in May but by August, Fred and his schooner were back in Marsh Harbour, Abaco.

Today, *Esperanto* sails on happily throughout the Bahamas with a new name and hopefully new luck. She has been re-christened *W. H. Albury* and charters in Abaco to the Boy Scouts and other charitable organizations.

* * *

On January 1, 1959, Fulgencio Batista fled Cuba for a life of luxurious exile in Portugal and Spain. He was driven off the island by the forces of Fidel Castro's "26th of July Movement," and the rest is history. During the first years of the Castro government, there were enclaves of anti-Castro activists, including an organization comprised of disenchanted ex-Castro rebels called "Alpha 66," formed in Puerto Rico at the end of 1961. It consisted of 66 ardent anti-Castro Cubans, most of whom were professionals. A training camp was set up in the Dominican Republic, and they used Bahamian islands as bases to collect arms and plan hit-and-run attacks against small government targets within Cuba. The Bahamian-owned Cay Sal Bank islets were only 30 miles from the north coast of Cuba, a perfect staging ground for the rebels. The Cubans, on the other hand, felt obliged to attack and destroy these "rebel" encampments wherever they might be. Of course, the Bahamians didn't want firefights breaking out on their soil, so the Bahamas needed a navy.

But the Bahamas had no navy and no money to buy one. There were no patrol or police boats of any kind. So periodically, *Aquanaut* was chartered by the government and effectively became Her Majesty's Royal Bahamian Navy charged with transporting raiding parties to the camps housing the rebels who were the targets of the marauding Castroistas.

A typical raid consisted of a British Marines captain leading an untrained and inept squad of 12 Bahamian police. The Keystone Kop character of the missions was not the fault of the officers, as there were no facilities or funds for training. Young Bahamians were recruited at starvation wages and thrown into situations for which they were totally unprepared.

When on a mission, Lou didn't even trust the Bahamians to run the shore boat.

"I couldn't trust any of them to run it. They'd smash it up on the beach or run it on the rocks or do something, so I looked after that. When they'd come back, they were inept with their rifles too, which was funny. They'd come back and the guns would be loaded and when they'd come to get in the boat, I said, 'Are they loaded?' They'd say 'Yes,' and I'd say, 'Well, unload them.' But they didn't know how to unload their guns. I had to show them how to do it."

One night when they were anchored in a safe harbor, a young Bahamian policeman asked Lou if he could borrow the shore boat to go fishing. Lou said, "Hell no." The entire crew wanted some fresh fish instead of the crummy rations that were brought aboard by the British Marines captain. He didn't bother to explain to them that the dinghy was the only means to get ashore, and if it were lost, it would be dangerous for the rest of the crew. Lou just repeated, "Hell no."

The commanding officer interceded on behalf of the crew, but Lou never budged. There was no way he was going to give the shore boat to an incompetent kid, and that was that.

Two years later, Lou was clearing customs at Nassau, and *Aquanaut* was tied up to the dock next to a brand new, pristine, 90-foot police vessel. A shabbily dressed Bahamian walked up and said, "Hi Skip. You remember me?" Lou looked at him for a second and said, "Yeah, you're one of the guys on the island raids. You wanted to take my shore boat out fishing." "Ya mon, that's me." Lou asked what he was doing now. "I'm on dat boat," the Bahamian motioned toward the shiny new police cutter.

"And he said, 'I'm on one of these.' There was a police boat at the dock. And I said, 'What are you doing aboard there?' And he says, 'Oh, I'm the captain.' And he was the captain of this ship, and I didn't trust him with an 18-foot whaleboat, heh, heh."

* * *

Castro's revolution took over Cuba's governmental affairs in 1959. Fidel Castro appointed himself Prime Minister of Cuba in 1961 and promptly expropriated something over eight million acres of plantations and private estates. He also postponed the promised general elections and broke off diplomatic relations with the United States.

A mass exodus of middle- and upper-class Cuban citizens began, and most of the refugees landed in South Florida. As soon as these expatriates stepped foot on U.S. territory, under the aegis of Alpha 66 and similar organizations, they hatched myriad plots to overthrow Castro's new government. The CIA set up training camps for them in Central America.

After the Bay of Pigs debacle in April of 1961, Alpha 66 was organized specifically to go it alone—to attack Cuban government targets without CIA help. Further, in the aftermath of the Cuban Missile Crisis that resulted in a U.S. guarantee to not invade Cuba, those anti-Castro Cubans still on the island lost faith that an invasion of liberation would ever take place. By this time, the only hope given to the anti-Castro forces in Cuba was Alpha 66's hit-and-run skirmishes, emanating mostly from the Bahamian cays and islets to the north.

After a few years of small but well-publicized attacks by Alpha 66, in a move he thought would backfire on the U.S., Castro accepted President Johnson's open invitation to welcome anyone who wanted to leave Cuba. Thus began the Camarioca Exodus of 1965.

Though the Cubans were welcome in the U.S., the catch was the U.S. wouldn't clear any vessels for Cuba to pick them up. So small boats simply made the trip at night, clogging the Veradero Docks at Camarioca in Matanzas Province on Cuba's north shore. The little vessels returned to Miami, and the Florida Keys jammed to the gunwales with refugees. They never cleared in or out, and after unloading their human cargo and refueling, the boats immediately returned to Cuba to haul another batch of Cubans to the Sunshine State. The Coast Guard stopped many of the vessels, but many more ran the blockade. The Cuban government feigned cooperation but in reality it was a frustrating hurry-up-and-wait experience once reaching Camarioca.

The media, especially in South Florida, was obsessed with covering the boat lift but couldn't get legal permission to travel to Cuba. The Bahamas, however, had diplomatic relations with Cuba. Theoretically, it was legal to fly to Cuba or clear vessels to Cuban ports from the Bahamas.

Time magazine and NBC learned of this hole in the fence and sent crews to Nassau to buy passage to Camarioca. Under pressure from Washington, U.S.-registered aircraft were forbidden to fly to Cuba even from the Bahamas, so that avenue was shut. Through quiet diplomatic channels, the U.S. government also insisted that the Bahamian government deny maritime traffic clearance for Cuba.

At that time, the Bahamas Development Board handled all press relations, and wanting to appear helpful to *Time* and NBC, recommended they talk to Lou Kenedy concerning passage to Camarioca. The news people were pleased when Lou accepted their generous offer for passage, but there was a catch: Though the Bahamas Development Board approved of a trip to Cuba,

Bahamas Customs and Immigration would not clear *Aquanaut* for Camarioca. Lou got around the problem by leaving Nassau during the pitch black of 0200 hours. He steamed non-stop and arrived two days later in Camarioca at 0800 on the 18th of October, 1965.

"Well, you never saw such a mess of officialdom. Everybody with guns, everybody clicking their heels. And they said there were no rules. You could use your radio, you could do this and do that. You could go anywhere you wanted. But when you tried to do the things they said you could do, it became a different matter."

The harbor had been cordoned off with chain link fence topped with barbed wire and was essentially a compound with access and egress only from the sea.

Lou, never one to accept any sort of confinement, decided he wanted a beer ashore. He called the mate and said, "Follow me." They strode to the gate, walked through, and started to amble toward the village a couple of hundred yards away. A guard pointed a rifle at them and gestured for them to stop. Lou just smiled and repeated over and over, *"Gracias señor, gracias señor, gracias señor,"* and walked right past. The guard was so angry he slammed his rifle barrel down in the mud and screamed, *"¡Hijo 'e puta—Párate!"** Lou just repeated, *"Gracias señor, gracias señor, gracias señor,"* and kept on walking.

"Then we got to a little village and as we went to it, a whole mob of Cuban populace gathered around us and started following us saying, 'Take me to America Yankee—take me to America Yankee'—hollering and yelling. And we got to a little place and I said I want a beer, me and my mate. Oh, I had asked them, what about Cuban money? And they said you don't need money for anything. And I said I'd have to change some dollars for some Cuban money. And they said, you don't need it. Anything you want here is free."

The bar was a simple room with a chipped and faded red and white ceramic tile floor. Some of the 10-inch tiles were missing but it was clean and uncluttered, with old wooden chairs and tables covered with shiny green plastic table cloths. At the bar sat a friendly, young Cuban Army lieutenant, and he struck up a conversation with Lou in English. It was the same officer who had cleared him into the port that morning. When Lou tried to pay for the beer with American dollars, the bartender drew his thumb across his throat,

---

* "Son of a whore—Stop!"

and the officer explained that if he accepted dollars, he would be severely punished.

After a couple of beers, the officer left only to return several minutes later, excited and out of breath. As he entered the cantina, a truck-load of soldiers in cleaner uniforms drove up outside. The lieutenant pointed at the truck and said urgently, "These are bad men, these are bad men. You must not be here." One of the new arrivals was the same guard who had pounded his rifle muzzle into the mud at the Camarioca gate. The obvious leader of the platoon was an officer who seemed pleasant at first and asked in lightly accented English if all was well, and Lou replied that everything was fine. Then the officer started screaming, "What are you doing here? What are you doing here? You can't be here." Lou calmly replied, "I'm having a good time here." "Get back to your boat!" yelled the Angry One. "O.K., I'll get back there as soon as I finish my beer," Lou answered. The Angry One, face reddening, yelled, "No, you will go now!"

"I've got to pay the bill first," Lou almost whispered to contrast his self-control with the hysterics displayed by the officer. Lou opened his wallet and withdrew a $10 bill and put it on the table. The bartender nearly fainted, and the Angry One blanched and stuffed the bill back in Lou's shirt pocket as fast as he could. "No American money here, no American money," shouted the officer. He looked around as if he had done something wrong and was afraid of getting caught.

Finally, the friendly lieutenant, who had retreated to the corner of the cantina, stepped up to the plate and paid for the beer and in Spanish told the Angry One he would take Lou and the mate back to the compound and guaranteed him they would not get loose in the village again. This seemed to mollify the Angry One and his blood pressure abated. The incident ended as quickly as it started when the Angry One turned to Lou and said, *"Buenos dias, Señor."* He clicked a heel and strode out of the bar.

The Nice One led Lou and the mate to a '36 Chevy four door. The two other common soldiers who were with them dove into the car through the broken windows. The officer looked sheepish and explained to Lou that the doors wouldn't open and everyone had to use the windows to get in and out. Lou said, "No problem," and went head first through the rider's side window like he'd done it a hundred times. In fact, he *had* done it a hundred times; the old canvas-covered Morris in Barbados had the same door-opening problem, and with the top up, the windows were the only ways in and out. Lou missed the Morris; it was aboard *Wawaloam* when she sank.

"But anyway that was the last time we got out of the dock area. It was some bunch of double talk. The movie and news magazine correspondents were taken to Havana where officials wanted to show how everything was going there, as a propaganda ploy. But that afternoon they were all brought back because the Cubans decided they didn't like them because they were reporting things as they saw them, not as they were told to report it. So that evening we left."

Aquanaut only spent one day and night at Boca de Camarioca—the official name—then left for Miami. Of course, the problem was they had not cleared out of the Bahamas and couldn't show American authorities their clearance out of Camarioca. But Lou had the answer. Cat Cay is a Bahamian port of entry, just across the Gulf Stream from Miami. *Aquanaut* entered Cat Cay ostensibly having arrived from Nassau and was now clearing out of the Bahamas for Miami.

"So I went in there and I said I'd come from Nassau and I wanted a clearance for Miami. So the Customs fellow gave me a clearance for Miami and we went across arriving at 4:00 in the afternoon. They were able to get their story on the 6:00 p.m. edition of the TV news."

As soon as *Aquanaut* arrived in Miami, a group of Cuban expatriates offered to pay Lou handsomely if he would return to Camarioca and pick up 100 refugees.

"So I said, well put the money down and I'll go. They put the money down and it was a good price too, I can tell you."

That same morning, October 26, 1965, *Aquanaut* cleared for Nassau but departed for Cuba, again risking legal action from both the U.S. and Bahamian government. Upon arrival, a storm blew in from the north, and as Camarioca is not well protected, a Cuban government skiff escorted the old patrol boat to a more famous and protected destination, Mariel, a few miles to the east. Mariel was a real marina that had been dredged and boasted docks and marine facilities. In the Hemingway days before Castro, Mariel was a favorite destination for the rich and famous to enjoy yachting and sport fishing.

Hundreds of boats were there, all with lists of the people they were to take back to the States. The Cuban government, however, never organized the lists, and after a week of cooling their heels, most of the 300 small boats were running out of food. No one had planned a week-long stay, and Cuba would not allow any provisioning from ashore.

Lou had only contracted for one week to retrieve those on his list. After the first week, he radioed his clients and explained that if he stayed for another week, he would have to be paid double. The deal was agreed upon, and the money was deposited into Lou's bank account in Miami.

After another week of inaction by the Cuban authorities, all the boats decided to call it a day and return empty-handed. The closest significant U.S. port to Mariel was Key West. Within 25 hours, a vast armada of small boats, including *Aquanaut*, descended on the little island. Customs officers were waiting for them and seized many of the vessels as they arrived. The number of vessels was so overwhelming that U.S. Customs had to call the state of Florida to help work the case load.

Upon arrival, Lou was notified that Customs, Immigration, and Coast Guard officials were coming aboard. The practiced official demeanor of the officers was bound to bring out the Lou Kenedy attitude:

"Well I decided to handle it a little bit different than the other fellows. They were giving right in and, of course, they were American and they were completely under their control. So I said, 'Now wait a minute. I can only handle one at a time.'"

Lou's demands took the officials by surprise, and since *Aquanaut* operated under the Bahamian flag, there was no end of confusion as to exactly how to handle the matter.

"...and I said, 'I'll take the customs first.' So we went through the customs racket and they said, 'Let me see your guns.' I said, 'Here. I got a gun and I have several pistols,' and I had rifles and I had one machine gun.' And they said, 'Well, if they're loaded, unload them.' I said, 'No, I don't like them unloaded on my ship. When I have a gun, I want it loaded. An empty gun is no good.' They said, 'Not if we seize them. We don't want them loaded.' I said, 'Where do you get the right to seize them? A perfectly peaceful ship with my protection here.' And he said, 'Well you've been to Cuba ...,' and so on. I said, 'What I did in Cuba is my business, not yours. I'm not under American rule when I'm 12 miles out.' And they thought that over and they found out that I was right. All they could do with the guns was seal them up. They couldn't take 'em off. I had to show them this in a maritime law book."

"When it was the immigration officer's turn, he simply washed his hands of the whole matter and without any questions, declared the crew legally entered into the U.S.; no passports or visas were requested."

When the Coasties came aboard, they considered themselves to have real power over the "outlaw" armada. They could cite the skippers for the smallest infractions and even impound a vessel when appropriate. If the fog bell was missing, citation; if there were not enough life vests, citation; if the fire extinguishers were out of date, citation; if the radio license was not displayed correctly, citation. So

"...the Coast Guard came aboard and they were going to stop all these boats by finding some imaginary or picayune infraction like not having a bell or a set of pilot rules or enough life jackets and all that kind of stuff. Well, of course, I had been fitted out with 100 life jackets for the people that I had expected to bring back from Mariel so here were two people aboard with 100 life jackets. I had a big bell. She had been an ex-Coast Guard patrol boat. She had all the equipment. Everything was right, and the head Coast Guard captain, I heard him say to one of the crew members, 'Boy, this skipper knows how to handle it. Boy, he's put the bee on those customs and the immigration guys.'"

The next day, *Aquanaut* sailed for Nassau on the clearance he received two weeks earlier in Miami. When she arrived, she was something of a celebrity in that *Time* magazine and NBC had covered the first voyage extensively and mentioned *Aquanaut* several times. This notoriety hit the local Bahamian newspapers, and Lou was summoned before the chief customs officer at Government House.

It was a somber occasion as Lou was formally accused of leaving Bahamian waters without clearance and going to Cuba when he was specifically prohibited from doing so.

Lou said he hadn't gone to Cuba directly but had cleared for Miami out of Cat Cay. The official didn't know Lou had gone to Cuba twice on the one set of clearance papers he received after the first trip. Lou said he had traveled from Nassau to Cat Cay, cleared for Miami, arrived in Miami, and cleared back into the Bahamas.

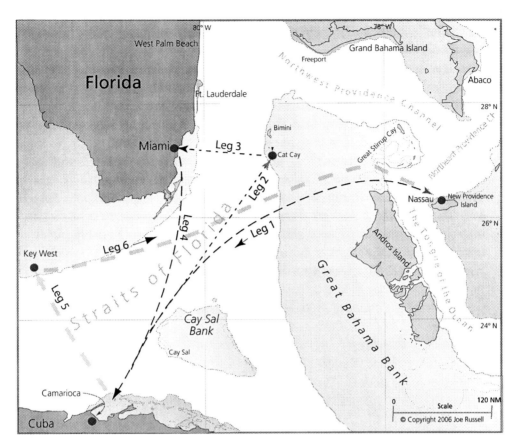

Figure 9-6. Chart: Route of *Aquanaut* during the Camarioca Boat Lift.

"So he said, 'How did you get out of the Bahamas?' I said, 'I cleared at Cat Cay for Miami.' And he swallowed hard. And I said, 'While I was in Miami, I cleared for Cuba and it was nothing to do with the Bahamas when I cleared from Miami.' And by God it all fell to nothing, but to this day he doesn't know I made two trips. He thought I just made the one, heh. But anyway that came to a happy end and that was quite an adventure and it was profitable. And we got out of it with a clean skin. But anyway we had to do some dodging on that one."

* * *

After the excitement of the Cuban trips, going back to government surveying of the Bahamas wasn't appealing to Lou. The work was tedious, but *Aquanaut* was the only vessel in the Bahamas that could do the job efficiently.

Some of the islands couldn't be approached closely with any vessel drawing more than six feet.

The new survey work was to be along the hot, shallow, mosquitoey west coast of Andros. The project was to be mostly accomplished in mangrove swamps and promised to be a miserable six months of sweating.

Lou yearned to get back into freighting and had begun negotiations on purchasing two little 80-foot cargo vessels from Newfoundland.

"But anyway I was making negotiations then to buy the Canadian freighters, Pikes Arm *and* Cobbs Arm. *They were in Newfoundland, and as luck would have it, another skipper wanted to buy* Aquanaut *and take over this job, which I didn't want. So we made arrangements and that's how I sold* Aquanaut. *I was glad to be out of it because I surely didn't look forward to that survey job on the west coast of Andros. It would be like surveying a great swamp which went for hundreds of miles."*

Lou sold *Aquanaut* and flew up to St. John's to inspect his new freighters.

So ends this day.

Figure 10-1. *Pikes Arm* **entering the Miami River.**

The ship: *Pikes Arm*
Year of Launching: 1962
Rig: Motor Vessel
Builder: E.F. Barnes – St. John's,
    Newfoundland
Engine: Single Caterpillar diesel

Material: Steel
Length overall: 80 feet 8 inches
Beam: 22 feet 6 inches
Draft: 6 feet (double bottomed)
Net Capacity: 230 tons

Chapter 10   *Pikes Arm*

Pikes Arm *and her sister ship,* Cobbs Arm, *were both built for trade between the small ports of the Canadian Maritimes, and Lou thought the shallow draft made them perfect for Bahamian waters. The vessels were named for narrow bodies of water on the western coast of southern Newfoundland*

* * *

The deal Lou struck to purchase *Pikes Arm* included her sister ship, *Cobbs Arm.* As he negotiated the purchase of the two vessels, he was already consummating the sale of *Cobbs Arm* to Bud Veenstra, an old professional footballer. *Pikes Arm* steamed down to the LaHave from Newfoundland, and

Lou took delivery. Lou asked the delivery crew how she handled, and after beating around the bush, they admitted that *Pikes Arm* was a dog. They couldn't average five knots in flat seas and she was even slower in a seaway. She had been laid up for years. Lou had her put on the ways in Lunenburg, where he discovered she was coated with three inches of mussels on the bottom, and over six inches on the sides. The mussel coating was so thick, Lou opined he could have opened a fresh seafood market. The job of cleaning the mussels off the slipway was a bigger job than scraping the hull, and a small front-end loader was brought in to push the bumper crop of mollusks into Lunenburg Harbour.

Figure 10-2. Taken at Smith and Rhuland, this photo shows both *Pikes Arm* and *Cobbs Arm* one behind the other on the same dry dock to the left.

After the cleaning, *Pikes Arm* steamed at a steady eight knots, seven and a half knots loaded. Three men could run her easily; the cargo handling equipment was efficient with a hydraulic ram to swing the boom, a powered conveyor belt for loading and unloading, and a Lunenburg Foundry winch, powered by an Acadia Gas engine.[*]

In Lunenberg, the bottom and decks were scrubbed and painted, but a prepaid charter popped up, and the rusty topsides were not tended to immediately. Not wanting to lose the charter, Lou decided to deal with the topsides after reaching the Bahamas.

The charter Lou had finagled was to deliver a broken-down carnival from Norwalk, Connecticut to Nassau. Along with 30 booths for the games, there were merry-go-rounds, Ferris wheels, a dangerously ill-maintained miniature roller coaster, and a Tilt-a-Whirl. The pick-up point in Norwalk was at a dock adjacent to a yacht club that sported a couple of tennis courts and an open-air restaurant. Lou received permission to pick up the cargo there, and the loading

---

[*] Motor built in Bridgewater by Acadia Gas Engines Company.

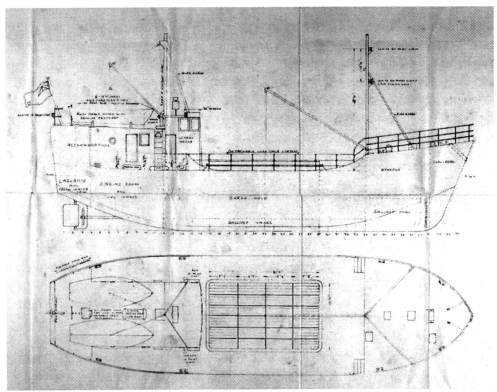

Figure 10-3. Original blue-line drawing of *Pikes Arm*.

process became the talk of the town. The carnival owner hadn't a clue as to how to load a vessel so Lou's crew did it for him—for a fee. The yacht club members and restaurant clientele spent hours sipping gin and tonics on the verandas discussing and pointing at the rusty old freighter being loaded with merry-go-round horses and other carny paraphernalia.

The loading was completed on a Friday afternoon and *Pikes Arm* was ready to sail. But Lou was not, under any circumstances, going to depart that Friday or any other Friday. This would fly in the face of one of his most deeply held superstitions—to never begin a voyage on a Friday. He didn't tell the carny owner about this superstition when he demanded the agreed-upon prepaid freight. The carny owner said it would take until the following week to get the money.

"I said, 'Well you'll have to pay demurrage.' He said, 'What's that?'
And I said, 'Oh you'll find out.'"

During most of the next week, Lou and his crew worked on *Pikes Arm*, enjoyed the yacht club, the short white skirts, the long tan legs, and the watered-down drinks until the carny guy finally said he had the money. He took Lou to the bank for payment, whereupon Lou again reminded him of demurrage, and the banker asked, "What is demurrage?" Lou explained it was the daily charter fee for every day the boat couldn't move through no fault of the vessel's owner except for an act of God. "Kinda like if you rent a car but don't drive it, you still have to pay the day's rent," Lou said. "Ah," the banker said and coughed up the demurrage which almost equaled the original charter fee. *Pikes Arm* sailed on a Wednesday and arrived uneventfully in Nassau a week later.

Lou's buddy Jimmy Porter was recruited as an AB for the trip to the Bahamas, and recalled it later:

> *"Early summer of 1967, I joined Captain Lou Kenedy, who had bought a little freighter in Newfoundland and needed crew to take her to Nassau. Over the next couple of months we prepared and provisioned the ship, sailed to Norwalk, Connecticut to pick up a cargo, and then went on to Nassau. Throughout the entire time we were enthralled by the infectious laugh, entertained by the yarns, and dazzled at the abilities of a true deep-water sailor.* Pikes Arm *had an impressive bow, a big cargo hatch with the wheelhouse directly behind it, and behind that—nothing. It was as if someone took a large knife and chopped off the back of the ship. The morning we arrived in Nassau we cruised proudly up the harbour straight to the pier where the captain's wife Pat was waiting. As we swung alongside the dock and Pat noticed the cut off look of the ship, she yelled up to Lou, "Where the hell is the rest of it?" causing great peals of laughter from the captain."*[*]

* * *

Though for years Lou had been smuggling relatively modest quantities of rum into the Maritimes and taxable goods down to the Caribbean, the story of *Pikes Arm* takes the art of smuggling to a heretofore unexplored level. Lou became the consummate smuggler and was mighty proud of it. This wasn't like the old days when secret hatches were cut into the fantail, casks of rum were disguised as chairs, or barrels of Mount Gay were buried on islets in the middle of the LaHave. No, these new techniques were sophisticated, sometimes more obvious, but always successful, profitable, and usually amusing. The yarns about Lou Kenedy's contraband runs into the Bahamas are among the most entertaining stories of an already entertaining life.

---

[*] Conversation with author.

There were a few other more mundane twists and turns during Kenedy's ownership of the little freighter, and there was a regular legitimate shipping schedule that was adhered to religiously, but the real money and fun for Lou was hauling taxable goods past the customs officials aboard *Pikes Arm*.

There is no income tax in the Bahamas. The government is run almost entirely on the 33-1/3 percent or more ad valorum duty imposed on imports. Some food items are excepted, and after particularly devastating hurricanes, the duty on building materials is temporarily lifted. Everything else gets taxed. This made avoiding taxes lucrative and presented Lou with irresistible opportunities for mischief.

Besides Lou's *sub rosa* profits from smuggling, his cargo shipping was becoming more and more lucrative. Hotel construction was booming in the Bahamas, and shipping construction materials was in great demand. Moreover, the upscale settlements at Spanish Wells and Harbour Island had no direct shipping from the American mainland. Every item arriving into these villages was transshipped in Nassau and suffered significant breakage and pilfering during unloading and reloading. *Pikes Arm*, on the other hand, would make a direct shot for North Eleuthera and clear customs in either Spanish Wells or Harbour Island; no transshipping was necessary.

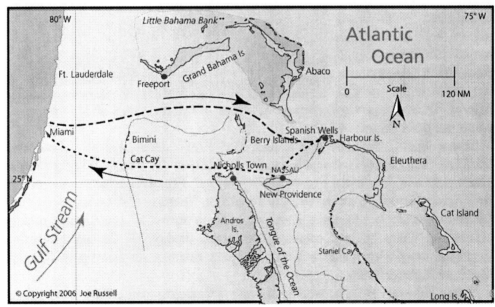

Figure 10-4. Chart: *Pikes Arm*'s biweekly course.

The secret to success was running a regular schedule so the businesses and approximately 2,000 relatively well-to-do inhabitants could absolutely rely on receiving their imported goods on a specific day. Everything except a bit of fish and some locally-grown vegetables had to be imported, including the frozen food for the tourist resorts and markets.

"So I announced that I would go every two weeks and make a run there and after awhile it was so successful that we went on and on and they sort of set their clocks by *Pikes Arm's* schedule. I would arrive every second Sunday and then on Monday, Tuesday, and Wednesday I'd discharge and they could count on it.

"I made 90 trips in all on this schedule and I never missed one trip, except when I was sick for two months and my daughter, Patsy, took over as captain of the ship."

* * *

Pikes Arm's original route began in Port Laudania, Florida and went wherever the freight took her. But within a few months, the regular schedule was established when Lou signed with a shipping agent, Johnson Shipping, with aggregation warehouses far up the Miami River. The new route ran from Miami to

Figure 10-5. *Pikes Arm* off Spanish Wells in 1968.

Harbour Island, Spanish Wells, and The Bluff. Soon a deep freeze was installed, and frozen food was brought bi-weekly to the Piggly Wiggly store at Harbour Island. Lou ran a two-week turnaround. Departing Nassau on Sunday or Monday, he would arrive early in Miami on Tuesday and have to wait until 0900 for the bridges to open, allowing passage up the Miami River. Loading started on Tuesday and continued through Friday. A Saturday-morning departure would have the freighter clearing customs on Sunday at Spanish Wells or Harbour Island.

Patsy Kenedy Bolling, who took over *Pikes Arm* while Lou was laid up after back surgery, explains that occasionally, the deck cargo was so high, Lou had to pay for a tug to take him down the river:

"...as he couldn't see very well, and negotiating the river with a single screw lump craft is a bitch on good days, what with a zillion *bridges to open, current, narrows, and Cuban boats all tied up to trees, hindered not only by poor visibility but poor maneuverability when you came to a bridge and had to hold position till it opened."*[*]

After arriving and clearing customs, *Pikes Arm* unloaded at Spanish Wells or Harbour Island, returning to Nassau for three days of maintenance and loading the occasional car as deck cargo for repair stateside.

On the bow of *Pikes Arm* sat the Acadia Gas "make-and-break" donkey engine, unique in a couple of ways. First, it looked like a steam engine. The rods and push-rods were out in the open and splash lubricated. Second, she was brightly painted, red with brass fittings and gold-painted trim. The engine never failed to start and always pulled hard. It looked so unusual and ran so well it became an object of reverence on docks throughout the Bahamas.

Refrigerators were a standard smuggled item. One day Lou arrived with a new fridge tied to the deck house of *Pikes Arm* and off-handedly reported the purchase to the customs man in Eleuthera.

Figure 10-6. Fiats as deck cargo for Harbour Island, 1970.

"And when I got there, I told the customs man in a matter of conversation how I had to buy another fridge because the one in the galley wasn't big enough and the ship wasn't well fitted with a fridge. So then I'd get to Nassau I'd put the fridge ashore, get over to the States, buy another fridge and put it on deck. And every trip she had a fridge on deck but it was never the same one. But sometimes it wasn't even the same color but there was always a fridge there and nearly every trip I brought in a new one. I must have brought in about 50 or more of them that way."

The main salon was always cool and comfortable, made so by an air conditioner that was, unbeknownst to customs, also new on every trip.

One of the favorite ways of bringing pricier items in without duty was to have the owner buy the item in the States ahead of time, then bring the

---

[*] Conversation with author.

registration or other proof of ownership over to the Bahamas. The next time Lou left for Florida, he'd produce the documentation to customs and have the item cleared out of Nassau. If it was mechanical like a boat or car, it would need to go to Miami for brake repair, perhaps, or just a tune up. The customs officers never checked to see if the item was actually aboard.

"Of course it wasn't aboard; it was still over in the warehouse or showroom in Florida. I'd get over there, load it aboard, bring it back, and I'd produce a bill. If it was a car, I'd produce a bill for repairing brakes or something like that and pay duty on the repair bill. And if it was oriental rugs or anything like that, it was over to be cleaned. I'd have a bill for that. Or if it was a boat, it would be something to put a new bottom end in the propeller housing or items like that. It was a foolproof method and it worked so easily we just went on and on doing that and nobody ever was the wiser.

"This is the first time I've mentioned it in public. I've mentioned it plenty in private. But I thought these methods should go down in history. People shouldn't forget all these items in case somebody else can use it in future, heh, heh."

At that time, auto license plates in the Bahamas were not issued by the government. The government issued the number but the car owner was responsible for getting plates made. The black background and metal numbers were available at local hardware stores. Lou simply bought the black background plate and some random numbers and made up matching tags and installed them front and back on cars he bought in Miami. When the customs officials saw the Bahamian plates, they never asked for the registration or any proof of ownership. As soon as Lou arrived in Spanish Wells, he'd sell the cars. Since it was already cleared into the country, the new owner just went to Government House and registered it in his name.

"And we'd sell 'em and get a receipt and the fellow would go down and just license them. It was not a very strict arrangement because they weren't thinking of what was going on and it worked very well. It was a challenge but it was fun."

One thing that should have been caught by the customs people was the fact that *Pikes Arm*'s fenders were tires. Most of them still had the labels on them, and the white walls still sported the green protective wash.

When Patsy Kenedy Bolling, the oldest daughter, was running *Pikes Arm*, Captain Lou was also aboard while convalescing after back surgery. About this time and for unknown reasons, the customs office began taking more interest in *Pikes Arm*. During one stop at Harbour Island, six customs officials boarded her and began a stem-to-stern search for contraband. While they were aboard, a friend of a crewmember who was visiting the boat was caught stealing one of the ship's pistols and fled down the dock. Lou was not too disabled to catch up to the thief, wrest the pistol from him, and proceed to beat the tar out of him. This, of course, caught the attention of the customs men aboard, and the search aboard *Pikes Arm* was intensified. They found and confiscated Lou's air pistol and .22-caliber rifle. But they never noticed the brand new refrigerator on the aft deck.

What they did notice were cases and cases of dog food. Lou explained that the dog food was horse meat and that's what he and his crew ate.

Rosie, the youngest Kenedy, recalls the story:

"The customs man said, 'You must have 20 cases of Alpo dog food here.' 'Right, but this is horse meat and I love to eat horse meat.' Then he went to a hand operated can opener and proceeded to open a can and started eating, offering some to the customs agent who turned away in disgust.

"Through the years I always thought that this story had been exaggerated. Some years later when I was living in Harbour Island and went through customs quite often, I once told them I was Lou Kenedy's daughter. One of the guys stepped forward, with a big grin on his face stating, 'I met your dad as a little boy on board Pikes Arm. *Customs were aboard at the time and I didn't believe what I was seeing, but he opened a can of dog food and started to eat it right in front of me.' I laughed then because I finally knew that it was a true story."*

Pikes Arm had a double bottom, and when she was in ballast, Lou would load 65 tons of water into bilge tanks to stabilize her. This came in particularly handy for his friends on Staniel Cay, in the Bahamas. His buddies ran a small resort there but had to make their own water with a tiny reverse osmosis system. They never had enough water for all the yachts, the guests, and kitchens. So when lightly loaded, Lou regularly took on a ballast tank full of fresh water in Miami to offload at Staniel for the Staniel Cay Yacht Club and the village. He never accepted money for the water but always enjoyed the meals and companionship of his friends. This in turn earned him free dockage as he traveled through in later years.

Figure 10-7. The captain with *Pikes Arm* at Miami Shipyard.

Always trying to save money, Lou thought the protected beach at Staniel Cay was perfect for careening *Pikes Arm* as she was slab sided and almost flat bottomed. The freighter's bottom along the keel was rarely covered with growth but the sides would foul after only a few months. On a spring high tide, Lou put a couple of tons of water in the bow tank and drove the little freighter up on the beach as far as she would go. As soon as the tide receded, the crew got busy with scrapers. By the time the water rose again, half the ship's bottom would be clean. After three tidal cycles, two coats of non-corrosive, ablative bottom paint would be applied. On the fourth high tide, the water was pumped out of the bow tank and she was reversed off the beach into deep water. Lou said, "It was a very efficient way of dry docking, and inexpensive."

* * *

The *Pikes Arm* days were formative for the younger girls, especially Rosie. Christmases were spent cruising the Exumas with all the friends that they could pack aboard the old freighter. Rosie recalls that the house in the Bahamas was always filled with friends:

"I remember that Mum and Dad attracted young people, our house was always full of young people, full of laughs, food, and drink. My favorite meal that Mum would produce was her curry, with raisins, fruit, vegetables, coconut, chutney, and all the good stuff to put on top of it. It seemed that this was a coming home meal for Dad, and I can remember hearing the gate open and running out to meet him. We'd embrace, have a good old-fashioned bear hug. I just loved that warmth that he displayed to me and my sisters."

* * *

After a few years of successful operation, Lou tired of the tedious bi-weekly trips to Florida. Even fooling the Bahamian customs officers was not as satisfying as before. Ninety trips were enough.

"Anyway it appeared now this was a fairly successful business and made a living but it wasn't making a fortune by any means, but it did appear to be a very efficient affair. But I was getting bored with the trips and I wanted to quit and this guy came along and made an offer through a broker and we accepted."

The sale of *Pikes Arm* followed the patented Lou Kenedy pattern of financial complication and, of course, those ever-profitable demurrage fees.

"He put up the check for 10 percent and then the balance was to be paid one-third down and then in another couple of months, another one-third, and in a couple of months, the balance. And then he would get possession of the vessel."

The deposit check bounced, which aggravated Lou to the point of distraction, and he considered bailing out of the deal. But he reconsidered and simply changed some of the details of the negotiation: Lou demanded one-third down payment. The buyer wrote the check but it bounced also.

However, within days, he made the second check good and the deal continued, albeit under a cloud. The second payment was a week late but did finally arrive and Lou then had two-thirds. The third and last payment was promised again and again but Lou didn't receive it.

"Every trip I'd be over in the islands, he'd telephone and say it would 'be here when you get back to Florida.'"

Trip after trip, Lou arrived but the money was not delivered. So, of course, Lou barred the prospective buyer from the vessel. The buyer was trying to get financing and he brought people to *Pikes Arm* to promote the investment. Lou would let the prospective investors aboard but not the buyer.

"I'd let them come aboard but I'd tell him he had to stand on the dock. And everybody thought I was pretty tough on him, but I was pretty fed up by this time."

Then Lou hit the buyer with the old demurrage gambit.

"So finally one of these weeks when he was going to pay when I arrived in Miami and he didn't, I said now we got a different arrangement. You got to sign a paper. You've got to pay demurrage, you're way overdue now, and you got to pay a demurrage of $200 per day for every day that you don't pay the final payment, and it's starting today."

"Oh, I'm going to have the money next week," gushed the buyer. Lou shot back, "Then you won't have a problem signing the demurrage agreement." The buyer nodded and signed. The agreement read that Lou would be paid every week, in advance for the succeeding seven days starting that day. If the buyer ever defaulted on a demurrage payment,

"...the whole deal was off. I kept all his money and the whole deal was off. And it was to be paid in cash—$1,400. So he said, 'Oh that's nothing. Within the week I'll have it and the few hundred dollars you get will make a little bonus for you.' And I said, 'That's very nice.'"

Remembering the *Pikes Arm* turn-around was a two-week process, the next week the buyer called and pointed out that since Lou would be back in Florida the next week, why didn't he pick up two weeks of demurrage when he returned.

"I said, 'No way. A deal is a deal; you got to bring it over here. Get it to me.' So he had to fly to Nassau and he brought his suitcase."

And just to annoy the poor guy, Lou demanded the money be brought in $100 bills, not "any chickenfeed. I don't want any $20 bills."

"And he hired a big taxi and came out from the airport and he came with his little briefcase looking very much the businessman. He opened his briefcase and started counting out $20 bills. And with tongue in cheek, I raised hell with him. I said, 'I don't want any damn chicken feed.' I told him I wanted $100 bills and when I said $100 bills, I meant $100 bills. And I wasn't going to waste all this time counting. So he said, oh he was very sorry and it wouldn't happen again. And he took it very seriously and I was laughing up my sleeve but I didn't give a damn if it was one dollar bills really. But anyway, I made my point."

As the weeks rolled on, Patsy Kenedy Bolling, who was born with a head for business, began worrying the whole deal would wind up in a lawsuit if the buyer demanded the return of monies paid to date. She made an appointment with a high-powered law firm in Miami to go over the agreement Lou had written. It was air-tight. The attorney said, "There's nothing he can do. He may have a battery of lawyers but there's no way he's going to get out of this."

Finally, while loading in Miami, after 96 days and over $19,000 in demurrage charges, the ship broker informed Lou the rest of the funds would be paid the very next day. "It's all set," he said. Considering the demurrage as part of the sale, the agent then demanded a percentage of these extra fees. Lou's reaction was predictable and swift, "Screw yourself."

The next day the agent called and said there had been a change and payment could not be made that day. Lou just shrugged.

"I said, look I've heard this every trip. So what? I don't give a damn. It can go on as long as he wants."

On the following Thursday, the buyer arrived on the dock and yelled up to the bridge, "This fellow wants to look over the vessel." Lou said, "That's fine, but you stay on the dock." While the man was inspecting *Pikes Arm*, the broker called and said the buyer had met the prospective investor in a bar the night before, and he was interested in buying into the venture and would put rest of the money up tomorrow, Friday.

The vessel was loaded early and cleared for the Bahamas, but if the deal fell through, Lou would waste a day in Miami, because he would never begin a voyage on a Friday. But the buyer insisted they would meet the investor at the bank at 4:30 Friday afternoon and consummate the purchase.

"I mean this buyer did everything in a big way, and I got in this monstrosity of a Lincoln that he rented, and after we took off he says, 'You don't mind if we stop and pick up my wife's dog at the vet's?' 'No,' I said, 'I don't give a damn what you do. Just get me back for supper.' I said, 'As far as buying the boat goes, I'll believe it when I see it. But just get me back for my supper.'

"So he stopped and went in and got his little white poodle and put it alongside of me. It was powdered and perfumed, had a pearl necklace around its neck and green ribbons in its ears and I looked at him. And he looked at me. Now I love animals but I wanted to make my point with him, and I said, 'Gr-r-r-r-r get this thing out of here, I don't want anything like that sitting next to me.' He said, 'What's the matter?' I said, 'I'll go home to my wife and she'll say I was in a French whorehouse.' I said, 'Get this goddamn stinking poodle off. Chuck it in the back.'"

The buyer threw the poodle in the back seat, and Lou feigned a shiver and asked the guy how he could stand being around a piss-ant animal like that? Lou was laughing on the inside, enjoying every minute of the buyer's discomfort.

It took a trip to an office, then to a bank in Pompano Beach for Lou to finally get his money.

"I had the bill of sale, which I had made out. I had it inside my shirt. I had no briefcase or anything. There was a great deal of confusion. At 10 minutes to seven he says, 'Here he comes, here he comes.' And the investor came with his son. Now this is a fellow that he had just met at a bar two nights ago, and the bank manager came to me and said, 'Have you got a bill of sale?' I said, 'Yeah, I got a bill of sale, and I want a bank draft. I don't want any check or anything like that. I want a bank draft from you, certified.' So he said, 'Well, we'll see what we can do.' So they went in a huddle around and then finally they came out and the bank manager gave me a bank draft, and I handed over the bill of sale.

"It was 7:00 then, and that's pretty late. So then I said, 'Let's go across the street and have a drink and settle this thing up.' And our friend the buyer said, 'Oh I can't do that. I got to go to another bank and put in some money against my wife's alimony or I'll be put in jail.' So I said, 'That's good.' I walked out and that's the last time I saw him. I said, 'Your boat's down there. Now go and take her.' And I had stripped everything, like her tools and equipment. I just went back to her and got a duffel of clothes and a few things and that was it."

Before the sale of *Pikes Arm*, Lou had purchased *Physalia*, a 68-foot motorsailer. He was aboard his new vessel two days after closing on the freighter when he received a phone call from the new *Pikes Arm* owner. He accused Lou of selling him a vessel with a bad clutch. The new skipper was a yachtsman and did not understand that *Pikes Arm* was a small ship, not a large yacht. Her clutch could only be engaged when the engine was at idle. The new captain, in order to keep her stationary while waiting for the bridges to open along the Miami River, alternately slammed her into forward and reverse to compensate for the current. Of course, the clutch quickly failed.

"...and I said, 'Well it's nothing to do with me; you bought her 'as is, where is,' and it was running when you got her. But today is Sunday and it's two days later and you broke her up and that's your problem. So call Caterpillar and get them to come and fix it.'"

Pikes Arm was subsequently seized as a marijuana runner, and Lou never heard of her again.

So ends this day.

Figure 11-1.

The ship: *Sea Fox* (ex-*Physalia*, ex-*Hal-Wan* II)

Year of Launching: 1940

Rig: Ketch–Motorsailer

Builder: Casey Boat Building, Fairhaven, Massachusetts

Engine: Superior Diesel 150 hp, replaced by GM 671 in 1961

Material: Mahogany planked over oak frames

Length overall: 62 feet 9 inches, lengthened in 1961 to 67 feet 9 inches

Beam: 16 feet

Draft: 6 feet 2 inches

Tonnage: 40

Chapter 11   Motorsailer *Sea Fox*

Designed by Furnan's Yacht Agency, Sea Fox *so resembled the famous Hand motorsailers that it is thought William Hand may have been working for Furnan's at the time of* Sea Fox's *original design. While she was based in Boston, several owners cruised her through New England waters. Robert Smith of San Francisco bought her and entered her in the charter trade in the Virgin Islands.*

Sea Fox *is still alive and well in Beaufort, North Carolina.*

* * *

On May 15, 1971, 60-year-old Lou Kenedy took possession of the 68-foot motorsailer, *Physalia,* while he was still running *Pikes Arm* during that seemingly-interminable escrow that lasted for over four months. He made sure work on *Physalia* had begun and took time to steam up the New River in Fort Lauderdale to Ellis Diesel for an engine rebuild.

Patsy's husband had done the survey on the ketch, and except for a worn-out 200-horsepower main engine and a frozen six-kilowatt generator, she was beautifully maintained. The interior mahogany joinery was magnificent, and the engine room was capacious. Being a motorsailer, she had over-sized fuel and water tanks. The ketch rigging was a little short, so Pat and Lou could easily handle her alone. She was mahogany-planked over sawn oak frames with bronze fastenings and teak decks and deckhouses. She drew only six feet two inches which perfectly suited cruising in the Bahamas, where the family was still based. Her below-water lines were much like a miniature fishing schooner; most dimensions were exactly half of those of the old salt-bankers. Lou had never lived ashore full time and wasn't about to start now; *Physalia* was to be his retirement home.

The machinations of the purchase of *Physalia* were vintage Kenedy. He made an offer on her he thought was ridiculously low. This offer was so low, the broker said it was an insult but was duty bound to present it to the owner who lived in San Francisco. The absentee owner quickly accepted the price so Lou rethought his offer and decided he must be paying too much. He called the owner and said he was taking $5,000 off the price under the guise that he had to rename the vessel and, of course, renaming a ship is bad luck.

"And I said, 'How the devil can a vessel be called Physalia*? You get it on the radio and say, 'This is the* Physalia*.' People would laugh and I'd laugh and I'd even be ashamed to say it.'*

And he said, 'Oh no. He says Physalia*—that's beautiful name! Don't you know what it means?' I said, 'No I don't know what it means.' He says, 'That's the name of a jellyfish.' 'Well I damn well don't want my vessel named after a jellyfish!' I said, 'I think I'll take more than $5,000 off.' Anyway, $5,000 came off, and I got the vessel, and I changed her name to* Sea Fox, *following on the tradition of the first* Sea Fox*."*

* * *

Pat and Lou got working. The diesel rebuild was quickly completed along with the installation of a new generator. By the middle of July, *Sea Fox* was seaworthy. Now that *Pikes Arm* was sold, the Kenedys loaded the ketch with food and provisions and headed across the Gulf Stream for Nassau. As soon as they arrived, they moved out and sold the Nassau house and stowed their belongings aboard permanently. Rosie was ensconced in the forepeak. In an extraordinary spate of extravagance, Lou signed a deckhand and *Sea Fox* cleared for Nova Scotia.

The trip is mostly remembered for the quantity of fish caught while in the Gulf Stream and Lou's blind navigation of *Sea Fox* to within earshot of the LaHave bell buoy after a day and a half of steaming in a pea-soup fog.

> "'Well,' I said to Rosie, 'At a quarter to nine we should hear the LaHave bell buoy.' And she said, 'What if you don't hear it?' And I said, 'Well, if we don't hear it at quarter to nine, we'll stop the engine and listen carefully to see if we can hear it then.' And she agreed, but she was kind of skeptical. And the other fellow was on the bow on lookout and Rosie said, 'Well, it's quarter to nine now, and I don't see anything.' And just then the man on the bow said, 'Vessel right ahead, vessel right ahead.' Of course, we were blowing our horn and everything, and we slowed down, and at 0846 we skidded 20 yards past the LaHave bell buoy. It wasn't a vessel he saw at all but it was the bell buoy, and Rosie said, 'Does that happen all the time?' 'Well,' I said, 'We won't go into that but it happened this time, didn't it?'"

A couple of weeks before, Lou had sent a postcard to a friend in Dayspring estimating this day for his arrival. As Lou continued working *Sea Fox* up the LaHave which was still thick-a-fog, Himmelman's wharf finally appeared through the mist. The skipper saw a man on the dock raising colorful ship's signal flags just as *Sea Fox* approached.

> "We saw somebody at the end of the wharf hoisting a bunch of code flags and all. And I thought, well I wonder what Lawrence is doing here with all those flags as I came along. I said, 'What are you doing with those flags, Lawrence? Are you having a yacht race or something?' He says, 'No, I'm putting them up for you.' I said, 'Well, what are you doing that for?' 'Well,' he said, 'we heard you would be here this morning.' And I said, 'Boy, you really took my word literally.' But he was hoisting those flags just as we were coming in. That was quite a thrill all right, arriving in LaHave with a welcoming party after all these years."

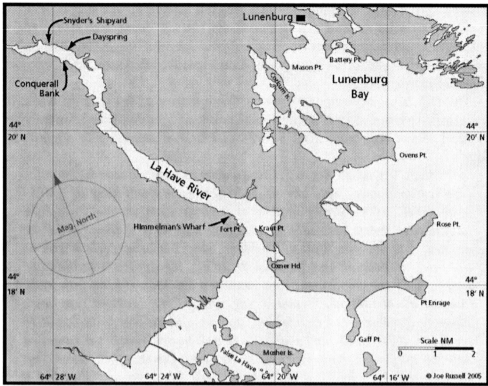

Figure 11-2. Chart: LaHave/Lunenburg area.

Lawrence Himmelman was famous for more than just free dockage; his chickens were famous with the Kenedy family, especially with Rosie:

"We were tied up at the Himmelman's dock in LaHave one summer and Mr. Himmelman was taking us to town [Bridgewater] unaware that there was a chicken in the back of his truck. Well, it fell out and I saw it fall and told Mr. Himmelman to stop the truck so we could rescue this chicken who was bleeding from his beak. We took the chicken back to Sea Fox *and was immediately informed by Dad that this chicken COULD NOT come aboard. I was crying and cuddling the chicken, so Dad relented somewhat and built a lean-to on the dock for this chicken. Everyday Dad wanted to know if the chicken was getting fat because he was going into Mumma's stew soon. I named him Mr. Stew. Worried that Dad really meant Mr. Stew for the pot, I would each morning bring out some eggs from the refrigerator and place them in Mr. Stew's nest. Then I would run to Daddy. 'Daddy, Daddy, Mr. Stew has laid some eggs.' Everyone would laugh and carry on. As I gave these eggs to Daddy, he would ask, 'Why are these eggs so cold?' I tried to explain*

how cold Nova Scotia is in the morning, et cetera, but one day there really WAS an egg and as I went running to tell Mum and Dad, with Mr. Himmelman there for coffee, they were all laughing, because Dad had put the egg there. He had pulled it out of the refer the night before!"[*]

Within a few days, Lou coasted over to Teddy Snyder's yard for some refitting and especially to build a workbench and chests for his tools and equipment. Maintaining *Sea Fox* in yacht condition was a full time occupation, and Pat and Lou took the job seriously. A Wood Freeman autopilot was installed during this refit. Lou considered the autopilot the same as an extra unpaid crewmen, because it steered all the time.

Figure 11-3. Pat and Lou at Teddy's Shipyard, Dayspring, Nova Scotia. Photo by Linda Mason. (Used by permission.)

Sea Fox under Pat and Lou fell into a cruising routine that was relied upon by scores of friends from Lunenburg to Nassau. Every year, *Sea Fox* departed the LaHave in late October and stayed just ahead of the cold air as it descended from the Canadian Maritimes. Then, during the spring, *Sea Fox*

---

[*] Quotations from the Kenedy family and friends in this chapter and the Epilogue are all from conversations with the author.

made the return trip just behind the warm air as it filled northward, and she arrived back in the LaHave to enjoy the summer and the local yacht club activities.

Every October, when starting south, if the weather turned nasty, the first stop was Shelburne, Nova Scotia to visit friends and wait for better conditions before crossing the Gulf of Maine to Cape Cod. After transiting the Cape Cod Canal, *Sea Fox* usually steamed up Narragansett Bay and tied up at a friend's dock in East Greenwich, Rhode Island.

Continuing to New York, Pat and Lou anchored off City Island or Sandy Hook—slips were too expensive—then proceeded down the Jersey Coast and up the Delaware Bay and through the Chesapeake Canal. The next stop was usually at Zahnaiser's Marine on Solomon's Island in Maryland, where they had friends. They usually stayed for a couple of weeks to visit with Brian and his family, who lived nearby.

Brian recalls a typical visit:

"Sea Fox *never arrived at the Solomon's Island dock that Dad didn't have some chore waiting for me.*

"One blustery day, Sea Fox *arrived when the water temperature was still about 45 degrees. As soon as we got there, he announced that he had hit a log or something out in the bay, and he felt he might have damaged one of the blades on the prop. He said he didn't want to spend the money for a haulout until he was sure that there was damage, and someone would have to go over the side and check it out. He said it was no big deal and that I should have no problem inspecting the prop and shaft. I told him it was cold and I damned well wasn't going over the side in freezing, murky waters where I couldn't see three feet in front of me. He said, 'You don't need to see anything, you can feel for the problem.' I said, 'No way.'*

"Five minutes later he showed up on deck with a quart of Mount Gay rum and said, 'Let's have a drink, son.' I said, 'OK.' He then kind of mumbled, 'Hell, me and Guy Earle went over the side in Carbonear, Newfoundland in December, by God, and that water was a damned sight colder than it is here.' By now, I had had two drinks of the skipper's version of a small toddy—a triple hooker of rum with a splash of water—but I still held out. Predictably, four drinks later I was over the side in a pair of pajamas feeling around the propeller and shaft checking for damage. Sure enough, a blade was bent. I came up gasping for air and made the announcement. He thanked me and said he only had one more chore.

"The masthead light was burned out, and he needed me to go aloft in a bos'ns chair and replace it. Still shivering from the last job, I went aloft in the chair—by now it was blowing 30 knots—and I hung on to whatever rigging I could get my hands on. He sent me up a cigar box filled with paraphernalia that looked like it came from the Smithsonian. Included in the box were about 50 light bulbs of varying sizes and wattage. I tried them all while hanging on with one hand. None of them worked. I yelled down, 'None of them fits.' So he asked me to drop the used one and also my car keys, which I did. Then he told me that he was going to the store to get a bulb and he'd be back in about 15 minutes.

"An hour and a half later he showed up. I had been dangling up there for what seemed like an eternity. He then announced that this bulb was pretty common but expensive, and he had to go to eight stores before he could find one that was reasonably priced. I finished the job, then the bottle of Mount Gay."

Deagle's Marine Railway in Deltaville, Virginia was the next stop. Patsy explains:

"Captain Deagle and the skipper would sit under the big tree in the yard and pass an afternoon reminiscing about the good old days, telling a few lies and sea stories."

The Intracoastal Waterway begins at Norfolk, and being blue-water sailors, the Waterway was an eerie change for the Kenedys. They sailed mile after mile with a shoreline close aboard, port and starboard.

"All our life was spent at sea, and this inland waterway was an intriguing change for us where we had land on both sides and close— right landlocked—something different than we had ever done before, so it was kind of a novelty and a challenge of piloting, because it's continuously weaving in and out of channels, rivers, bays, and things, and it was appealing to us."

One of Lou's favorite stretches of the Waterway was the trip through the Great Dismal Swamp Canal. This, the oldest operating canal in the United States, connects the Chesapeake Bay near Norfolk to Albemarle Sound in North Carolina. Albemarle Sound is a broad body of water that, along with Pamlico Sound, makes up a significant portion of the north end of the Intracoastal Waterway. George Washington had logging interests in the area

Figure 11-4. Navigating Great Dismal Swamp Canal. The canal runs from outside Norfolk to Albemarle Sound in North Carolina.

and visited the Great Dismal Swamp. He was apparently one of those who suggested it be drained for the construction of a canal to connect Virginia with North Carolina. However, the popular tale that the first president-to-be directed the surveying and excavation apparently is not true. The canal was initially 22 miles long, 60 feet wide, and 6.5 feet deep.

On one trip through the swamp, *Sea Fox* was already 15 miles into the canal when Army Corps of Engineers personnel informed Lou there were sections being dredged where the depth was only 4.5 to 5.5 feet. This area was well known for shoaling due to drifting sand. When Lou reached the area where little boats were doing the dredging, a skiff came alongside and a worker handed the captain a sketch-chart of what had been dredged and what had not. The drawing looked like a snake inside of a snake with lines for each shore and a serpentine line between them showing the right course to avoid grounding.

This little chart indicated there was one spot that was too shallow for *Sea Fox,* and the canal was too narrow for Lou to turn her around. The Corps of Engineers worker said that the shallows were very soft sand.

"So I said, 'Well there's no way I can turn around and go back so I'm going to give her a try.' So we edged up to this one place, the way they had it charted, we had to go right up against the bank on one side so that her topsides were brushing the grass. And we got through, but very slowly, and then we came to where it was this 3.5 to 4 foot area. It seemed to be the way they showed it, in a ridge. So I opened her wide open and pounded into this thing, and I figured if I got stuck I'd put my anchor chains out to trees ashore and heave her with the windlass as well as the engine."

Sea Fox worked slowly though the sand with the engine at flank speed, churning up the bottom and making a muddy mess of the canal.

"But anyway she worked slowly, slowly along. We wiggled through this thing at about half a knot and just before we got clear of it, the mate

hollered, 'Look astern!' And astern they had these flat boats and rowboats and the wash from my propeller swamped them and turned them upside-down. It was a great mess. I was glad we got through and kept on going, before the owners of these boats came running to find out what caused all this devastation. But we certainly pushed through some bunch of sand that time. I'll never forget that."

After Elizabeth City at the end of the Great Dismal Swamp, it was down to Beaufort, North Carolina. Beaufort is a seafaring town adjacent to Moorhead City. There were no fees to use the old Beaufort Docks on Taylor Creek in Lou's time aboard *Sea Fox*, but today they sport all new floating slips, Internet access, loaner cars for running errands, and three-phase 100 Amp power. Today, Lou would pass up Beaufort Docks.

The rest of the trip to the Bahamas was much of the same—day tripping all the way to Florida and tying up at friends' docks, or any dock that was unattended, then crossing the Gulf Stream over to Nassau.

Several times during the 14 years the annual migration took place, Lou signed on crew to help out. These crewmembers were rarely paid, but were given the chance of working for the "experience." One such poor bastard was a talented dentist named Bill Munton. He was signed on specifically to work on Lou's teeth during the month-long trip up to Nova Scotia. The skipper's teeth were in dire need of a deep and thorough cleaning. Bill or Doc, as he was called, looked forward to the trip. In between seeing to Lou's dental problems, he wanted to help in the galley and perhaps take a trick at the wheel. Patsy recalls:

"Well, the skipper had him up at the crack of dawn to wipe down the varnish and get the coffee going, help get underway, steer most of the time, make engine room checks, do some painting and varnishing, and then get to the teeth... if there was time. It was about a month trip north in the Intracoastal, stopping at various places to visit friends. Doc really enjoyed the trip, meeting new people and seeing new places. Arriving in Nova Scotia, with the teeth all better, the skipper didn't even give Doc plane fare home."

The interesting subtexts of this yearly trek are really the countless ways Lou avoided paying dockage, and the annual family reunions Pat and Lou attended, reunions that now included grandchildren. These winter reunions with Pat and Lou aboard *Sea Fox* are still among the cherished recollections of the Kenedy clan.

Tiffany, Gabrielle's daughter, remembers learning to tie her shoes and tell time. But best of all,

"Granddaddy was the best jokester and it was always exciting when April Fool's rolled around. One year he called to tell us there was a polar bear drifting down the LaHave River on a piece of ice that had broken off...what should he do? We were beside ourselves, and we soon called back to give him our advice only to get the greeting 'APRIL FOOL.' One year, he placed a phony can of spilled oil on the cabin sole; it looked real, but wasn't. It was positioned so that everyone coming aboard thought they tipped it over, and he would pretend to get mad at them for knocking over his oil can. We all got good laughs from that one. We all loved our special Valentine's cards that he hand made, and he never missed a year."

* * *

Figure 11-5. *Sea Fox* **tied up at Jones Fruit Company dock, Wabasso, Florida.**

When *Sea Fox* tied up, it was always at a friend's wharf, or else Lou expertly timed his arrival to tie up at a marina after business hours, to avoid any unpleasant attempts to extract moorage fees. Of course, *Sea Fox* always set sail before the harbormaster's office reopened in the morning.

Just north of Vero Beach, in Wabasso, Florida, Jones Fruit Company allowed yachts to tie up free if they bought some fruit. Lou always bought a couple of oranges and then spent the night. In later years, the fruit company abandoned the free-dockage policy for all vessels—except, of course, *Sea Fox*.

Once, south of Charleston, Lou tied the ketch up for the night at a private dock with a home on the shore behind it. Lou had surreptitiously moored there for years. Since he never saw a light on in the house, he figured it was abandoned. One spring evening, on a north-bound trip, an unknown couple sauntered down the dock and the man said, "Do you use this dock often?" Lou gushed, "Yes, we love this dock, found it several years ago, and overnight here every year on the way down from Nova Scotia and again on the way back." "Well, that's interesting. We own this dock," the elderly man said. Lou didn't skip a beat and said, "Well, this is a damn fine dock you have here and we thank you for building it." The man replied, "We're not here much but we love for you to enjoy the dock as we love looking at your vessel. Give us a little notice, and we'll leave the electricity on for you each year when you arrive." They exchanged addresses, and Lou slipped through the noose again.

* * *

Up many of the rivers and other sections of the Intracoastal Waterway there are bridges that adhere to restricted opening times. Commercial vessels, like tugs in tow, however, do not have to wait for the scheduled opening time, and the bridge is opened upon request. So as Lou Kenedy was wont to do, he always scheduled his arrival at the bridges to coincide with the raising time. If he missed it, he would wait for another vessel, get together with the skipper, throw him a line, and tow him under the bridge as though he was a commercial tug. That way, they both got under the span before the scheduled opening.

* * *

When stressed, Pat Kenedy had the habit of silently stealing below to her cabin, lying down, and sprinkling 4-711 Cologne on her forehead. Closing her eyes, she breathed in the scent and thought of better places. Maybe Isla Aves and her baby turtles would come to mind. Knowing what we now know of Lou Kenedy, Pat's anti-stress procedure seems perfectly logical.

A favorite Bahamas destination for *Sea Fox* was Sampson Cay. Daughter Rosie and her husband, Marcus, owned the island and, of course, always provided free dockage. One year during a departure from the Cay, the crew were at stations. Pat was at her usual post astern with a boat hook to fend off the dinghy as Lou reversed *Sea Fox* from the berth. After reversing clear of the slip, Lou gave a heavy burst of forward power with hard left rudder to kick the bow to port, followed by more reverse. This time, however, this back and fill maneuvering stretched the dinghy painter as tight as a fiddle string that slackened as the small boat shot back toward the stern of *Sea Fox*. Trying her best, Pat jammed the barbed end of the boat hook against the dinghy's bottom, wedged it under the seat, and she braced the other end beneath *Sea Fox*'s rub rail. The boat hook punched through the bottom and a geyser erupted from the dinghy's sole just as *Sea Fox*'s engine inexplicably stalled. Luckily, Teddy Snyder, of Dayspring, was aboard and he threw a line to an idler ashore and *Sea Fox* was slowly hand-lined back to the dock. The captain and crew collected at the stern and found the dinghy and its outboard were sunk, her painter firmly wrapped around *Sea Fox*'s shaft, and the boat hook floating away. Pat was below in her berth, dabbing 4-711 on her forehead.

This early, homespun aromatherapy was always effective; in an hour or so she cheerfully returned to the deck refreshed and regrouped.

Another example of Pat Kenedy's independence and resolve was recounted by Lou's grandson, Brian Jr.:

"When I was 16, circa 1976, I went to visit Granny and Granddad in the Bahamas. While fishing, I caught a good sized fish, and as I brought it to the surface, a barracuda followed it up. When the barracuda struck the hapless fish, Granny stood up. Taking an oar in both hands, bringing it overhead, she smashed the oar down on the barracuda with tremendous force. As the oar struck the barracuda across its back, water exploded everywhere and she exclaimed, 'You son-of-a-bitch!' And from that point forward, we had no more trouble with barracuda on the reef."

* * *

From Gabrielle we get the following insight into these *Sea Fox* days:

"The absolute, most memorable times with my girls, Tiffany and Sabrina, was when they ran down the dock in December to greet Dad and Mum on Sea Fox *as she arrived in Nassau. This was usually around December 18, Mum's birthday. Then we prepared to spend Christmas day at our house. On occasion, Bill and Patsy, Dad, Mum, Rosie, Marcus, and their kids—Melissa, David, Lauren, and Amanda—along with Tiffany and Sabrina gleefully opened presents that were piled high as a mountain. Good friends would drop in for some morning bubbly and later we'd cook up a storm while arguing with Mum about when to put the turkey on or finding out if Patsy will burn the sweet potato pie this year, all the while keeping Rosie's children from eating all the smoked salmon and sipping on the bubbly.*

"Every year for 10 years, my husband, our two daughters, and I left aboard Sea Fox *the day after Christmas for a week in the Exumas, mostly on Staniel Cay. There was no greater holiday before or since. New Year's Eve at the Happy People Marina on Staniel is an experience never to be missed. Our whole family has great friends on Staniel Cay and a deep love for the beautiful people there.*

"There were several occasions that the girls and I met Sea Fox *in an easy-to-get-to port and cruised with Dad and Mum for awhile. It was a great learning experience for the girls as Mum always had a kiss ready and, "Let's play dress up." And there was the ever-present smell of*

Edgeworth tobacco coming from the deckhouse, where one might run in for one's favorite bear hug from Dad."

Lou considered the Bahamas to be the ideal cruising grounds. It was his idea of heaven for those who enjoy boats and solitude.

Figure 11-6. At anchor in the Exumas, Bahamas.

"We'd catch plenty of fish, either hand line, fish-pot, or trolling, and that would be our main staple. The wife is a good cook and she enjoyed making pies and bread and all those things, so we lived a great life, and we had two daughters living there married with their children, one of which, Rosie, ended up owning Sampson Cay and flying about in their own airplanes.

"In the Bahamas, where there were boat building centers, it was really quite a life, quite a bit different from when we were going to sea. People think sailing in the Bahamas is 'going to sea,' but to us that wasn't going to sea, it was just enjoying ourselves with boats, just all inshore work as far as I was concerned."

Though his enthusiasm for sailing, exploring, smuggling, and drinking never waned, even the incredible Captain Kenedy had to finally accept the natural processes of aging. After a second hip replacement, he admitted he needed additional crew for the annual treks north and south. Of course, competent crew members were hard to come by as the skipper refused to offer wages. He would say, "It's for the experience, you know." Then, he would work them to death.

Frank and Debbie Knight of Vineyard Haven spent several winters in the Bahamas aboard *Sea Fox* "for the experience." By the time they moved on, they had completely stripped, painted, and varnished the entire interior of the ketch. At the same time, they stood watches at the wheel, cleaned up the galley, and kept the deck area in Bristol fashion.

* * *

Figure 11-7. Lou and ship's dog Thor riding in dinghy. Photo by Dick Juppenlatz, February 1980, near Staniel Cay, Exuma. (Used by permission.)

At age 75, the circulation in the captain's legs was beginning to give him trouble. He found it hard to maintain *Sea Fox* in yacht condition. He would never allow her to be in any condition less than perfect. Caulking decks and painting the topsides became more and more difficult as time went on. And finally Pat and Lou put *Sea Fox* on the market, but without a broker. The winter of 1985 was spent in Marathon, Florida, with dockage courtesy of Patsy and Bill. They all worked together to bring *Sea Fox* up to top notch condition and began removing Pat's and Lou's personal gear in anticipation of *Sea Fox*'s sale.

"A man came along and I did my pitch and I said, 'As is, where is, and that's it!' And I had another fellow looking at it at the same time and I played one against the other and the one who came first got it, and that's what happened. And I agreed to deliver her up to Deltaville, Virginia."

* * *

A few miles north of the Wolf Trap light, after passing Gwynn Island, he turned into the channel at green marker #3. Lou moored the big ketch at Deagle's in Fishing Bay at Deltaville. The problem now was unloading 14 years of gear, tools, and memories. There was enough gear left aboard to fill a Volkswagen van. They loaded it so full that the springs were completely compressed; it was a rough ride from Virginia to their newly-purchased home in Dayspring.

So ends this day.

> *For the longest time, I thought everyone's grandfather captained three-masted schooners. Granddad actually looked the part of the Sea Captain: tall, weathered, and strong.*
> Jennifer Kenedy Lohnes
>
> *You could see the sea on his skin and the days of work in his calluses.*
> Sabrina Lightbourn

Epilogue

After selling *Sea Fox*, Pat and Lou settled into their house at Dayspring. Lou began having serious difficulty maneuvering, for his diabetes was taking its toll. But the captain's cantankerous personality, maritime superstitions, and sense of humor never waned, not a bit; neither did his love of ships and the sea.

"People often asked me about my favorite ship, and I guess it would be like asking a man who has been married 11 times which of his wives he liked the best. He probably liked a lot of them, and I certainly liked Abundance. *She was my first, and I guess she'd be about my favorite. But then, of course, I liked* Sea Fox—*the one I had so much adventure with, Two-Gun Cerulli and all, and she was such a marvelous sailer. The only thing against her was that I liked bigger vessels, but at the time, she was just right for the trade and for making a living during the Depression. I was very fond of* Wawaloam *because I put so much personal work into her, re-rigging her and re-decking her and restoring her. And, of course, then again every one had a different charm.* City of New York *had the ruggedness and the strength of an ox, and when you're out to sea in her, you were in walls of oak. You felt that you were in perfect security. She wasn't the fastest, and she wasn't the prettiest, but she surely was the strongest. So it's pretty hard to say. I never had* Vema *long enough to get attached to her really, but she was big and she was doing funny work, this scientific work. That kind of work I wasn't too keen on. But I loved them all as long as they were sailing vessels."*

Sea Fox's sale was timely as Lou encountered more and more difficulty getting around the house on the LaHave River. But his sense of humor was still evident when according to daughter Patsy:

"We were up from Florida for a visit in the summer of 1986 celebrating Mum's and Dad's 50th wedding anniversary. Daddy suggested we drive over to the cemetery in Lunenburg so he could pick out a couple of plots for Mum's and his final journey. We arrived at the cemetery's modest office, and a little troll-like caretaker scuttled out to the car. Explaining what we wanted, the gnome grabbed up a vacancy listing, mounted a bicycle, and signaled us to follow. Not far up the road he stopped and dismounted. Halting at some available real estate, he began extolling its virtues. Shortly, Daddy said, 'Stop! Listen.' We all stood still. 'Hear all that traffic noise?' said Lou, 'Far too noisy, this'll never do.' So we continued our quest until two peaceful plots were presented."

Figure E-1. Pat and Lou's 50th anniversary celebration aboard 120-foot *Albert* in the LaHave River, Nova Scotia.

Later that fall, a tax bill arrived for the house in Dayspring. Lou called and complained, explaining to the tax assessor the increase couldn't possibly apply to him, as his property was in Lunenburg, not Dayspring, and giving the assessor the cemetery's address. He never heard another word from the tax collector. Amen.

Diabetes finally cut off the circulation in his left leg and amputation was required. Awakening after the surgery, he called for the attending doctor immediately. "Whadya do with my left leg?" he growled. The doctor started a surgical discourse which Lou interrupted. "No, I mean where is it?" The sawbones said it would be disposed of properly. Lou snapped, "The hell you say. I want that leg delivered to the Lunenburg Cemetery for burial exactly north and south, or I'll be all fiddled for the rest of my days!" His wishes were obeyed, and he maintained a steady course, telling sailing yarns to the many well-wishers who visited the house.

The only real lament of Lou Kenedy's life is expressed in a discussion with a friend before he died:

"It is real sailing vessels that you won't see anymore. Any that might be built and sailed, will be all play-acting boats. They won't be the real McCoy, that run on grit and economy and hard work. They'll all have to be subsidized with no money worries. And they won't be run by men who were brought up in the Age of Sail. There won't be anybody to teach anybody, so how will they ever learn? Because that tradition is gone. But the essence of it—now what should I say?—the spirit of it will carry on by the dedicated men in the museums, especially the Fisheries Museum. That will keep the memories and the essence of this stuff going for future generations to read about, but they will never be able to experience it again, and they won't see the ships on the sea anymore, which is all too bad. But that's the way it goes."

Captain Lou Kenedy signed articles and cleared for Fiddler's Green July 25, 1991 at age 81.

So ends his days.

Acknowledgements

People are pleased to help with research when writing about a giant personality like Captain Kenedy. Nonetheless, many individuals went yet another extra mile to make sure this book is factual, interesting, and conveys the essence of Lou Kenedy and his times.

First, of course, are Patsy and Bill Bolling. Without them, this project simply wouldn't have happened. Patsy in particular spent months researching questions I had about inconsistencies in the retelling of 70-year-old events. She and Bill also kept me abreast of schooner nomenclature that was unique to Lou's ships.

Howard Brady, my editor, molded the original manuscript and in so doing, made me a better writer.

Family and friends of the captain were generous with their time. They sent me many of the stories that make retelling Lou Kenedy tales a quay-side tradition from Nova Scotia to Barbados. I'll simply list them here, well aware that I will accidentally omit many who deserve mention:

Gil Plumb, who supplied details and a drawing of *Wawaloam*'s 6-71 being started with a rope; Raynell Smith, curator of the Deltaville Museum, and her husband, Kaptain Krunch; Gloria Greco, for allowing me to use her wonderful painting of the sinking of *Wawaloam*; Ralph D. Getson, curator of the Fisheries Museum in Lunenburg whose interviews with the captain before his death were instrumental to this project; Linda Mason, who wrote several articles about Lou for newspapers in both Bridgewater and Halifax, and who contributed several important photographs; and Emily Johnson at *The Saturday Evening Post*.

Many others contributed, some without knowing it: Barry Rofihe, Jimmy Porter, David Himmelman, Skip Zahniser, Jim Robars, John Rumsey, Frank Knight, Barbara and Sherman Zwicker, Dr. William Munton, Captain Joe Maggio, Jeff Thomas, Peggy Crimmins, Sonny Pryde, Patrick Morris, and Roger Vaughan.

Special thanks to *The Barbados Advocate*, Barbados Yacht Club, *The Stamford Advocate*, *The Quincy Patriot-Ledger*, and *Southern Boating* for historical documents and insight.

I thank Sue Combs for her unflagging support of this and many other projects; of course, Lola and Harold Russell, my folks, who always encourage my efforts no matter how far afield they might take me; and all those who crossed Lou Kenedy's path to become part of his life and sea stories.

Glossary*

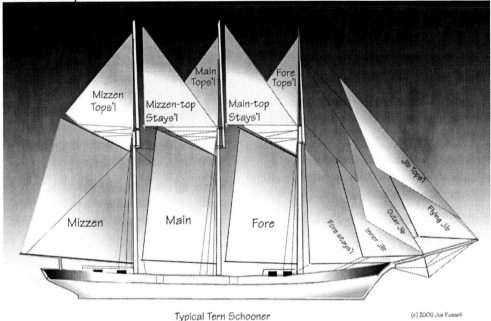

Figure G-1. Tern schooner sail nomenclature.

Ablative paint. Bottom paint that prevents marine growth by sloughing its layers as compared to a copper-based paint that poisons the organisms as they adhere to the hull.

Articles (of Agreement). A contract between ship owner (or owner's agent) and seaman stating terms, wages, etc.

Athwartship. Across the ship from one side to the other.

Bajan. (rhymes with occasion) n. A native of Barbados.

Baldheaded. Said of a *schooner* when she has no *topmasts* or has removed them.

Batten. On large *schooners*, pieces of sawn lumber used to secure hatch tarpaulins. In modern sailboats, thin battens are inserted into pockets sewn into the *leech* to preserve the sail's shape while under way.

Beam. The extreme width of a vessel.

Beaufort wind scale. The mariner's system of quantifying the sea state and the force of the wind. Stated, for example, as "Force 4 winds" or "A force 10 storm." (See Appendix 1.)

Before the mast. A reference to the position of common sailors who reside in the fo'c's'le, forward of the foremast.

*Words italicized in definitions appear separately defined.

Bend. v. To rig sails on masts, *boom*s, or *gaffs*. n. A type of nautical knot.

Block. A mechanical device for moving an object, consisting of a frame, pulley, pin, and cheeks.

Bollard. A large, well-secured post for making fast *hawsers* and mooring lines.

Boltrope. A rope sewn into the edge of sails to aid in resolving wind and running-rigging loads.

Boom. *Spar* for extending the foot of a sail in *fore-and-aft* rigged vessels.

Boom lift. (Topping lift) A line extending from the top of the mast to the end of the *boom*.

Bow. The forward end of a ship or boat (usually the pointy end). (See s*tern*.)

Box the compass. Recite the 32 points of the compass (each point is 11 ¼ degrees apart) starting from north and proceeding clockwise. (See Appendix 2.)

Breast hook. A "V" shaped timber or iron installed at the *bow*s to reinforce the connection of each side of a vessel.

Bristol fashion. The highest quality standard of workmanship and organization aboard a vessel.

Broach. To turn a vessel broadside to seas and weather. In heavy weather, broaching can cause her to capsize.

Bulwark. The part of a vessel's side that extends above the weather deck.

Bumboat. A small boat that sidles up to ships at anchor to sell supplies and provisions and sometimes shore boat service.

Cabotage. Literally, "coastal navigation and trade," it has become the term used for a country's system of protecting its shipping industry by not allowing foreign vessels to run trade or passenger routes from one port of the country to another.

Careen. To ground a vessel to perform maintenance on the exterior of the hull before refloating her at next high tide.

Careenage. A shallow where a vessel is grounded to expose her bottom and sides for maintenance or repair. Or a quay designed specifically for vessels to moor in order to perform maintenance on the bottom when the tide recedes.

Cathead. A *beam*, fitted with a sheave projecting from the bows of a vessel, used as a crane to lift the anchor. Thus the term, "catting the anchor."

Chandler. (Originally pronounced "candler") A store that sells ship's supplies and provisions.

Clew. After corner of a *fore-and-aft* sail.

Coamings. Vertical flanges around cargo hatches to keep water from passing into the hold or cockpit verticals.

Companionway. Stairway leading below decks.

Cranky. Said of a vessel that is unstable and unresponsive to the helm due to bad design or improper loading, usually overloading.

Cruzan. (rhymes with contusion) A native of St. Croix.

Davit. Crane or arms with rigging to lift a small boat, anchor, or accommodation ladder aboard.

Ded reckoning. The manner of determining a ship's position by deduced reckoning, using course steered and distance run. Also known as "dead reckoning."

Deadeye. A wooden *block* with several holes to accept and adjust the lower ends of standing rigging.

Demurrage. Penalties paid to a ship owner for delays caused by the charterer.

Depth of hold. The vertical measurement of the cargo compartment from lowest point to the underside of the weather deck.

Donkey's breakfast. A traditional sailor's mattress stuffed with hay.

Draft. The measurement of the depth from a vessel's waterline to the lowest point of her keel.

Droger or Drogher. A slow, usually ill-found cargo vessel commonly used for carrying low value cargos (e.g., cattle droger or lumber droger).

Dunnage. Material used to facilitate proper stowage and protect cargo during the voyage.

Flake. Organizing rope or chain on deck or ashore by laying it out in rows of equal length for maintenance. (Sometimes confused with "faking" which is to lay line or rope in a figure eight pattern to insure it runs freely.)

Flat. Expanse of low ground over which tidal waters flow.

Fleet. Not only does "fleet" describe a group of vessels controlled by the same entity, but it also, among other things, defines incremental movements or shifting of position of a vessel.

Fo'c's'le. (Fōk′səl) Contraction of "forecastle," a forward cabin that is traditionally a common sailor's quarters.

Foot. Bottom edge of a sail.

Force #. See *Beaufort wind scale*.

Fore-and-aft rigging. A sailing vessel rig, with all *booms* and *gaffs* connected at one end to the *masts;* thus the sails run parallel to the length of the ship.

Forepeak. Deck area at the bow, or more commonly, the small compartment immediately aft of the stem.

Forestaysail. A triangular sail set on the forestay, sometimes fitted to a *boom.*

Freeboard. The area of the hull above the waterline; distance from waterline to the deck.

Gaff. A *spar* including *jaws* which spreads the upper edge of a *fore-and-aft* sail.

Gaff rigged. A ship on which the large, lower sails are configured as in Figure G-1; the tops of the major lower sails are attached to a *gaff*.

Gaskets. Lines used to hold a furled sail to a *boom*, yard, *gaff*, or *spar*. A "gasketed" sail is furled and tied in place.

Glass. The nautical term for a barometer.

Gripes. Ropes or canvas used to secure deck gear, especially boats, to prevent them from coming unshipped in heavy weather.

Gudgeon. A metal eye or socket attached to the sternpost to receive the rudder *pintles*.

Gunwale. (pronounced, GUN-el) The uppermost heavy plank on the side of a hull.

Halyards. A single rope or purchase by which a sail is hoisted or set.

Handy billy. A short *block* and tackle (one single *block* and one double *block*) for general use about the deck.

Hawser. A large diameter line used for towing, warping, mooring, or tying up a vessel.

Hawsepipe. A lining in the opening in bulwarks of a vessel to allow cables or *hawsers* to lead to anchors or moorings.

Hog. To droop at both ends as a structurally strained vessel.

Hove to. Stopped with bow into the wind, maintaining this position with a sea anchor or by trimming sails.

Inwale. Interior longitudinal stringer running the full length of a vessel just below the rail.

Jaws. Forked end of a *gaff* or *boom* loosely gripping the mast.

Jibe. Changing the *tack* of a sailing vessel by bringing the stern through the wind. If sails are not carefully controlled, they can shift position violently as the direction of the wind's force on the sails changes.

Keelson. Structural stiffener above keel.

Kittitian. A native of St. Christopher, known in the Caribbean as St. Kitts.

Lazarette. A storage area aft, accessible through a hatch in the deck.

Leech. The trailing edge of a sail.

Length between perpendiculars. A cargo vessel's midline waterline length when fully loaded.

Lighter. A vessel used to load or unload a ship.

Logy. Slow, labored movement of a vessel.

Luff. n. The forward edge of a *fore-and-aft* rigged sail. v. To lose wind in a *fore-and aft* sail which causes it to flap.

Mast. Vertical *spar* that supports a sail and gear for spreading sail and working cargo.

Minister's eyebrows. The shredded bottoms of black storm clouds.

Mizzen. Aft-most *mast* on most *schooners* and all ketches and yawls.

Padeye. A ring attached to a reinforcing plate mounted to the vessel, usually used to attach a *block*.

Pan. An evaporation pond for the production of salt; a radio distress signal one step below SOS indicating a vessel is in danger.

Parcel. To wrap treated canvas, as if a bandage, along the lay of a rope or splice to prepare it for *serving*.

Peak halyard. Rope or purchase used to raise the outer end of a *gaff*. (See *throat halyard*)

Pin rails. Racks, often at the ship's side, built to hold belaying pins to secure *running rigging*.

Pintle. Vertical pin mounted on rudder that slides into a ring or socket (see *gudgeon*) attached to the rudder post. This combination of pintle*s* and *gudgeons* hinges the rudder.

Poop deck. A raised afterdeck.

Port tack. Sailing with the wind coming from the port (left) side of the vessel.

Pratique. Permission to go ashore after clearance by medical and sanitary officers. Hoisting the yellow "Q" flag is the recognized method of requesting the health officials to come aboard.

Puncheon. A wooden barrel or cask holding 84 U.S. or 72 Imp. gallons, which is twice the capacity of a standard wooden beer barrel.

Pungy schooner. A small, fine-lined, fast work boat developed in the eighteenth century for use on the Chesapeake Bay.

Quarter. The side of a vessel from amidships to the stern, or the direction quadrant from *beam* to aft.

Ratlines. (rát-lins) Permanently installed web of small ropes across a vessel's *shrouds* forming a series of steps providing a means for climbing aloft.

Rattle down. The installation of *ratlines*.

Road or roadstead. A place less sheltered than a harbor where ships may ride at anchor.

Rode. Cable, chain, and/or line for an anchor.

Rub rail. The external protective protrusion around the outermost part of a hull to prevent chafing.

Rudder head. The upper end of the *rudder stock* to which the tiller or quadrant is fitted.

Rudder stock. A vertical member to which the rudder blade is attached.

Running rigging. *Halyards*, sheets, and other lines used to readily adjust the sails during the normal course of sailing.

Saban. A native of the Caribbean island of Saba.

Salt-banker. A fishing *schooner* often used on the Grand Banks. (Term originated from salt carried aboard to preserve the catch.)

Samson post. (King post) A very sturdy post (bitt) in the bow to which lines may be attached (e.g., for towing a vessel).

Schooner. Various sailing vessels rigged *fore-and-aft* with two or more *masts* of the same height. In the case of a two-masted schooner, the fore *mast* is generally shorter than the main *mast*. Most schooners are *gaff-rigged*.

Scupper. An opening in the *bulwark* to allow water to drain from the *weather deck*.

Seize. To connect two lines or two ends of the same line together by wrapping *small stuff* tightly around them.

Serve. Twine or small cordage wound tightly around a splice, rope, or wire keeping the turns close together as protection against weather or chafing.

Sheers. An "A" frame used to *step masts*.

Shooks. A set of wood staves and heads needed to assemble a barrel or keg.

Shrouds. Rope or wire rigging that gives support to a bowsprit or *mast* in a *thwartship* direction.

Small stuff. Yarns and lines of less than one inch in circumference. (General term for small cordage used for light lashing.)

Sole. Floor of a cabin or cockpit.

Spanker. Nautical slang for the aftermost sail.

Spar. The traditional name for a rounded piece of lumber that makes up a *mast, gaff,* or *boom*.

Stanchion. A vertical member usually installed to hold man-lines or to retain cargo on deck.

Starboard tack. Sailing with the wind coming from the starboard (right) side of the vessel.

Stay. Rope or wire rigging that gives support to a bowsprit or *mast* in a *fore-and-aft* direction.

Steerageway. The minimum amount of headway necessary for a vessel to answer her helm.

Step. n. The fitting that carries the lower end of a *mast*. v. The act of installing a *mast*.

Stern. The extreme after end of a vessel. (See *bow*.)

Strand. The edge of the land by the water; a beach. Of late, it has been used to describe the water's edge in a town, and many English speaking islands have a Strand Street in their main villages.

Sternsheets. In a dory, the space aft of the aftermost *thwart*.

Stops. See *gaskets*.

Tack. n. The lower forward corner of a *fore-and-aft* sail. v. The act of turning a vessel's bow through the wind.

Tern. A down-east term for a three-masted *schooner*.

Tholepin. A wooden or metal pin set into the *gunwale*; a pair are used as rowlocks.

Throat halyard. Rope or purchase used to hoist the foremost end of a *gaff* (the end next to the *mast*). (See *peak halyard*.)

Thwart. A board that spans the *beam* of a small vessel lending lateral strength and seating. In sailing dinghies the *mast* thwart will have a hole through which the *mast* is stepped.

Thwartship. See *athwartship*.

Topmast. A vertical extension of a *mast*.

Topsail. On a *schooner*, the sail spread between the *gaff* and the *topmast*.

Topsides. Portion of the hull above the waterline.

Truck. A metal cap covering the top of a *mast*, used to secure blocks and other gear.

Trysail. (trys'l) A small, three-cornered sail lashed to the *mast* and secured at the *clew*, used during heavy weather.

Tween deck. Deck or decks between the *weather deck* and the hold.

Ways. Short for a railway used to haul vessels out of the water.

Weather deck. Deck wholly exposed to the elements.

Wildcat. Sprocket wheel of a *windlass* that positively hauls the anchor chain.

Windlass. A winch or capstan specifically designed for heaving the anchor and warping *hawsers*. In the days of sail, the windlass could also be used for raising sails.

Worm. To put string in the cantlines (grooves between *strands*) of rope or wire to be *parceled* or *served*.

Yawl boat. A vessel's small work boat.

Appendix 1
Beaufort Wind Scale

Beaufort Wind Force	Wind Speed in Knots	Description	Sea State
0	0	Calm	Seas mirrorlike—smooth
1	1-7	Light Air	Small wavelets, without crests
2	8-11	Light Breeze	Short waves, with crests
3	12-16	Gentle Breeze	Waves short & more pronounced, crests begin to break
4	17-20	Moderate Breeze	Small waves; numerous white caps
5	21-24	Fresh Breeze	Waves more lengthy, white foam crest—sea breaks
6	25-30	Strong Breeze	Large waves form, white foam crests, breaking seas
7	21-35	Moderate Gale	Sea heaps and spindrift begins
8	36-42	Fresh Gale	Dense foam reducing visibility—(sails reefed)
9	43-49	Whole Gale	Wave height & crests greatly increase, sea begins to roll
10	50-56	Strong Gale	High waves, overhanging crests, surface turning white
11	57-65	Storm	Seas rolling, become shock like, poor visibility
12	66 & up	Hurricane	Hang on—under bare poles

Appendix 2
The 32 Points of the Compass

Scope	Degrees	Points
North to South Clockwise	0°00'	N
	11°15'	N by E
	22°30'	NNE
	33°45'	NE by N
	45°00'	NE
	56°15'	NE by E
	67°30'	ENE
	78°45'	E by N
	90°00'	E
	101°15'	E by S
	112°30'	ESE
	123°45'	SE by E
	135°00'	SE
	146°15'	SE by S
	157°30'	SSE
	168°45'	S by E

Scope	Degrees	Points
South to North Clockwise	180°00'	S
	191°15'	S by W
	202°30'	SSW
	213°45'	SW by S
	225°00'	SW
	236°15'	SW by W
	247°30'	WSW
	258°45'	W by S
	270°00'	W
	281°15'	W by N
	292°30'	WNW
	303°45'	NW by W
	315°00'	NW
	326°15'	NW by N
	337°30'	NNW
	348°45'	N by W
	360°00'	N

Index

Abaco, 187, 188, 191
abandoned ship, 31, 41, 86
Abundance. *See* Chapter 1
Acadia Gas Engines, 202
Adams. *See* Chapter 2
Adams & Knickle, 9, 14, 15
Adams, Harry, 9, 14, 15, 16
Agnes Norton, 158
Allan's Cay, 176
Alpha. *See* Chapter 8
Alpha 66 anti-Castro group, 191, 193
Amanda F. Lewis, vi, 2, 7, 100
American Museum of Natural History, 8
Amundsen, Roald, 112, 113
Antarctica, 114
Antigua, 159, 160
Aquanaut. *See* Chapter 9
Argentia, Newfoundland, 96
Arthur, Robert, 183
Atlantic, 142
Atlantic & Chesapeake Canal, 1
Atlantic Bridge Company, 134
Atlantis, 146, 147, 157
Atlas Diesel, 133
Azores, 89, 90
baby turtles, 160, 161, 162, 225
Bahamas Development Board, 193
Bar Harbor, 13
Barbados, vi, 22, 23, 26, 39, 56, 57, 58,
    59, 62, 63, 64, 65, 75, 76, 81, 105, 119,
    120, 121, 126, 137, 235
    Bridgetown, 22, 26, 36, 39, 56, 60, 76,
        78, 104, 121, 123
Batista, Fulgencio, 191
Battle of *Sea Fox*, 48
Battson, Bert, 21
Bay of Fundy, 9, 35
Bear of Oakland, 114
Beaufort, North Carolina, 223
Bell, Alasdair, 132
Bennett, Floyd, 114
Bermuda, 40, 55, 88, 89, 91, 105, 117
Berry Islands, 189
Blairesk, 40, 42, 46

Bligh, William, 112
Bluenose, 44, 187
Boca de Camarioca, 196
Bolling, Bill, v, vi, ix, x, 178, 235
Bonavista, Newfoundland, 129
Boudreau, Walter, 117
Bounty, 112
Boxing Day Race, 63
Brennan, John, 53
Bridgewater, Nova Scotia, 35, 78, 83, 152,
    218
Butch (ship's dog), 84, 87, 89, 93, 94, 95,
    97, 98, 106, 107, 129
Byrd, Admiral Richard, 113
C.A. Larson, 114
Cabot Straits, 148
Caicos, 24, 37, 58
Caledonia, Nova Scotia, 138
Californian, 110, 111, 112
Camarioca, Cuba, vii, 193, 194, 195, 196,
    199
Canfield, A. Cass, 45
Cape Cod, 220
Cape Horn, 112
Cape LaHave, 35
Cape Race, 85, 89, 149
Cape Sable, 35, 40, 152
Carbonear, Newfoundland, 137
cargo
    aluminum and copper, 102
    dynamite, 76
    lumber, 7, 119, 120, 137, 138
    rum, 105
    salt, 24, 40
Castro, Fidel, 191, 192
Cat Cay, 196
Cay Sal Bank, 191
Cerulli, Nicholas, 49, 50, 51, 57, 231
Chomedy, 106
Christophe, Henri, 171
City Island, 8, 19, 46, 47, 54, 55, 100,
    143, 152, 220
City of New York, 150, *See* Chapter 6
Clark's Harbour, vi, 22, 26, 35, 39, 76, 77

Coast Guard, 12, 13, 180, 182, 193, 197, 198
Cobbs Arm, 201
Columbia University, 147
Combs, Sue, 236
Connecticut River, 154
Conquerall Bank, 81, 82, 85, 98, 99, 100, 102, 115, 134, 137, 147, 158, 159, 165, 166, 175
Corkum, Captain Howie, 21
Crimmins, Peggy, 235
Curry, Socks, 167, 169, 170
Dauphinee, 166
Dayspring, Nova Scotia, viii, 102, 115, 133, 145, 153, 157, 159, 165, 166, 217, 219, 225, 229, 231, 233
Deagle's Marine Railway, 221
DeCarlo, Yvonne, 162
DECCA, 180
Deltaville, Virginia, 221
Detroit Diesel, 74
Dickens, Colonel, 60
diesel, rope starting, 77
Dominican Republic, 28, 38, 191
Dönitz, Admiral Karl, 83
donkey engine, 40, 71, 78, 129, 207
Dorman diesel, 152
Dr. Ballard's dog food, 129
Duck Island, 156, 157, 164
Duff, Howard, 162
Duvalier family, 170
E. C. Adams, 21, 22
E.F. Hutton, 141
Earle, Guy and Fred, 137
Easton, Maryland, 3, 99, 100
Eastport, Maine, 34
Edward VII Land, 114
Eleanor Bolling, 114
Elephant Island, 112
Elizabeth City, 223
Endurance, 112
Esperanto, vii, 187, 188, 189, 190, 191
Estimé, President Dumarais, 170
Evans, John, 21
Ewing, Doc, 145
Exumas, viii, 165, 171, 176, 210, 226
Falkner's Island, Connecticut, 20

Father Goose (motion picture), 183
Fisheries Museum, xii, 4, 233, 235
Flame of the Island (motion picture), 162
Flipper (motion picture/TV series), 182
Fort Lauderdale, 180, 182, 189, 191, 216
Fosse, August, 110
Furnan's Yacht Agency, 215
Galveston, 147
Geldert, Captain Dawsie, 62
Gertrude L. Thebaud, 33, 44, 187
Getman & Judd, 49
Getson, Ralph D., 235
Gloucester, 6, 34, 35, 44, 187
Gonaïves, 171
Gonave Island, 28
Goose Islands, 20
Gotlik (ship's dog), vii, 142, 143, 146, 147
Gray Marine, 74, 77, 86
Great Dismal Swamp, 223
Great Inagua, 171
Greco, Gloria, 235
Guantanamo, 106, 146
Gulf of St. Lawrence, 102, 104
Haiti, 27, 28, 38, 170, 171, 173, 174, 183
Halifax, x, 16, 17, 18, 19, 20, 21, 22, 35, 39, 78, 84, 85, 102, 103, 106, 124, 126, 127, 134, 135, 139, 175, 235
Hand, William, 215
Happy People Marina, 226
Harbour Island, viii, 167, 205, 206, 207, 209
Hayden, Sterling, 44
Hebb, Boomdie, 166
Himmelman, David, 235
Himmelman, Lawrence, 217, 218
Hocher, Joe, 187
Hog Island, 95, 106
Hubbell, John, 13, 19, 21, 22, 26, 31
Huguenot Yacht Club, 6
hurricane Carol, 155
Hussar, 141
Île Brion, 102
International Fisherman's Trophy, 44
Intracoastal Waterway, 175, 221, 225
Irish Rose, 95, 96
Isla Aves, 159, 160, 162, 165, 180, 225
Ivan Tors Productions, 182

Ives, Burl, 170
jail, 169
Jamaica, 28, 172
    gang of robbers, 31
    Kingston, 28, 29, 30, 31, 32, 185
    Rocky Point, 29
James Caird, 112
Johnson, Emily, 235
Johnson, Paul (Mate), 41, 46
Jones Fruit Company, 224
Jones, Peter, vi, 61, 68, 70, 72, 84, 85, 86,
    98, 100, 101, 116
Kaptain Krunch, 235
Kelson, Captain William H., 34
Kenedy, Brian, vi, vii, 65, 66, 69, 72, 73,
    79, 80, 87, 96, 98, 115, 118, 119, 129,
    130, 148, 152, 153, 154, 157, 158, 165,
    166, 180, 220
Kenedy, Gabrielle, vii, 118, 135, 136,
    167, 175, 224, 226
Kenedy, Jr., Brian, 118, 226
Kenedy, Patsy, vi, vii, ix, x, xi, 8, 78, 115,
    118, 119, 131, 132, 133, 165, 166, 167,
    174, 175, 206, 208, 212, 216, 221, 223,
    226, 228, 232, 235
Kenedy, Rosemary, ii, vii, viii, 158, 159,
    166, 167, 174, 175, 187, 209, 210, 217,
    218, 225, 226, 227
Key West, 197
King, Admiral Ernest, 182
Klausner, Karl, 161
Knickle, Johnny (photographer), 78
Knight, Frank, 235
Knight, Frank and Debbie, 227
Kosmos, 114
Lady Boat, 61
LaHave River, 9, 12, 80, 81, 127, 164,
    202, 217, 219, 224, 232
Lamont Geological Observatory, 145, 147
Latele River, 34
Laura Annie Barnes, 55
Le Bon Papa, 173
Lightbourn, Sabrina, 231
Lincoln, 33, 34, 43, 213
Liverpool, 153
lobster, 129
Lohnes, Jennifer Kenedy, 231

Loran, 159
Lord, Captain Stanley, 110, 111, 112
Loveland, Sam, 68
Lunenburg, vi, vii, viii, xii, 4, 9, 13, 14,
    26, 44, 47, 48, 76, 116, 123, 125, 133,
    150, 165, 166, 202, 218, 232, 233, 235
Lunenburg Foundry, 202
Lupino, Ida, 163
MacFayden, Captain John, 40
MacLeod, John, 132
Madeira, 21, 22
Maggio, Captain Joe, 235
Magloire, General Paul Eugene, 170, 171,
    172, 173, 174
Mahone Bay, 11
Man-o-War Cay, 188
Marathon, Florida, 228
Marcus, Isabel, 159
Marian Belle Wolfe, 63
Mariel, Cuba, 196, 197, 198
Marsh Harbour, 188, 189, 191
Martha's Vineyard, 157
Mason, Harvey, 18, 19
Mason, Linda, 219, 235
Mason, Windy, 16, 18, 49, 51, 54, 57, 59,
    60, 137
Massasoit, 49
Maughers Beach Light, 19
Mersey, Lord, 111
Meteghan, Nova Scotia, 35, 73, 74
Miami, vii, viii, xi, 174, 196, 201, 206,
    208, 209, 211, 212, 213, 214
Mona Marie, 63, 65
Monti Cristi, 28
Morris, Patrick, 235
motorsailer *Sea Fox. See* Chapter 11
Mount Gay Rum, 80, 105, 121, 130, 138,
    161, 204, 220, 221
Mount St. Vincent Academy, 175
Munton, Dr. William, 223, 235
Muzzio, Frank, 46, 47, 48, 49, 51, 52, 53,
    65
Nantucket, 157
Narragansett Bay, 6, 12, 220
Nassau, 120, 163, 166, 167, 170, 174,
    176, 192, 193, 198, 204, 205, 206, 207,
    208, 217, 219, 226

NBC, 193
Neville (ship's cook), 39, 41, 129
New Haven, Connecticut, 154
New London, 21, 46, 166
New Providence, 183
Newport, Rhode Island, 12, 175
Norwalk, Connecticut, 202
Olin, Colonel Andrew, 171, 172
Oyster Bay, Long Island, 154
Oyster Wars, 3
P.J. Kenedy & Sons, 6
Patricia Greenidge, 62
Pentz, Clarence (mate), 142
Pikes Arm. See Chapter 10
Plumb, Gil, 78, 235
Point Morant, 28
Port au Prince, 27, 28
Port of Spain, Trinidad, 106
Port-aux-Basques, 107
Porter, Jimmy, 204, 235
Pratt, Dallas B, 46
Pryde, Sonny, 235
Pryde, Walter (engineer), 142, 143
radio, marine two-way, 157, 174, 188,
    194, 216
Reid, Reginald, 23, 32, 35, 46, 86, 87, 124
Rice, Captain Gus, 2, 100
Ritcey, Willoughby, 126
Robars, Jim, 235
Rofihe, Barry, 235
Rum Row, 12
Rumsey, John, 235
Russell, Lola and Harold, 236
Sabin, Ed, 142, 164, 165, 166, 168, 171,
    175
Sampson Cay, 225, 227
Samson, 109, 110, 111, 112, 113
San Juan, 162
San Juan, Puerto Rico, 159
San Souci, 171
Sarah E, 5
Schug, Walter, 67, 82, 83, 84, 86, 87, 88,
    89, 90, 143
Sea Fox. See Chapters 3 and 5
Seaman's Institute of New York, 10
Seawanhaka Corinthian Yacht Club, 45
Sewall's Point, 34

Seymour, Gordon, 125
Shackleton, Sir Ernest, 112, 113
sheers, 71
Sheet Harbour, Nova Scotia, 137
Shepard, Dr. Sam, 162
Smith & Rhuland, 164, 175
Smith, Raynell, 235
smuggling, 180, 204, 205, 227
    car, 208
    dog food, 209
    refrigerators, 207
    rum, 125
Snyder, Teddy, viii, 115, 128, 134, 145,
    153, 165, 166, 175, 219, 225
Snyder's shipyard, 102
Snyder's Shipyard, 219
Sober, Leonard, 81
Solomon's Island, 220
South Georgia, 113
Spanish Wells, viii, 167, 205, 206, 207,
    208
St. John's, Newfoundland, 84, 85, 96, 98,
    106, 200
St. Lucia, 159
St. Mary's Bay, Jamaica, 184
St. Nicholas light, 28
St. Vincent, 159
Stafford, Captain John, 180
Staniel Cay, 187, 209, 210, 226, 228
Staten Island, 139, 142
Stewart, Commander Alexander, 182
Storey, Arthur D., 33, 34, 35, 43
stowaway, 23, 32, 35, 46, 86, 124
Sullivan, John, 139
Sullivan, Tiffany (granddaughter), 224
Taylor, Blake, 138
T-Bone, 171, 172, 173, 174
The Bluff, 206
The Man Who Loved Schooners, 117
Thomas W. Lawson, 130
Thunderball (motion picture), 187
Time magazine, 193
Titanic, 111, 112
Todd's Shipyard, 146, 147
Tongue of the Ocean, 183
Tors, Ivan, 183
Tortuga, 28

Turks Island, vi, 22, 24, 26, 27, 36, 37, 39, 41, 58, 76, 78, 117, 119, 124, 129
Turks Island., 22
Tusitala, ix, 8, 46
U.S. Navy, 99, 123, 180
U-86, 82, 83, 84, 85, 86, 87, 88, 89, 90, 91
union labor, 121, 137
Upham, Mrs. R. D., 46, 47
Vaughan, Roger, 235
Vema. See Chapter 7
Vetlesen, George Unger, 142
Vineyard Sound, 157
W. H. Albury, 191

Wawaloam. See Chapter 4
Weddell Sea, 112
Wendell, Jerry, 48, 51, 54
Whittier, Fred, 187, 188, 189
Windward Passage, 183, 184
Wolf Trap, 2, 229
Wreck Commissioner's Court, 111
Xavier College, Nassau, 167
Yarmouth, vii, 13, 72, 73, 119, 131, 140
Yelcho, 113
Zahniser, Skip, 235
Zinck, Captain Ammon, 12, 52, 53
Zwicker, Barbara and Sherman, 235

Captain Lou Kenedy's Lifeline

1910	1920	1930	1940	1950	1960	1970	1980	1990

- **1910** - Lou Kenedy is born.
  - **1920** - Owns first sailboat *Tilky* at age 10.
  - **1924** - Owns first sloop the *Sarah E.* at age 14.
  - **1928** - At 18, leaves university to work as a cook aboard the *Amanda F. Lewis.*
  - **1929** - At 19 leaves home to sail on the *Tusitala* out of Baltimore.
  - **1931** – At 21 graduates Seaman's Institute of New York.
  - **1931** - Buys tern schooner *Abundance* in Nova Scotia, his first command.
  - **1932** - *Abundance* shipwrecked in Jamaican hurricane.
  - **1933** - Buys tern schooner *Adams* – one of the last U.S. wooden, three-masted cargo schooners.
  - **1934** - *Adams* sinks in storm near New York City.
  - **1934** - Partners with Frank Muzzio in the Sea Fox Shipping Co. and buys yacht *Sea Fox* in NY.
  - **1935** - Sails *Sea Fox* out of New York to Barbados before Muzzio could sell the ship's lead ballast -- "Battle of the Sea Fox."
  - **1935** - Converts *Sea Fox* to freighter for local shipping runs in Barbados.
  - **1936** - Meets and marries Pat Greenidge, from a rich Barbados family.
  - **1937** - Rents house in Barbados – first shoreside home in five years. Grandmother buys out Muzzio and all charges from "Battle of Sea Fox" in America dropped.
  - **1939** - Find buyer for *Sea Fox* in Baltimore and sails back to U.S.
  - **1939** - Buys steel-hulled *Wawaloam*, stuck on a mud flat in New Jersey.
  - **1940** - Refitting and repairs completed on *Wawaloam.*
  - **1941** - Jury-rigged way of manually starting *Wawaloam's* diesel engine becomes standard teaching for American G.I.s in World War II.
  - **1942** - Buys home for family in Nova Scotia due to U-Boat threat in the Caribbean.
  - **1942** - *Wawaloam* sunk by U-boat. Crew escapes in lifeboats and rescued at sea by freighter *Irish Rose.*
  - **1943** - Lou buys back *Sea Fox* in Maryland.
  - **1943** - Buys *City of New York* for $1,000.
  - **1944** - Sells *Sea Fox* to a captain in Barbados.
  - **1944** - *City of New York* refitted near his home in Nova Scotia.
  - **1944** - As war winds down, family begins living aboard *City of New York* off and on for 10 years.
  - **1945** - Loses two crewmembers in a storm on way to Halifax.
  - **1949** - Diesel engine installed on *City of New York* marking the end of sail-only cargo shipping out of North American ports.
  - **1952** - Sells *City of New York* and buys *Vema*, a schooner slated for destruction on Staten Island.

1910	1920	1930	1940	1950	1960	1970	1980	1990

Captain Lou Kenedy's Lifeline

1910	1920	1930	1940	1950	1960	1970	1980	1990

• 1953 - *Vema* ready to head to Nova Scotia for refitting.

• 1953 - *Vema* becomes research vessel for Columbia University in Gulf of Mexico.

•1954 - Buys 80-foot iron ketch *Alpha* in New York.

•1954 - Runs charter trips around Maritimes and New England. Daughter Rosemary born.

• 1954 - Hurricane Carol swamps New England. *Alpha* rides it out, passing through the eye of the hurricane in Long Island Sound.

• 1954 – *Alpha* chartered as supply ship for research expedition in Caribbean.

• 1955 - *Alpha* used as prop in movie filmed in Nassau.

• 1955 - Runs charters in Maritimes and New England out of Connecticut. Son Brian enlists in Navy.

• 1955 - Moves family to Bahamas to pursue charter work.

• 1956 - Experiences revolution in Haiti while running a charter.

• 1958 - Family sails back to Nova Scotia to refit *Alpha* and enroll Patsy in school; sails back to Bahamas.

• 1959 - *Alpha* blown ashore in Exumas.

Works for U.S. Navy antisubmarine program. 1960-1961 •

Buys *Aquanaut* in Ft. Lauderdale. 1962 •

Hired by U. S. Government to survey ocean near Andros Island

Sells *Alpha*. 1963 •

Aquanaut used in film *Father Goose* in Jamaica. 1964 •

Back to Bahamas' hydrographic work. 1964 •

Aquanaut chartered for use in film *Thunderball*. 1965 •

Takes part in Camarioca Exodus from Cuba. 1965 •

Sells *Aquanaut*; buys two freighters. 1967 •

Sells *Cobbs Arm*, keeps *Pikes Arm*.

Runs contraband and cargo shipping in Bahamas. 1967-1971 •

Sells *Pikes Arm*. Buys ship in Florida, renames *Sea Fox*. 1971 •

Sails home to Nassau. Sells house & moves 1971 •

aboard *Sea Fox* for trip back to Nova Scotia.

Family spends winters in Nassau, summers in Maritimes. • 1971-1985 •

Sells *Sea Fox*. 1985 •

Skipper dies at age 81 – "The Last Schoonerman." 1991 •

1910	1920	1930	1940	1950	1960	1970	1980	1990

About the Author

Joe Russell was raised in the San Francisco Bay area. After a serious hydroplane racing accident in the early 1960s, he switched to sailing, which led to a yacht delivery job from Alameda, California to the Virgin Islands.

While in the Caribbean, Joe sailed to most of the countries in the area and wrote features for *Cruising World* magazine. A year in the South Pacific skippering the 38-foot cutter *Christina* led to the publication of *Exploring the Marquesas Islands*. He is also the author of *Exploring the Virgin Islands*.

During a research trip to the Bay Islands of Honduras, the author met Lou Kenedy's family which began an enduring friendship and was the genesis of *The Last Schoonerman*.

Printed in the United States
64990LVS00005B/29-30